Social Smarts Strategies That Earn Free Book Publicity

Social Smarts Strategies That Earn Free Book Publicity

◆

Don't Pay to Market Your Writing

Anne Hart

ASJA Press

New York Lincoln Shanghai

Social Smarts Strategies That Earn Free Book Publicity
Don't Pay to Market Your Writing

Copyright © 2006 by Anne Hart

ASJA Press
an imprint of iUniverse, Inc.

iUniverse books may be ordered through booksellers or by contacting:

iUniverse
2021 Pine Lake Road, Suite 100
Lincoln, NE 68512
www.iuniverse.com
1-800-Authors (1-800-288-4677)

ISBN-13: 978-0-595-39221-6
ISBN-10: 0-595-39221-0

Printed in the United States of America

Contents

1

How to Earn Free Book Publicity from Non-Profits' Publications & Schools Using Social Smarts

Do you want to earn free book publicity? Start book readers' groups nationally in places where book readers, book buyers, and book sellers gather. Let the local chapters appoint a leader and send them copies of your books that you pre-sell to the group members and/or leaders.

Connect with people on a larger scale and locally. Instead of some pyramid scheme, think of how social intelligence is made up of empathy, charisma, and observation. Empathy and social smarts help you earn free book publicity by connecting you with key people, media, schools, and the publications of nonprofit agencies. As a writer, you can promote your own book and earn free book publicity by connecting key people, media, and nonprofits' newsletters with schools.

Social intelligence used in book promotion is like a three-ring circus. Use empathy, that is people smarts, as a catalyst to bring together schools, nonprofit agencies, and authors. Observe, simplify, and offer commitment as charisma.

Query editors of nonprofit publications. These nonprofit agencies often publish high-circulation newsletters and sometimes also publish sizable, glossy magazines. Some produce videos or documentaries. To connect with the nonprofit agencies' editors, use your social intelligence skills to make connections in the nonprofit agencies' public relations and communications departments.

Join public relations societies, national associations, and help out the nonprofit agencies or organizations of your choice focusing on what gets published in their magazines or newsletters. If you want to earn free publicity for your book, supply these editors with facts, findings, and trends.

Bring the nonprofits in contact with schools. When you talk to school assemblies or classrooms, relate your book topic to any specific work or project done by a nonprofit association for whom you could write an article for that association's newsletter or glossy magazine.

Use social intelligence to connect to people. What you need to earn free publicity is self-awareness and an understanding of how the main topic of your book influences your own behavior and how others perceive your behavior.

In short—do you immediately connect with others when you speak about your writing? Can you become charismatic for the 45-minutes you spend speaking to a school auditorium? Or are you unable to speak in public at all or travel to promote your book?

Back in 1995 Daniel Goleman wrote a book titled, *Emotional Intelligence: Why It Can Matter More than IQ*. Then in 2006 Karl Albrecht wrote a book titled, *Social Intelligence: The New Science of Success*. How do others experience what Goleman calls your social radar? Many writers are too introverted to promote their own books with social smarts if they are asked to speak in public.

For those without this ability to connect face to face and stand up to deliver a 45-minute presentation, what else can you do to earn free book publicity? You can write articles for the magazines and newsletters of nonprofit agencies. You can visit schools and show a topic-related video. Then answer questions and mention your book without having to give a formal speech. Ask the students to discuss the video with one another.

Then have a table 'captain' or lead person from among each group of students stand up and discuss feedback from their group about the video. Relate the video to your book. Make sure the school pre-orders your book for each student. Hand out flyers and comments about the content in your book and how it relates to the similar topic of the video. If you score low on emotional intelligence due to genetic anxiety or lack of energy, health issues, or disabilities, don't fret. Keep videos handy to speak for you as you hand out your book and information you've prepared about what's inside.

What if you can increase your social intelligence with practice, at least to the limits of what your genes dealt you versus to what sensitivities the environment conditioned you? That's where writing for the newsletters and magazines of the nonprofits can help you get your word across.

Without emotional intelligence applied to book public relations, alternatives that you have include your free book publicity with Google Search (engine) on the Internet and your own Web site. You also have your own flyers and brochures sent to librarians and coordinators of authors in the schools programs.

Don't fret if you are unable to speak in public. You can always write to the distributors and reviewers or review books yourself for various online or in print publications working with other authors. Ask an author to review your book in exchange for you reviewing his or her book if that author also writes book reviews.

Also check out Freelance Success at: https://www.freelancesuccess.com/classes/bookpublicity.php. And see the Web site at: http://www.bookpromotion101.com/bp101/ for Book Promotion 101 (Workshops & Consulting for Authors. There are numerous books on how to write press releases, how to persuade the media to read, publish or re-write your media release, and how to plan, pitch, and present your book.

The goal is how to get as much free book publicity or project publicity as possible. You can even write a grant proposal to get funding for your project. Include a budget for publishing, promotion, or marketing. How do you get non-profit agencies to give you free book publicity in their newsletters and other publications, seminars, or conferences?

Working with Nonprofits' Newsletters

Allow excerpts from your book or project to be published in nonprofit associations and organizations' newsletters when there is a good link to your books. The publications of nonprofits may be able to increase your sales in the long run.

Choose an organization with a purpose related to the information in your book or project. Free book publicity also can be extended to free documentary video or audio project publicity. Make sure the nonprofit's newsletter is widely distributed. Call the newsletter editor as your primary contact.

Since your article or book excerpt would be offered free, most of the editors would be glad to have informative content with good resources, and you would in turn not be charged for advertising. The publicity for your book, documentary, or other project would be free. These newsletters value credible, informative writing that would help readers form decisions and make choices based on researchable, checkable facts, trends, and news. The details need to be so current or hidden that the mainstream media may not have seen it. Such facts could include findings of studies or trends.

How to Write a Media Release for the Editor of a Non-Profit Association Seeking Good Resources

Nonprofit agencies look foremost for excellent resources—credible and current. Send a media release to the editor. Content would run a page and a half. Choose topics related most closely to the current projects or themes of the particular month. The newsletter may have guidelines as to what topics are chosen each month.

Follow that calendar when you choose what topics to cover in the content you send to the newsletter with your press release. Work your book into the press release by covering the topic of the month for that newsletter.

For example, if the newsletter of the nonprofit agency is circulated to persons with mobility-related disabilities, and your book is about travel, emphasize what new technology is provided to make travel accessible, available, and affordable to those with mobility-related disabilities, such as rough terrain wheel chairs, accessibility to transportation, or tours and hotel rooms equipped for use by persons with mobility-related disabilities.

Emphasize tours for those who walk slow, use walkers or wheelchairs or related topics. Use the same theme to write for mainstream magazines. Most information from your press releases can turn into query letters destined for mainstream magazines.

How to Begin

When you're writing an article for a nonprofit's newsletter, the content would be different than when merely sending a press release about your book. An article has more of a chance to be published than a press release. Customize the article to run about a page and a half, which is the same size in length as a media release. Here's where the difference kicks in. Your short article has a title that gives specific information. One example would be *Ten Tips on Avoiding Elderly Abuse.*

When I wrote a paperback book on the topic of preventing elderly abuse, a section in the book mentioning 60 points to become aware of related to preventing elderly abuse easily could be condensed into ten tips on avoiding elderly abuse that would fit the tight space requirements of a brief nonprofit newsletter. The 515-page paperback book is titled, *How To Stop Elderly Abuse: A Prevention Guidebook* (ISBN: 0-595-23550-6, Published: Jul-2002-View and peruse the book at: http://www.iuniverse.com/bookstore/book_detail.asp?&isbn=0-595-23550-6).

It is important to include a tagline in the article before sending your content to a nonprofit association's newsletter editor. The tagline should include information on your book and two sentences showing your expertise. Offer tips, and inform the editors that they can publish your tips on how to do something that's in your book—as long as they include the entire tagline mentioning your book.

Nonprofit newsletter editors prefer articles giving 10 tips on how to do or prevent something important that they are emphasizing that month in their newsletter. It works most of the time also with magazine editors.

Not all nonprofit agencies publish only one type of publication. In addition to a newsletter, there may be glossy magazines, employee newsletters (called house organs), and other publications. The glossy magazines published quarterly or even monthly by some of these nonprofits usually pay for content. Additionally, some newsletters also pay for press releases, unlike newspapers. After your articles are published, ask if you can become their regular columnist if you're looking for freelance writing that helps your book publicity as well.

Prepare a dozen columns to fit the length of the glossy magazine published by some nonprofits and send it out to the editors. Do the same for the newsletters, restricting the length to what's usually published in those brief newsletters. Send a cover letter with the columns and tagline about your book at the end of each article, media release, column, or other content material you send. Never send anything too long for the publication. Count the words in the newsletter's monthly columns, articles, or press releases.

Connect To People

What can you expect when you try to connect to people with empathy in mind? Give useful, current, or hidden facts that help people make more informed choices. Ask how you can serve your audience by solving problems and getting results through your research and writing in future books, interviews, or articles.

Focus on how you can help other authors or publishers sell more books by visiting schools to talk about writing, age-appropriate topics, current events, history, health, or storytelling. It's the empathy and social smarts that makes you charismatic as a writer and speaker who does research that easily can be fact-checked by readers. The thoroughness of your research earns you credibility points. And credibility is publicity.

Emphasize positive points. Charisma is about connecting to people in a positive atmosphere.

The more that you understand what people want from a book or article about your specific topic, the better you can connect. Do feasibility studies and market research before you decide what kind of book, article, or media release to make public.

Talk to editors and publishers at national associations' meetings or conferences. Ask why editors choose to publish or reject similar, equally qualified books on specific trendy subjects in a particular year.

Ask them what book and/or article topics are 'in' or 'out' this season and why. Examples include memoirs books, angel books, or ethnic books being in or out of fashion for a specific season.

Are their choices based on sales potential? Who does their feasibility and market research and what questions are asked to *predict* future sales?

How often are they accurate? Who chooses or predicts 'hot' topic books that are 'in' for the next year? Interview those people.

Write an article about how they arrive at their predictions. What sources and trends do they research?

Show how their conclusions are based on improving sales figures of books pointing to products with high sales and popular culture trends or high-demand needs and requests. What types of marketing surveys are used?

Offer the article to writing-related publications. Connect new writers with trade journals related to the *business* end of publishing.

Empathy is about walking in the other person's shoes. Practice social smarts by connecting people in one business to people in another business for current, practical, and transferable reasons.

Physicians and physicists may not have the time to communicate enough, but both could be interested in your new book researching what 25 diverse, credible scientists say about why spontaneous healing occurs.

To sell books, develop relationships. You have to make people want to buy your books by inspiring and motivating them with concrete facts, details, and new trends or resources.

Your books must inspire commitment in readers. The only thing that will sell in books is to inspire people to be more committed to what they do or what they enjoy. To sell your books, sell commitment and simplicity. People want facts and instruction that are easy to understand and at the same time makes them want to be more committed to what they enjoy doing either in their work or in their relationships or in fixing, decorating, and cleaning up their homes, meals, or environments. The same formula applies to making workplaces better through commitment and making the complex easier to understand—making life simpler.

That's how you sell your book—even if your book is about how to build dog houses. To sell your book, develop vision. Become a visionary at selling your book using social radar. As a writer, it's better to have social smarts. Tell readers where to get expert information in depth on the subjects you cover.

Writers seeking free book publicity need to start by developing better relationships with the people who can buy and sell their books. Include the associations that move those books. Develop relationships with some of the small publishers' associations and nonprofit agencies emphasizing the subject matter in your books. Review the books of other authors. Ask authors to include a comment or quote from your book in their books and not only in their bibliographies.

Free book publicity is upward mobility. It's like a promotion, and it only comes about when you develop a strong relationship with editors and publishers of topic-related newsletters and magazines, including online audio and video content.

To get free publicity, you need to develop working relationships even though you may be a freelancer/independent contractor. Teach online. Start columns for print distribution. If your article or column appears in print, you can get permission to put it online if you ask for your copyright or publishing rights. But if your article or column first appears online at your Web site, it could be rejected by print publications as having appeared as distributed content. Then its status is reprint only, and you might not get paid.

Skills and high IQ in writers often lose out to high social smarts, which consists of the working relationships you have with editors and publishers and also with your audience of readers, which includes school librarians, coordinators, and teachers who order the books 45 at a time for students when you speak at school assemblies.

What is the best move a writer can make to sell a book and get free publicity? Get the tools of your trade. Imitate a great politician. Build relationships with those who buy or promote your books. Street smarts or social intelligence is one tool among many. If you are unable to travel or speak in public, you have many other tools available that include the written word disseminated to audiences interested in your specific topics and corporate, family, newcomer, travel, or institutional gift baskets. If you're selling a book on fad diets and gum disease, you might wish to inform manufacturers of health food products or holistic dental aids to package your book with orders of certain products.

To earn free book publicity, you can't stand still. You have to move your book forward just as you did in its plot. And you move the plot forward by actions of the characters. In the same way, you move the sales of your book forward by the actions of people with the power to promote or buy your work.

How you accomplish moving your work forward is to measure the range of change in attitudes toward your book by those you contact. If you are empathetic enough towards your readers, you'll come up with a book that answers their questions, fulfills their needs, solves problems, and offers results. Before you write a book, ask potential readers what they want to see in a book and what information and resources the topic should include.

People know what they want if you ask them. They want instructions on how to solve specific problems, step-by-step guides to follow, and results to measure. Put empathy first before you write your book and before you write your articles, columns, or press releases about your work.

Put yourself in the reader's shoes before you write anything. People want empathy, commitment, and simplicity in a book that solves problems and gets measurable results. People want information they can check, use, and apply to make better choices. All these answers need to appear in your book publicity, your book, and any columns you write for nonprofits or when you present or show a video while visiting schools, clubs, community centers, senior centers, children's camps, parent organizations, houses of worship, creative writing boot camps, libraries and bookstores.

Understand and be empathetic with your readers and editors. You can learn to understand them by walking a mile in their roles. Look at the world from their eyes before you write the first query letter.

What do they want most in their busy day? Some editors often are so busy that they tell writers not to write to them more than once a year because it clogs their email box. They get this way from hundreds of writers emailing in stories each week. Your job is to find out how to make yourself more than a total stranger without clogging their email box. Your best bet might be a press conference where you invite the editors to brunch. You can do this by teleconferencing as well as in person.

When an editor is not busy, you can talk. This is accomplished at clubs where the editor sits at the same table as writers as in professional associations conferences and meetings.

Social radar in the world of publishing is about targeting those with the power to publish, promote, or sell your book. Often other writers will not help you if their own books are not selling. Instead, they will use a disguise of sending you email telling you what you did wrong in your book or on your Web site to cause you a lack of sales.

They think they are helping you. They do not buy your books or promote your books. They wouldn't have emailed you in the first place if you hadn't told them your books weren't selling. They look for a weak spot and open the wound of negativity further by showing you what you are doing wrong. This is not empathy, and they are not committed to a working relationship with you. If they did, they would buy your book. The real culprit is that they don't have high-speed Internet, and your Web site opens too slowly and has too much information, and they will email you that you have done something wrong. They will inform you that you need to change your whole Web site architecture. This will only lead you astray. The real issue they will avoid because the real issue is that the topic of your book is of no interest to those persons. What you need at this point is praise, prayer, and promotion. What other writers will give you is a laundry list of what you are doing that's wrong.

Then you will remember them as not the warm, fuzzy mothering and comforting creatures that you eagerly need, but only as the critical colleagues who do not buy your books. Is it jealousy hidden under the cloak of wanting to improve you? Are you their competition? Some writers will help and mentor other authors. Find out whether your mentor is competing with you.

There are various levels of social smarts, also called emotional intelligence, social radar, or social intelligence. As a journalist or writer, you are good at observing people. Then observe how others treat one another at meetings and when competing at work. Why do writers act the way they do with one another?

Why do editors and publishers treat staff and freelance writers differently, or treat writers in general in the ways that they do? Observe how editors and publishers treat writers and switch roles with an editor for three months—either for real as in a game show or in your imagination. Write down what the editor sees each day from writers, including you.

You can make a documentary video about switching roles—writer and editor or publisher. Keep track of the information that comes in and write about it. Use it in your book promotion. Process the information. Build your relationship with the editor you switched roles with for a short time.

Writers make their livings explaining the complex to people looking for simple answers. You are going to write for people much smarter than yourself, and you will write for those with lower IQs. To communicate, to share meaning is about making a commitment to empathy, observing, and sharing. You're worried that others won't value your information. As a writer you have to work with people, and commitment is the beginning.

To develop your social skills in writing so that those smarter than you and those not as informed will value your information, begin to promote your book by writing columns that help people observe others, solve problems, and get measurable results. Check to see how simple you have made your information so others can follow your writing step-by-step without confusion. Write to share meaning.

Begin by writing a column made up of brief excerpts your book or documentary project. Send out the excerpts to a variety of publications. Inform the editor that the article may be run free in free in exchange for a credit mentioning the book. Anything you offer free in exchange for mention of your book in a national publication is excellent exposure and free publicity for your projects.

Which Quarterly Club Tabloids Should You Target?

Choose a nonprofit newsletter, magazine, or tabloid that is mailed out to more than 45,000 members of a national or international club. Ask the editor whether you can lay out the publication. Or talk to the person who does lay out the newsletter or magazine. One example is the Sierra Club that uses excerpts of environmental books with permission from the authors. As a freelancer, you can pitch the editor if you do work for any similar group with similar goals. For example, if you do volunteer work for any type of environmental group, you still can pitch a different environmental organization because all the environmental groups have in common the goal of working to make the environment healthier.

The Sierra Club, for example, has editors in various regions. So instead of contacting one editor in one region, you can pitch to another editor in a different region. Research how many other organizations have local chapters with their own newsletters for different regions. To look at a variety of association, your local or university library has Thomson's Encyclopedia of Associations. Information on these reference books is found at: http://library.dialog.com/bluesheets/html/bl0114.html.

Speaking to School and Library Audiences and Storytelling

Free book publicity is about storytelling to library and school audiences, giving interviews to the media, speaking about what's in your book, and reading in public and on CDs or DVDs, broadcasting on Web sites, and doing book store appearances, and book tours, if you are able to travel. Virtual book tours are helpful if the stress of travel is too much. You can publicize your book in food court malls and shopping centers or in libraries, university auditoriums, or even teacher's lounges and at national and local associations, clubs, or houses of worship.

If you are writing children's books, purchase your state's public school directory. Contact schools and school librarians. Charge a fee from $400 to $1,000 to visit schools. Select the appropriate age group to speak to assemblies about your book(s) if they are suitable for that age group. Talk to the coordinator or librarian to set up your speaking engagement to talk about your children's book. The books will be pre-ordered for each student by the school.

Also look at parochial and Montessori schools. Visit some of their Web sites. Contact your state's School Library Association. Look for Career Days at schools and Authors' Day at schools to make your appearance with information about your book and some copies of your book.

After you have spoken, ask for a letter of recommendation from each school. Use these letters to obtain assignments to speak to another school. You also can apply for the poet-in-the-schools or poet-in-residence scholarships to appear for a semester or year in various elementary, middle, or high schools.

When you speak at a school, ask to be paid. You can also volunteer without pay at a school, but generally, authors are paid expenses, usually around $400 or more for each day you appear in the school and speak to children, usually at assemblies. If you stay overnight, your hotel and food expenses would be covered if you ask for payment to cover these expenses.

The pay could be for one day $400 or $500 if you are not staying overnight. Some speakers ask for $1,000 and do get it if their books are well known by teachers or librarians. For a beginner, $400 or $500 per day is appropriate.

Before you contact any school you'll need to make an information and contact sheet. Here's the template for such a sheet. This would be one page in length. Fill in your personal information:

Contact Sheet for School Coordinators and Librarians:

Page One:

Name:
Address:
Telephone:
Fax:
Email:
Web site:
Contact by: Phone, Fax, or Email

Age, grade, or level of school audience:

Type of Presentation:
Length: (usually 45 minutes for elementary, middle, and high school, less for kindergarten)

Display for Illustrations:
Storytelling for each age group:
Writing discussion
Illustrations
> Editing
> Revising
> Printing
> Story sources
> Publishing
> Self-Publishing
> Distribution
> Promotion
> Overlays and color, stamps, graphics
> Question and Answer time

Writing Type/Classification:
Honorarium: $ per day, $ with overnight
Number of Presentations: (How many presentations per day—one, two, three four?)
Usually four presentations per school day are appropriate.
Grades:
Size of audience desired: Are classes to be combined? Will you go into classrooms or work with assemblies in an auditorium?
Equipment: (Microphone, video equipment, table, or other presentation machinery).

Books: (Name your published books and have the book covers printed on your contact sheet. Include a small photo of yourself.)

Page Two

Enclose the Second Page with Your Contact Sheet:

List your books by title. Show book covers on this sheet. Include a one-paragraph summary of your book's story or plot. At the bottom of this second page include a student order form and a presentation date that can be filled in by those who hire you to speak in public and private schools.

Have an order form at the bottom that teachers, librarians, parents, or students can fill out and return to the teacher. Include sales tax. Sign the books that are pre-ordered for the class. Include an inscription if requested. Make checks payable to you. If you have published your book print-on-demand, you can buy them at a discount from your publisher after the books are pre-sold or pre-ordered by the school.

Usually print on demand books will be sent within ten days of orders received. Teachers and librarians or students can order the book directly from your publisher. Or you can purchase the books and sell them directly to the school. At the bottom of your order sheet, include a space for the student's name, teacher's name, the total amount being paid for the books, and your address or your publisher's mailing address, Web site, email address, and telephone number.

Author in the Schools Presentation Check List

Before you appear at any school to speak to an assembly or do storytelling in classrooms, create a presentation check list. It should look like this template:

<u>Date</u> Sent   <u>Date</u> Received

Accounts Receivable
(Include all check numbers
& amounts)
Address
Books donated
Books mailed
Books sold
Brief biography
Confirmation Letters
Contacts
Date of Presentation
Fliers/Students
Fliers/Teachers
Fliers/Librarians/Coordinators
Institution
Lesson Plan for Day of Presentation
Letters of Recommendation

Order Forms
Phone
Query Letters to each school
Students
Telephone numbers, addresses of each contact
Thank you follow-up letter to contacts and students
Fee charged

How to Use Social Intelligence to Earn Free Book Publicity

How many copies of your book will sell is often tied to social intelligence. To sell your book, your first tool is a social radar detector. Your book needs to understand what it will do to readers and also what it will do to attract readers. What type of reputation of credibility and excellence does your book have before anyone will read it or even be told the title?

How many other areas are influenced by emotional or social intelligence? You have a variety of high IQ societies for those passing a test of intelligence. But how many associations do you have for those who score high on emotional intelligence, regardless of IQ? Who would join, and what would their purpose be?

Could your book use social intelligence, emotional intelligence, or behavioral intelligence to improve its promotional and marketing ratings and sales figures? Can social intelligence aimed at booksellers, review publications, or consumers increase your book publicity and sales?

Let's compare free book publicity in the media to self-awareness. If social awareness is all about how people start and keep relationships, then emotional intelligence when applied to book publicity is about showing people how to be more self-aware. When pitching your book, you need to help others understand how their feelings influence their behavior (including book buying behavior). Most of all, to sell your book, your high social intelligence score will underscore interpersonal relationships. And most community colleges offer classes on interpersonal relationships in the public speaking and in the psychology departments. Perhaps it's time you offered a course for book authors, publishers, or editors on interpersonal relationships.

What if your book has nothing to do with this subject? For example, if your book is a how-to build some project, your own interpersonal relationships with the media and editors of newsletters, magazines, and newspapers is important.

You need to get on the right side of the media by using emotional or social intelligence skills. Just be polite. You learn this in preschool. Work on external relationships to publicize your book at no cost to you.

What's social intelligence all about without psycho-jargon? It's simply connecting to people. If you can connect to people, your book will sell more copies. If you don't connect to editors and consumers, you will remain hidden. It's all about getting charisma from your book publicity.

If people describe you as charismatic, and your book also is charismatic, you get free publicity. What gets you free book publicity is working with small groups of people who work together for a common goal that also includes your book in that common goal as a main tool of information and resources.

You can't sell your book if you remain in a vacuum. The only way to sell your book is to connect to people who will most likely buy what you have to say. The same goes for any article you write, a video, audio, or documentary. Empathy is the one behavioral *tool* that connects you with those who would promote or buy your book.

2

How to Promote Your Writing without Paying for Publicity, Marketing, and Advertising

Don't pay to promote, publicize, and market your book. The quickest ways to get free publicity for your book are to work at a writing camp (a boot camp for creative writing) and query a magazine editor to ask whether you can get a go-ahead to write an article titled, *"How to Write a Syllabus for Teaching a Course In* ____. (Fill in the topic of your how-to book).

Ask how-to or research-based publications' editors whether you can write an article on *how to solve a problem* (step-by-step) for readers. Showing results, advice readers can follow, and solving problems gets you free book publicity.

Use your credibility and experience to sell your books—the notion that people take you *seriously*. Show honesty and charisma in your writing. Motivate others to buy your book by showing them why they can trust your credibility, commitment, and stability. Being serious and convincing, even in comedy, promotes your book by 'branding' your reputation with a familiar symbol, proverb, or slogan related to your skills, life experience, or expertise.

Showing readers how to teach a skill or craft quickly attracts the attention of magazine editors who might assign you to write articles where you can mention your book. Ask some of the *how-to* or research-based publications whether you can write an article on how to write a course syllabus for the particular specialty of the magazine.

Writing a course syllabus as part of a feature article on the topic of how to teach a course in_____ (fill in the subject) is one way to find free publicity for your book. It's acceptable to some genealogy research publications, history magazines, and with publications in the fields of fitness/health, folklore, nutrition, cooking, crafts, self-help, and niche (specialty) areas. Free publicity for your book is given when you train a group with similar interests or offer expertise in fields where instruction is welcome and readers wish to teach what they practice—such as research, repair, and lifestyles.

If you've published a book and want to generate some publicity beyond the usual paper media kit that busy reporters may not read, try recording numerous one-hour or half-hour 'lectures' helping people solve particular problems. Then save the video and audio recordings to a CD and to a DVD.

For example, you can put 16 one-hour MP3 audio files on one CD. Then take a DVD and place not only your 16 MP3 audio files on it, but also place eight videos saved as either Windows Media Video files or MPEG movie files. Keep the videos about one hour or a half hour in length. Don't exceed the hour on one file. Nobody will watch a talking head for more than an hour. Forty or 50 minutes for each video is even better.

If you don't have the audio and video rights to your book, make audio and video files with different information, but on the same subject as your book. Use it as supplementary material or course lectures that help people solve problems or achieve results. The material can add to knowledge and information that you didn't include in the book. Use your Web and DVD or CD 'pod casts' or broadcasts for online distribution to promote the important messages, solutions, or pointers in your book.

Not everyone is able to speak in front of groups or on the radio, but those who can talk to a camcorder while alone in a room, safe at home, can use a remote control to turn the record button on and off and record by putting the camcorder on a tripod, then adjusting your desk chair. Hook your camcorder to your TV set so you can watch yourself as you speak. It will help you move to the correct position for a well-centered image of yourself talking to your audience.

Video and audio files book format works well with time capsules and memoirs books, hen-lit, (chick-lit for women over age 50), and non-fiction books for Boomers. One of the best ways to promote your new book in addition to the standard press kits or talking in front of groups is to offer your broadcasts online, at your site, or through Google video, and to offer some information free. You can sell your audio books on eBay or similar sites or your own Web site. Each week you can put your audio book for sale on eBay. If the buyer likes the lectures, they can email you link your Web site to theirs if there is a similar interest in subject matter.

However you choose to publicize your books, it helps to have a CD available with several MP3 audio files that people might listen to while in transit. They can download the MP3 files to an iPod or similar mobile device and listen while at the gym, driving, walking, jogging, or to pass time spent on a bus, cruise, or plane.

Not only can these MP3 files increase your listeners, but you can make valuable contacts to help move your paperback books and other writing. Audio files are easier to sell on a CD than video files on a DVD that requires people to sit still and watch a talking head. For videos, bringing pets into the picture can help.

For example, instead of doing a documentary on Yoga or fitness dancing, try a documentary on belly dancing with your dog (or cat) for fitness or some other involvement with a friendly pet, usually a dog. It has been done with the wonderful show on satellite TV titled, *Canine Karma*, where a woman and a dog work out in a Yoga studio as well as follow the dog through other situations. Scenes include a Yoga studio filled with women and their dogs all doing Yoga postures.

If you want to market a book, try a documentary on writing with your dog or some other pet involvement to move the interest, especially when your book is one of many on the same subject. If you have a paperback book to promote, buy some Web space and upload a few lectures that you can offer free as audio and video files. People can either download the files free, which include mentions of your book, or you can save the files to a CD and/or a DVD and combine audio and video on one disk.

I've recorded my videos originally with Windows Movie Maker and my camcorder. At first the files were saved as MPEG files. I then clicked on "finish movie" and "save movie" and imported the movie from the original MPEG file into Windows Movie Maker, saving it again as a copy now saved as a Windows Media File that easily plays at first click on Windows Media Player (that comes with Windows XP software).

To make the audio files without having to record them again in audio, I played the video files while recording them at the same time with Total Recorder software. I used Total Recorder developer edition. After the audio files picked up the sound from the video files, I saved the files as MP3 files in Total Recorder.

Because MP3 audio files are compressed, you can fit many of them on one CD. I easily fitted 16 one-hour lectures on one CD saved as MP3 files. Total Recorder software is very affordable and available from High Criteria. The company's Web site is at: http://www.highcriteria.com/.

In this way I am able to produce interviews, infomercials about my books, radio shows, lectures, seminars, and courses in both MP3 audio files and MPEG or Windows Media Video files. The files are on my Web site at http://www.newswriting.net, and also at http://www.newswriting.net/writingvideos.htm.

I have uploaded two of these files to Google video and offered them free. I also saved all these files on CDs and DVDs and sell them on eBay for $5.00 plus postage. All these lectures are part of my course in how to be a personal historian and record the highlights of people's lives or write plays and skits from people's life stories or current events.

The broadcasts are designed to promote my paperback books on the strategies of writing plays, monologues, and skits from life stories, or to promote my genealogy books on subjects from DNA-driven genealogy to finding specific ethnic genealogy records and starting home-based online businesses. My latest books on video pod casting careers and businesses to start and on how to write and publish memoirs gift books and corporate success stories.

Don't stop there. Your radio broadcasts can promote your specialized fiction to niche markets. I began posting my radio shows on Web sites and on CDs or DVDs after doing one radio show. I found the regular radio shows that ask authors to come on for a talk to restrict your use of the interview. First of all, the radio shows are copyrighted by the radio. So everything you said is now the property of the radio show and station. However, when you record your own lectures or seminars, everything you say is copyright in your own name if you want it that way. You're the owner of your recording, and you can put it on your Web site or save it to a disk.

Instead of the radio show being in one city, your Web site broadcast stays up there for as long as you have your Web site. On a CD or DVD, you are able to sell a collection of talks you record on one subject or on a variety of subjects. This works well with comedy writing as well. Make sure you copyright your material and get an ISBN (number). One Web site that allows you to buy one ISBN at an affordable price is Bar Code Graphics at: http://www.isbn-us.com/. Check out their frequently asked questions page at: http://www.isbn-us.com/isbnfaq.htm. You can buy an ISBN and get a barcode number with it.

After doing radio and TV interviews many years ago, I decided to do my own radio shows at my Web site. It costs very little to record your voice using a computer microphone. You can save your audio file as one or more MP3 files using Total Recorder software. Then upload your audio file to the Web. A video file from your camcorder may be saved as an MPEG video or a Windows Media Video (WMV) file. Then save your video to a CD or DVD. It's a good idea to not let audio or video files go for more than an hour. A half-hour or 56-minute file is fine. Unless you have a complete hour-long or 90 minute documentary, keep the talking-head types of video and audio files to about an hour or a half hour each. Make note of the average attention span watching a video of a talking head type of lecture. Lecture-type videos and audio seminars should consist of several short audio or video files. Otherwise, attention span drifts, and people can't take notes for long lectures. Number your files or arrange them in an order. Use an index so people may choose which lecture to view or listen to first. A copy of the menu or index of file titles may be inserted inside the CD or DVD case. The side facing the viewer may be the title and a graphic. The outside back case should have the ISBN number, a bar code with the price, and instructions on how to play the disc. For example, if you have 16 MP3 files on one CD, a label on the outside back cover can be a sticker telling the owner to only play on an MP3 player, iPod-like device, or personal computer.

If you have a data DVD containing a mixture of MP3 audio files and Windows Media Video files or MPEG files, tell the owner where to play the material, such as on a personal computer. If the MPEG files are able to be played on most new DVD players, let the owner know this.

Another way is to play your video file while capturing only the audio using Total Recorder. Or use Windows Movie Maker to save just the audio file or the video and audio files. Then save your separate video and audio files to a CD or DVD.

Several years ago I answered an ad or flyer asking authors to come on a radio show. I did a few minutes interview and had to pay a small fee to get on the air. The broadcast came from a city on the East coast. As a result of the show I had one email asking for further information on my book. No actual book sales occurred as a result of my radio interview. The female interviewer was wonderfully insightful.

After the 5-minute interview was over, the male radio personality made a comment on the air which the audience might have interpreted as a bit skeptical. I understood this had been his usual role to take an opposite side of opinion. I felt this comment of disbelief on the subject I discussed in the interview lopped off some credibility points of my talk. I wondered whether the audience actually took me seriously enough to email me about my book. On the positive side, the female interviewer did give out my Web site.

I wanted something more practical in the way of "giving a talk." By putting up 40-minute or 56-minute talks, seminars, courses, or lectures, at least I preserved credibility and respect for my research, charisma, and writing. In this way, I created my own "radio shows." If I choose to have someone interview me and record the 'infomercial' in video and audio, at least I have a script as to what questions I want to be asked. My air time then becomes my Web bandwidth, but I can control what information, resources, and references I offer to help my listeners or viewers find solutions, answers, or experts to go to for more information or additional resources.

More information can move across the airwaves with broadcasts or interviews on a Web site, CD, or DVD. With 64+ paperback books to promote, and travel time limited, I'm making use of the airwaves as far as Internet audio and video are possible, and my Web site bandwidth cost is still affordable. It's amazing how much may be said or shown on the Web, in a documentary, or on a disc, and then offered as an audio book or documentary when edited. Possibilities are expanding daily.

Success Stories—Corporate

Promote your book by writing corporate case history success stories related to the content of your book. Success story books are one possibility to include in the occupation of book packager and book publicist. You'd put together success stories of a company and create a book targeted to the media. This type of book is called a media book. You'd interview satisfied clients of a company, ask them why they switched from one company's product to another company's product, and then collect success stories for the perusal of select media. Your interview questions would focus on what step-by-step procedure was taken to solve a problem or achieve results. Ask about benefits and advantages. An excellent example of a "media book" available to the press is titled, *Media Guide on Food Safety and Nutrition 2004-2006.* It is published by the International Food Information Council. See the Web site at: http://ific.org.

Why did they switch? Software is an excellent product to interview satisfied customers about, emphasizing why they changed software and what they liked about it. This success story approach can be done with interviews about many other types of products, from cars to pet food. Choose a product that's individual enough. Some products have different labels or distributors, but all come from the same manufacturer.

As a freelance case history manager, you'd collect the success stories from satisfied clients and record interviews by phone. Then you'd write a series of news releases about one and a half pages in length.

Each success story would be put into a book to be presented to the press as part of the company's public relations and marketing communications department. The collection of success stories should be consistent in length and presented in book form and/or electronically to select media. It would be up to the public relations director of the particular corporation to select which media would get a copy of the "media book" that you'd publish for a corporation.

To drum up business, contact the director of media relations, the marketing communications manager and the public relations director of each corporation that interest you. Then pitch to each corporation that you would like to write a media book for select reporters based on you being allowed to interview satisfied customers on why they switched to a particular company's product.

Emphasize details and benefits. Most likely to hire outside publishers and book packagers are new software firms that have public relations departments used to hiring independent contractors. Have some 'mock' sample media books published already to show them your work. You may focus on a particular niche such as mall grand openings.

You'll need a portfolio of your work as an interviewer, writer, and publisher. Practice working with software that controls text and imaging. Then approach potential clients. Have good samples to show.

If you need to use hired printers and interviewers, have your team help you create some samples to show of your memoirs books, gift books, or business case history success story books. You can work entirely in text and photos or vary your output with video and audio multimedia productions or slide presentations for business meetings and conventions.

If you want to publish memoirs books, work with genealogists, family history researchers, wedding or event planners, oral historians, librarians, and publishers. Contact associations related to genealogy or DNA-driven genealogy. Memoirs books can be combined with the design of keepsake albums.

You also can branch into digital scrap booking using photo-imaging software and text with other graphics to produce gift books. Emphasize events, celebrations and commemorations for different stages of life, graduations, and rites of passage if you want to work with families or schools and hospitals instead of manufacturers.

E-Books (Electronic Gift Books)

Promote your book with a much shorter electronic booklet (E-book) containing material about your lengthy book. Readers let you take your favorite books and magazines in digital form, usually saved as PDF files. These types of books are lighter to carry than the average paperback book. Most clients asking you to publish a memoirs book will not want an E-book or electronic book. However, in addition to a printed paperback or hard cover book, you might want to put an electronic book on a CD or DVD and send it along with the book for those who like to read electronic books (E-books) in handheld devices.

To create an E-book, all you need to do with your written book that says it's copyrighted in your name with the year, is save it in digital format such as a Microsoft Word document cut and pasted into Microsoft Front Page software (that creates files compatible with Web sites).

You then save the document as a Web page. When you've finished creating your Web page in Front Page software or used one of the free Web site services online, you just upload or send your book to the Web page. You can view it there or download it and save it on a disk or in your computer.

Use your search engine to find which sites offer free Web space for your book. Also you can contact an e-publisher online that already provides a Web site to showcase the memoirs book. If you use a print on demand publisher, the charge can range from 300 to 700 dollars to set up your book.

Some publishers also charge you a monthly or annual fee per book just to host it on their Web site or keep it posted with major distributors online. To avoid these types of costs, buy your own print on demand equipment and publish one memoirs book at a time for each client. If you have only a few clients at one time, you'd only have to print a few copies for each client's circle of family and friends.

You control how many clients you want to take at one time, like a literary agent or event planner. If you are a wedding planner or genealogist you might want to add a sideline of publishing memoirs books. People who work with older adults also might have an interest in interviewing and presenting life stories in life long learning settings from senior centers to extended studies programs at universities for active people in retirement.

Adult continuing education classes and gerontologists as well as family historians may all have an interest in memoirs books. It's not only for older adults, but for new parents documenting a child's growth stages or teenagers marking the taking on of responsibility. All these life stages can be incorporated into such a gift book.

E books are read with E-book readers. These are usually free, downloadable software that enables a viewer to read an E-book. Examples of E-book readers that are free and available on the Web include Adobe Reader, which is free and downloadable at: http://www.adobe.com/products/acrobat/readstep2.html. Microsoft E-book reader is at the Web site: http://www.microsoft.com/reader/default.asp.

Many popular and/or best-selling books have been formatted to be read by E-book reader software. You can use the free E-book readers online by downloading them or buy professional-type E-book reading software such as eReader Pro for Palm Os. That Web site is at: http://www.ereader.com/products/ereader/pro.

Some people use hand-held devices such as Pocket PC to read electronic books. Other people prefer to listen to an audio book instead of reading text on a computer screen or on a hand-held device's small screen. Audio gift books may be narrated and saved as MP3 files so that people can buy the book to download on an iPod or other mobile listening or viewing device.

Audio books may be saved on a CD or DVD or uploaded to the Web as an audio podcast which is an audio file under compression. The MP3 audio file takes up less bandwidth space online than other types of audio files. There are numerous E-book publishers online, but you can obtain E-book publishing software and circulate your own gift books. The most popular way to market a gift book is to have text and photos that can be handed down to future generations as keepsakes and heirlooms.

3

DESCRIPTION OF BOOK PUBLICITY BUSINESS
Creating Free Book Publicity Infomercials Online and On Disc Home-Grown Broadcasting of Online Book Publicity Techniques

The Video Book Publicity Infomercial

What's the newest trend in book publicity? Books are in demand on specialized memoirs, chick-lit, hen-lit, and crone-lit. Men's adventure and how-to remain stable. The average man commuting or traveling listens to the radio, audio recordings, or reads newspapers. Most publishers do research on the demographics of who is reading their books and other publications. For example, research done by Penguin books found that "men who are seen reading a book are more attractive to the opposite sex." This tidbid appears at: the British online publication, Guardian Unlimited, at: http://books.guardian.co. uk/departments/generalfiction/story/0,6000,1233121,00.html in an article titled, "You Couldn't Make it Up," by Jonathan Heawood. The article is on the subject of getting men to read fiction.

Regarding women's literature, publishers and agents currently are looking for women's reading material and the variety of factual, adventure, and how-to men's interest reading, especially audio books that men listen to while driving. For the women's markets, chick lit is written for female readers up to age 30. Hen lit targets women in their forties and fifties.

Chock-lit is directed at women over age 60. (Chock-lit usually reaches women in the age group 65 to 85+ as consumers of "bitter-sweet and dark books that can be habit-forming, yet as anti-aging as pure, anti-oxidant chocolate without the added 'butter fat.' Books in the chock-lit category concretely (without theory) detail commitment and faith. Chock-lit books are about putting food on the table—pulling one's weight, and keeping the family together.

Like real chocolate, the hidden element in chock-lit feels like a dose of oxytocin. That's the hormone best known for its role in inducing labor that influences our ability to bond with others, according to researchers doing a preliminary study in 1999 at the University of California, San Francisco.

That oxytocin study appeared in the July 1999 issue of *Psychiatry*. Researchers looked at the biological basis for human attachment and bonding. Oxytocin is associated with the ability to maintain interpersonal relationships and psychological boundaries with other people that are considered healthy. Chock-lit is about continuing or establishing healthy boundaries about integrity, independence, and joy.

Chock-lit moves women from despair to integrity. The genre of healthy interpersonal relationships and boundaries is of great interest to women over age 65 that read or listen to audio books. Self-help books as well as fiction and memoirs also may be in this category. Chock-lit books reveal a lasting, a pure kind of love, stability, and commitment.

Men's lit is cock-lit, referring to rooster power and the alpha male—human or animal. The genre includes adventure-action 'cock tales' showcasing mixed cocktails of popular brews from sports, adventure, travel, spy stories, science fiction, horror, competition, business, science, and winning technology to how-to lit, whether fiction or nonfiction.

How do you publicize and promote your chock-lit genre book? The post-retirement aged female stereotype caricature is supposedly interested in reading large-print books, viewing informational or armchair travel documentaries, or viewing DVD documentaries in a specialized area of expertise, such as fitness aimed at the age group, history, local history, archaeology, gardening, hobbies, recreational vehicle living or travel, volunteer work, life-long learning opportunities, religious, retirement and vacation real estate, political clubs, history, nutrition, and leisure activities books.

Audio book selections include instruction on world affairs, genealogy, historical facts, weird news, religious and inspirational books, respite activities, friendship groups, music, art, care-giving, and other subjects of interest to this age group. You find the hidden markets and interests by taking surveys at senior community centers. Find the hidden and niche markets based on interests of special groups. Ask people what makes them laugh and what answers they want to find from books or videos.

Talk to people at senior centers, assisted living apartments, and retirement homes, including the realtors. Interview people on what they like to read, listen to, or watch. What information do they want in your local area? Book purchase information by zip code and age demographics are kept by many publishers. Make use of this information before you start a campaign to reach your intended audiences.

Be sure to research the interests of this age group for what they really want to read by visiting leisure, travel, nutritional, informational, residential, and fun-and-hobby groups for this age group. Not all of them want the usual senior publication news on healthcare information because they read that in other publications. What escape literature do they want? What other informational literature do they read? Is it history? What type of entertainment do they want to experience? Look at the trends, recreational spending, and hobby markets.

If you have a new angle or a hidden niche market for these types of books, such as self-help directed to women of a particular age group, try publicizing your book using the online infomercial, a new type of Web log (blog) that also appears for direct mail marketing on DVD or CD. Study the current trend in book buying by book sellers before producing your video and/or audio book infomercial.

For free book publicity use compressed video files of your book publicity and marketing home-grown infomercial that is made available to small mobile players such as cell phones and iPod-like devices. You upload it free of cost to you to your Web site. Your target market downloads it. Any video or audio file uploaded may also be saved to a DVD and CD and sold on your Web site or on most online auction sites such as eBay. These files could be turned into a documentary video if you have a collection of files or interviews of authors or can offer a course in a subject in which you have expertise—such as the subject of your book.

You can list your book with an online print on demand publisher. Or publish it yourself as an 'e-book.' Use PDF software to create e-books. For paperback books, have a printer make you a few paperback copies to test market how your books sell. Don't invest money in publishing your book unless there's a demand for the subject in a specialized, niche, or hidden market. If you want almost free publicity, promotion, or marketing, your own Web site and a few DVDs or CDs will get you started. Compare what this costs to the average $21,000 a publicist might charge to promote your book on a variety of TV and radio shows. One good DVD or CD (or tape) sent to a radio or TV station along with a paper press kit can help you learn and use the strategies of an expensive book publicist.

What you're actually paying for is not the simple, low cost of making press kits or getting a person to mail your CD, tape, or DVD to a radio or TV station. You're paying primarily for the contacts that the expensive publicist has—the connections. Anyone can duplicate press releases and mail them out, even you, the expert and author. It's the connections that count.

Your job is to make those connections yourself. It doesn't take money to make connections, unless you have to buy fancy clothing to work the room at meetings the expensive publicist attends. It's far less expensive to join the professional associations the publicist belongs to and work the room yourself. If you want to avoid paying the fees to join the organizations, or if you don't qualify, but still have expertise in the area of your book, then offer yourself to organize and/or to speak on panels at meetings at those associations. Nobody will notice you or take you seriously if you only sit in the audience and listen. Get on the panel or organize a panel.

When you are booked to speak, you're taken seriously. If you're sitting in the audience, you're equal to everyone else at the meeting, and you have to prove your credibility in 20 seconds. Speakers don't have to defend their credibility. If you can't speak in public, offer to organize the panel and recruit the speakers. While interview them, you can mention your book and slip them a CD or DVD of your promotional material or documentary about your book and/or the subject in your book.

Promote your book at low or no cost with a video pod cast on your Web site. Anyone with a digital video camcorder, microphone, computer and some technical savvy can launch an Internet video pod cast show to inform, direct or enlighten. You can offer foresight, insight, or hindsight. Open a business or find a job delivering digital video recordings—usually free—as pod casts.

If you want to make money with video pod casting, offer to sell a sponsor's publicity and advertising on your video, or an author's creative works, interviews, or sermons. You can even show people how to fill out tax forms using a video pod cast as instruction on most any subject people can learn independently.

People who subscribe to video pod casts usually want to view for free. You can charge for a course to train or teach a class by video lecture and/or demonstration, but what if you want an actual paid job in video pod casting? And can you make more money in video than in the older, audio MP3 file 'radio' pod casting?

Check out the RSSJobs Web site at: http://www.rssjobs.com/index.jsp?cid=10. Careers in video pod casting are beginning to bloom as seen by a variety of pod casting associations, news publications, and career information. Even job listings unrelated to pod casting are 'broadcast' by RSS feeds. You can create your own job in pod casting by showing others how to find passion in their careers and making motivational video pod casts, but what if you want to use video pod casting to actually get hired? Are there jobs in video pod casting yet? Or is the field still primarily for entrepreneurs on the Web?

Any job you'd get right now would be as a content producer for a large news corporation, as an online journalist, or in the technical end of setting up pod cast technology for larger corporations in information dissemination and news broadcasting or at colleges that offer courses online.

To get into the field, you might start with your own video pod casting Web site offering to help others find highly valued hard-to-find information or data so new the media hasn't seen it yet. Video pod casting is a font-loading ancillary like a newsletter-type trade journal particular to a specific industry. An example would be a video pod cast about the latest news on XYZ widget manufacture concerning what deals the competition are signing or what's new in a specific industry. The difference between a slow, paper print industrial newsletter or trade journal and a video pod cast is the speed the news is delivered, fresh from an RSS feed.

When you use RSS feeds to look for any type of job, you use an RSS Reader to make Web browsing less time consuming. An RSS feed researches every RSS capable site you want to read at one time. The feed gives you a list of everything on the site. The RSS feed also lets you know which items you've already read. Then it highlights the updated and new Web sites that you haven't seen.

Not only can you search for a job, but you can find a job, make a career, or open your own business writing, producing, and syndicating video pod casts. What's in it for you? And how can you compete with the huge news TV conglomerates already distributing free news video pod casts on the Web? Pod casting also is a global pulpit. Churches are using video pod casts.

Aren't the news organizations merging, downsizing, and employing fewer newsgathering personnel in favor of expanding news syndication channels? Video pod casts are not only for news and opinion. Compressed video files on Web sites that can be downloaded to mobile players such as video iPods and comparable devices are wonderful tools for learning and creative innovation. Video content finally has been democratized.

Pod casting, a term originally based on the name for Apple's portable media player and similar devices from its competition, allows customers to download audio and/or video segments for free to their computers and portable devices. The popularity of home-grown broadcasters is revolutionizing movie making. In a parallel information dissemination industry, print-on-demand publishing revolutionized the ability of freelance journalists to become published book authors.

Here are the steps you can follow to learn how to open a business producing short video segments that can play on viewers' mobile players or personal computers. These video segments can be how-to information, interviews with authors, courses, tutorials, religious sermons, life stories, animation/cartoons, games, plays, narrated, dramatized novels, science, travel, parenting skills, children's programming, music, dance, poetry, infomercials, reality TV, historical, news, opinions, health, nutrition, exotic, ancient, or traditional ethnic weddings, rites of passage celebrations, reviewing movies, books or other creative projects such as architecture, housing, or virtual reality, sports, competitions, job interviews, exercise, comedy, or financial advice.

Broadcast commentary or conduct interviews about business, politics, global trade, environmental science, organizational communications management, or anything that is popular culture, high-brow, ethnic traditions, folklore, comedy and humor. Research what topic is most in demand by niche audiences compared to what is requested by the general public.

Your video pod casts about your book for publicity purposes may be aimed at various age groups, children, adolescents, parents, honeymooners, young married couples, middle-aged empty nesters, or mature adults and gerontologists. If you do your market research before you start, you'll find an audience or special interest group for your expertise or field of concentration.

Offer an alternative from the usual cooking shows seen on satellite TV, such as special diets or vegan cooking, or ethnic and holiday cooking not seen on TV, such as cooking without added trans-fats, salt or sugar, or cooking for metabolic syndrome. Or offer after-school tutoring or home-schooling with videos of trips to local museums. Perhaps you want to show video segments of what's it like to be old or how parents can solve problems with new babies or pet training. You're the expert in the topic. Videos can serve hobbies such as scrap booking and quilting or hiking local trails. Show what work life is about in different careers aimed at young people deciding on what college major to choose.

The popularity of home-based entrepreneurial broadcasting revolutionized the creative expression industry. Home-grown radio shows, called pod casts are saved as audio MP3 files and uploaded to the Web. Bandwidth-saving video compression software takes up far less space than the usual .mpeg or Windows Media Video (WMV) files uploaded to the Web.

Following in the steps of the largest news conglomerates that feature online video news segments, home-grown audio broadcasting soon evolved into online, downloadable video. From school lectures, politics, and pet training to music, comedy, and life stories, video segments can be compressed and saved to small, mobile players such as video iPods.

News programs are among the most popular pod casts, but amateurs have changed pod casting into a global phenomenon. Video pod casts can help you learn a foreign language, plan travel, or entertain kids with movies or games in an auto's back seat while you drive.

What sells best to the general public in video pod casting is how-to information specific to very specialized niche areas. Examples would be how to knit a certain type of garment, how to home-school children in a specific subject, how to build a tool shed, dog house, or repair a broken toilet, sink, or other appliance.

If you think video pod casting will follow the type of entertainment that's on satellite TV stations, you're correct. The music videos, the talking-head lectures from distance learning universities, and the general fare that you see on TV and pay TV will be what will also be offered on video pod cast. However, you'll see the niche, underground, and hidden markets as well.

What' you'll see on video pod casts are tutoring in high-school or middle-school subjects as well as university courses, weddings and funeral eulogies, pet training and house-sitting, numerology and astrology, psychic readers, the usual pornography videos, and religious programming. You'll also see more distance learning and home schooling alternatives, more travel and extreme telecommuting to one's job or business from anywhere on the globe with Internet access on the go.

Video content competes with the entire entertainment industry and schools. To sell your video content, you need to market your video clips as if they were self-published books competing with all the books on bookstore shelves. But even in the book industry, a little more than 55% of books are lined on the bookshelves.

The rest are sold in niche, hidden markets. Examples would be sports, gift, and specialty stores, book fairs, school librarians, and in specialty catalogues. School librarians buy contemporary controversies and issues in the news books and pamphlets that students use to research term papers.

Follow the market that school librarians buy from. Lead with video pod casts. Provide research and resources that help students organize their assignments, term papers, and debates. Follow the money and the markets used by self-published book authors that are successful in marketing their wares. Market your video pod casts—to niche audiences and markets by launching your content in the media.

Educators, preachers, advertisers, counselors, consultants, lawyers, doctors, dancers, artists, musicians, politicians, historians, librarians, movie producers, documentarians, life story videographers, chefs, knitters, crafters, dog trainers, house remodelers, contractors, strippers, pornographers, social scientists, radio talk show hosts, demographers, novelists, scientists, lecturers, travel agents, professional travelers, resort owners, publicists, public speakers, activists, infomercial producers, journalists, playwrights, parents, students, sales representatives, song writers, rappers, and poets (and anyone else with video content) have equal access to video pod cast production and content creation.

The common denominator of what might sell as video pod cast content and become a viable business is whether the content offers the audience what the specific audience wants to see. Some of the best markets are how-to videos that show people how to solve a problem and get results step-by-step so the viewers can follow.

Here's how to start a career, get a job, or open a variety of businesses in video pod casting. It's about putting up on the Internet's Web video content that anyone with a device such as a video iPod can download video content. If you want a job in video pod casting, you can work for the companies that make the equipment—hardware or software, or those who produce the video content. Or you can start your own business by putting your own video on your Web site. All you need is a camcorder, a computer, and a software program that edits your video so you can create a video pod cast online.

Content is in demand now, that video pod casting is still in its infancy. So there's room to jump in at any age and from any niche.

You can still go the relatively "old fashioned" route for your latest music television productions (MTV) if you're a musician by looking at the content available through music stores online such as the iTunes Music Store. Or you can put your own content online for streaming video that's downloadable to devices such as iPods and its competition.

School lectures, foreign language learning, and anything that can be taught are ripe for video pod casting. You can open your own school and teach what you're expert in, without having to show your degrees and licenses, as long as a license or degree is not required for the subject you're teaching. An example would be on how to knit dog sweaters or how to publicize your book. You can interview authors and put up a speaker's panel that people can download on life experiences.

Examples of a video pod cast movie would be *Crookz*, a video pod cast (iTMS link) spoof of *Cops*, is offered at the iTunes Music Store. View what's out there, and then make your own movies, documentaries, or other video offerings.

What you need to start your own video pod casting production business is a Web camera called a 'webcam' and a digital video camera, called a "DV camera." Creating a video pod cast is the first step in becoming a video producer on a neighborhood budget.

Pod cast listening is not for music fans any more. Students want to see lectures in video. Older adults want to see their life stories on an iPod or other small, lightweight, mobile device. Children want to see video while they sit in the back seat of cars when on long vacation rides. Adults want to see automobile travel videos showing them where they are going.

So by democratizing video content on the Web with video pod casting enterprises and services, the whole movement of video production for all is following in the path of print on demand published authors. And you need to market your video pod casts much in the same way as print-on-demand published authors market their books to specialized, niche audiences and markets.

It's a revolution that you want to join, moving from print-on-demand text books whose content is not controlled by copyeditors from major publishing houses to public speakers whose content is not controlled by major news media conglomerates. Now we have video content producers whose visual imagery is not controlled.

This has all come about because there are far more book authors and video producers in the masses than there are room for the converging publishing houses and large video production corporations to allow every author or producer publication or dissemination. Now everyone potentially has a voice and video content that can be heard around the world.

Blogging isn't enough because many video blogs lack credibility in the mainstream media. Video pod casting now has become simple for non-technical people to publish creative projects online. With less people reading books, and more books being published by print-on-demand authors, the door is open for businesses to step in and offer what people want: visual learning.

Video offers those who want to learn by seeing, or see how hands-on learning is actually done. Text almost always moves to audio and then to video in a learning situation.

You're still competing with the entertainment industry just as computerized interactive learning modules of the 1996 era competed with textbook publishing. According to the Apple Insider article titled, *Apple Files For Pod casting Trademark*, September 14, 2005 posted at the Web site: http://www.appleinsider.com/article.php?id=1271om, Apple has applied for trademarks relating to the word iPod cast.

If you're starting a business or looking for a job or career in the world of video pod casting, you need to list as many forms of video entertainment, learning, and leisure that would make money as video pod casts. It helps if you can find celebrities to endorse your how-to, entertainment, or infomercial video pod cast.

You can produce and upload video content for other entrepreneurs, including vendors at trade shows and expos. Let's look at how to product a typical 28 ½ minute video pod cast infomercial for a Web site, DVD, or CD used to market a product.

If you're going to make money working in the field of video pod casting, one of the most commercial ways related to schooling or training is the infomercial for a product. Although no audience would pay to watch an infomercial, your advertiser certainly will.

Your book publicity clients could be corporations, advertising agencies, publicists, book authors, doctors and other healthcare professionals in practice with advice to sell, and manufacturers as well as technical and business training schools. Here's how you begin to develop your video pod cast infomercial.

The Video Pod Cast Book Publicity Infomercial

1. Produce Video and MP3 Pod-casts and DVDs: Internet Video Infomercials Solving Problems, Revealing Results & Showing People Benefits and Profits

2. Let the viewers follow your instructions step-by-step

3. Show Advantages

Keep everything you show in a video grouped in threes. People remember three items grouped together. Information given in threes impacts the memory and stays within the average attention span for watching a video segment.

Infomercial pod casting is do-it-yourself online radio, which can also be put on disks such as DVDs or CDs. You create video pod casts as well as backup MP3 audio files that people can download from CDs, DVDs, or their computers through your Web site. Pod casting also is about listening to your infomercials on iPods and other audio players. Making videos for pod casts as well as MP3 audio files are easier and cheaper to produce than recording videos. If you want to go the video route, choose an industrial-quality camcorder, not an amateur quality.

According to the October 18, 2005 article, *Creating a Video Pod cast on Mac Os X,* Apple has added a tutorial at http://www.apple.com/quicktime/tutorials/ videopod casts.html to its site giving directions you easily can follow to create a video pod cast using Mac OS X and QuickTime Pro. You'll learn how to use QuickTime 7 Pro to make an .m4v file that has H.264 video and AAC audio, compatible with iTunes and the latest iPods.

To produce professional-quality pod casts, you need an RSS feed. Check out the site at: http://www.masternewmedia.org/news/2005/03/22/ where to find the right.htm. There are search engines and directories entirely devoted to the indexing of RSS feeds. Read eWeek at: http://www.eweek.com/. Build your own RSS feed for your Web site. Go to *Feed for All RSS Feed Creation Tool* at: http://www.feedforall.com/. Pay attention to the *FeedForAll* Web site if you want to learn how to create, edit, manage, and publish RSS feeds.

According to the site, RSS is the standard for content distribution and syndication. The reason you create an RSS feed is to keep visitors to your Web site informed of current material. New RSS feeds can be quickly and easily created with *FeedForAll.* Advanced features enable you to easily and rapidly create professional looking RSS feeds. Also, read the informative book titled, *Syndicating Web Sites with RSS Feeds for Dummies* by Ellen Finkelstein, ISBN: 0764588486, published 2005.

Learn about pod casting because you can build your business around your own pod casts. This is one more way to show people how to cut expenses. Your audio books also can be pod casted as MP3 audio files and narrated as video pod casts saved as Windows Media files or mpeg, or any other file extension commonly accepted by the audience for video pod casts. Where you find this information is in the numerous video pod casts magazines and e-zines on the Web. In your search engine use the key words "video pod casting how-to publications" and take your pick of this burgeoning information industry.

Another way to publish audio books as narrated video pod casts is to promote business clients by having dramatizations and public speakers or panels and interviews as video pod casts. Author interviews are a good way to start interviewing people on video or dramatizing documentaries from real life or life story applications. Streaming video and DVD multimedia also are other possibilities.

You can use pod casting to create travel or neighborhood walking and touring guides, talk about any subject, or show people by example how to cut expenses.

It's about making your audio files mobile. People not only listen to current information at Web sites, but also can listen to advertising at trade shows. Pod cast online or on disk infomercials and instruction on any subject, including how to start niche-market businesses.

Show others how to save money by shopping for shelf-pulls and overstocked items at hidden markets. Help your audience find little-known opportunities. Offer tips for making non-toxic cleaning products from basic household ingredients, spices, or natural scents.

Sure, you can record to CDs, DVDs, or your Web site, but pod casting is the current trend—broadcasting news from your Web site or downloading the audio MP3 file to an iPod or other audio device.

Downloading video via portable devices is here now. Pod casting in MP3 audio to Web sites is like 1940 radio compared to current high definition television. Video is as mobile as audio is mobile. People listen to talk or music pod casting and radio while driving, but view video pod casts when at school lectures, in libraries, while hiking, and when riding public in transportation. An example would be while taking a long overseas or cross-country flight.

Use pod casting for training sessions. Put travel guides in the pod casting formats so people can download the video MP4 and/or audio MP3 files as they walk through various neighborhoods. The pod cast video promises mobility of viewing dramatizations and documentaries or listening to hundreds of songs or lectures, books, or training materials, even learning foreign languages saved in the MP3 file format and also pod casted from your Web site as news or easy listening. Anything that can be recorded in video can be viewed as a video pod cast and used as instruction or entertainment. Combined, you get 'edutainment.'

Your next step is to develop direct mail copywriting on pod casts or DVDs to show people how to cut expenses. Infomercial producers can write or hire a freelancer to write infomercials sharing information with people on how to cut expenses and get higher quality goods from hidden markets such as shelf pulls and overstocked items or wholesale items that may be ordered by anyone.

Video pod casting infomercials are similar in production techniques to the "cable TV" and trade show-style infomercial. These 28 1/8 minute-in-length ads broadcast direct mail marketing programs and track TV-shopping audiences. Direct mail copywriting and producing for video telemarketing is one of the highest paying freelance writing available. The manufacturers of the product pay you to pod cast the infomercial or produce it on a DVD.

Writers who specialize in writing direct mail copy for print mail order and video infomercials headed for cable, Internet, or Satellite television can create thriving writing and production businesses catering to telemarketing and mail order corporate clients and copywriters. Another career track is to write in-house for firms who manage telemarketing.

For those who enjoy the music business, contact musicians, and open a business that sells their music to the movie industry. Another venue is medical marketing. Write reviews of audio books and videos online or for magazines.

You have a choice of either writing or producing an infomercial or doing both. An infomercial is a long commercial video, running to a half-hour in length, but usually precisely timed at 28 1/2 minutes. It's created to sell by telemarketing. The best infomercial producers use around 400 cuts with music. Many people are interviewed in the infomercial.

Infomercials wait for audience response. The viewer orders the product or service by phoning a toll-free number or sending money to an address flashed on the screen to order the product.

A demonstration video script that solicits audience response through telemarketing on cable stations, or a videobiography script for non-broadcast television personifies and proves a point. Read the book Response Television, by John Witek, Crain Books, Chicago, IL (1981), to get an idea of how response television works. Also read Television and Cable Contacts, Larimi Communications Associates, Ltd., 5 W. 37th St., New York, NY 10018 (212) 819-9310.

INCOME POTENTIAL:

Video producers of infomercials charge by the hour plus production expenses. The current fees vary with location and complexity of job required. Some producers charge $35 and up an hour plus expenses of production. Check the current rate in your area charged by your competition. Check the current rate in your area charged by your competition. Others create a budget with all expenses first, including cost of tape and crew's requirements, then add an hourly fee, plus the post-production editing and distribution expenses.

BEST LOCALE TO OPERATE THE BOOK PUBLICITY BUSINESS:

Infomercials can be produced on-site at any location of a business. Being near your clients helps. Big centers for production of infomercials include Los Angeles, San Francisco, San Diego, New York, Chicago, and Orlando, Florida. San Francisco is the hub for multimedia and interactive infomercials, including the San Jose/Silicon Valley area for the software book publicity infomercials.

TRAINING REQUIRED:

It's best to take courses in video production or read books on how to produce infomercials before you begin. Join professional associations and volunteer. Attend trade shows for infomercial producers and watch a variety of infomercials. Study the number of cuts in popular infomercials.

GENERAL APTITUDE OR EXPERIENCE:

Creativity, imagination, and experience with a variety of sales and marketing alternatives are beneficial. You're always offering the benefits and advantages of a product. Therefore, sales and marketing training combined with video production experience or coursework is best. It will save you money if you can write your own scripts as well.

EQUIPMENT NEEDED:

You'll need your Internet or digital video camera attached to your PC and hooked into your Internet Service Provider, narrator, host, editing equipment or access to video editing services, your video crew, and a good sound stage or work area to tape the commercial. There should be an audience, and special effects to show the phone number and address where television viewers can phone or send in the order for the product. You'll need to hire operators who take the call on a 24-hour basis.

Ask your client whether it is appropriate to charge phone expenses to your client's budget for the type of contract you have to promote your own book versus your client's books or videos. It depends on what you have been asked to do for your client. If you're only publicizing your own book, you pay your own phone, postage, and package handling expenses. Are you acting as a literary agent or offering editorial services? Or are you publicizing someone else's books? Or simply promoting and marketing your own book?

You'll also need a computer to track your customers so you'll have a list of television viewers who shop after watching infomercials. Watch infomercials and note the special effects used.

OPERATING YOUR BUSINESS:

Escape doesn't work in a how-to infomercial. A viewer watching a tape on on how to buy real estate doesn't want to be swept away to a castle in a fantasy setting for long. It might work in an infomercial selling a general idea or theory that applies to many people in many jobs, such as how to get power and success in relationships or careers.

Infomercial scriptwriters don't resort to gimmicks. They give information for decision-making by presenting the points in as straightforward a manner as possible for intelligent decision-making. The questions of who, what, how, why, where, and when are answered as in an in-depth straight news article.

The viewers want to be well-informed before they spend their life-savings, their "blood money" on a cable television advertisement. They are wondering whether they can buy it cheaper in a store or at the swap meet as they dial the phone.

Will they be hit with a handling and shipping charge that raises the cost another ten dollars? The customer wonders what happens when they give their credit card number to a total stranger on a toll-free number across the country. Who else will have access to that credit card number?

Some beginning infomercial writers turn out scripts that use the techniques of a Hollywood filmmaker to make people watch. Instead, they should be writing to make people buy one brand over another. There's no correlation between a person liking an infomercial and being sold by it.

Use direct, tough commercials because they work. Hard hitting, informative infomercials and commercials sell a product where the customer is watching solely to get information. Soft-sell imagery doesn't work in infomercials like they do in 30-second commercials selling the imagery of the pleasure of eating a bar of chocolate.

Infomercials emphasize believability, clarity, and simplicity over creativity. Don't write confusion into a script by putting in too much dazzle, sensation, and entertainment that overpower the information and message. The emphasis is on helping the customer make a sensible purchase.

Small budgets often do better than big ones in the infomercial for cable T.V. production. TV's longest-running commercial which offers a record set of "150 Music Masterpieces" through mail order by phoning a toll-free number, was made in 1968 for only $5,000. It sold millions of dollars worth of records through mail order because of this one television advertisement.

There are a dozen types of infomercials. They include the following:

1) Product demonstration.

Scripts are used for trade show exhibition and continuous loop playing.

2) Testimonials.

Real people on tape add credibility for a product.

3) The pitchman.

A straight narrator delivers a sales pitch on the product to give vital information in the shortest period of time. This is a talking head short that should only be used for brief commercials or a scene in an infomercial of less than 10 seconds.

4) Slice-of-life.

This is a dramatization between two people and a product.

In an infomercial or training script, the dramatization is a container that can be used to portray true-life events to teach people how to make decisions or how and where to get information.

5) Socio-economic lifestyle.

The social class of the user is emphasized to show how the product fits into a certain economic class such as blue collar, yuppie, new parent, career woman climbing the ladder, or senior citizen retiree.

Examples are Grey Poupon, the upper-caste mustard selling to social climbers and Miller Beer dedicated to blue collar workers celebrating the idea of the working man and woman being rewarded for hard labor with a cold beer.

6) Animation.

Cartoon infomercials sell to children in school and at home. Adults become impatient watching a cartoon demonstration. Animation is expensive to produce for cable television. Use it only to sell to children or to sell supplies to professional animators in non-broadcast demonstration video tapes used to sell products through mail order or at an animator's trade show or exhibit.

7) Jingles.

Lyrics work in short commercials because they are remembered. A best-selling board game called 'Adverteasements' makes players recall all the advertising jingles and trivia information from their past. Ask any person in the street to sing the jingle of an advertisement, and chances are he or she will remember the jingle.

8) The mini-feature film with visual effects.

(Case studies don't report that action set in fantasy 'scapes' sells more products.)

9) Humor.

In short commercials humor works well as in "Where's the beef?" In long infomercials, it distracts from the information. Some humor can be used to prove a point in a long commercial. Infomercials sell credibility. Humor distracts from believability.

10) Serial characters.

A fictional character appearing in print ads and short commercials, such as Mr. Whipple or the Pillsbury Doughboy, is very effective.

In a longer commercial, viewers will soon tire of the fantasy character and change the channel. Infomercial viewers want to see real people's testimonials, people like themselves with whom they can identify. Keep the fictional character out of a true-story informational commercial. People want references. Give them references who testify why the product works so well.

11. Tell-me-why infomercials.

Give people reasons why and how the product works as it does and why they should buy it. In an infomercial for cable, obtaining "tell me why" information is the reason people watch in the first place. Viewers want the writer to go ahead. Make your information convincing by providing credible facts with resources that can be checked and verified.

12. Feelings, Intuition, and Sensation.

Tug at my guilt-strings. Persuasive infomercials use feelings backed up by logical points that prove a point about a product. Move the viewer by writing genuine emotional copy. A dramatization showing a person shedding tears of joy that someone has telephoned long distance is persuasive. It makes viewers feel guilty they haven't called their mother in years. Infomercials emphasize demonstrations, testimonials, pitchpersons, and straight-sell formulas.

A little emotion within a dramatization can be very persuasive. Either it will sell the product or evoke guilt and anger in the viewer for not having lived up to expectations. The viewer could have conflicting feelings.

He may not want to call someone he dislikes because of having suffered emotional abuse in that person's presence. A whole slew of nasty or sentimental feelings totally unrelated to selling the product can be unleashed by one emotional scene in a commercial.

The emotional, "tug at my guilt-strings" 'approach' works when selling nostalgia. Emotion persuades people to make more telephone calls, or send more candy and flowers by wire.

Using the emotion strategy in infomercials works well for selling sentiment, communications products, craft and knitting machines, charm bracelets, products for the elderly, or greeting cards. Look at the success of the long-running AT&T commercial, "Reach Out and Touch Someone." Who doesn't remember that command to extravert?

To write an infomercial that sells, first find out the producer's budget. Then deliver a selling message within the budget and time limits. Turn the sound off. Can you still understand what is being sold? Sight and sound works together. Use sound only to explain what the picture is demonstrating.

Keep the pictures simple. Use words to make an impact, the fewer the words, the better. The more complex the graphics, the few the words are used to explain them. Computer graphics, special effects, and animation are expensive. The stand-up presenter and demonstrator cost much less.

Ninety words can be spoken in 60 seconds. Forty-five words can be crammed into 30 seconds. Many 30 and 60-second commercials contain far less words so the viewer can really get the information. Compare this to the print ad which usually runs 1,500 words in a 30-60 second read.

Sell every second the script is on the airwaves. The first four seconds of an infomercial are the same as the headlines of a print ad. The viewer takes four seconds to decide if he/she will sit through the rest of the infomercial or commercial.

Open the infomercial with a real-life situation. It must hook the viewer in those first four seconds. The music and visuals can add the background. The opening is called the cow-catcher. It's supposed to grab the viewer. After seven minutes, the average attention span wanes quickly.

Use motion to keep attention riveted. Show the syrup pouring, the machines working, the demonstrator moving. Let the viewer hear the whirr of the machine as it moves forward. The sound is more appetizing than the look.

Use titles superimposed over the picture to reinforce a sales point not covered in the narration. The address and phone of the company are always superimposed in addition to the narrator's spoken words. What if the viewers are deaf or blind, can they still read or hear the infomercial? Have titles superimposed on the info-mercial saying "Not available in stores," when applicable.

The market for Spanish language infomercials is skyrocketing in the South-west and in California and Mexico. Bilingual video scriptwriters are in demand. In some of the major cities such as Los Angeles and New York, infomercials in several foreign languages are broadcast on cable television's ethnic and foreign language programming stations or on radio.

Some video magazines to sell products are made in two languages, especially to reach the huge Hispanic market in California and the Southwest. Every infomer-cial repeats the product name and selling point several times. Most viewers aren't paying attention when the infomercial comes on. A repetitive script is necessary in this case. The product name and selling point is repeated at the beginning, middle, and end of the infomercial.

Viewers of infomercials get bored quickly if the presenter isn't somewhat different. Use a child who looks five years old, for example, to sell a product emotionally. Have an adult present the points and logic behind the demonstration for credibility.

Show people using the product constantly throughout the infomercial. Product neglect is the primary reason why infomercials don't sell. Show people demonstrating, talking about, and applying the product to many different uses. Proven techniques in print ads also work in television infomercials, such as color reversals, black background with white letters superimposed over a photo, etc. In infomercials, viewers call or write to order the product.

Announce this at the beginning with something like, "Get your pencil and paper ready to take advantage of this one-time offer." Few people sit down in front of a T.V. set with a notepad. It's entertainment time.

The infomercial is an unwanted intrusion that angers a lot of people. Late night infomercials interrupt late night films. People may be grumpy at 3:00 a.m. or 5:00 a.m. when many infomercials are broadcast. Prime-time cable infomercials interrupt the entertainment. Give people a chance to get out of bed or away from the graveyard shift desk clerk slot and get paper and pencil.

Use a celebrity to do a voice-over or on-camera narration. Identify the celebrity by name and superimposed title. In local retail infomercials, give the directions or address of the store.

Short T.V. and radio commercial basic lengths run 10, 30,60, and 120 seconds. Infomercials run 5, and 30 minutes. The 30 minute length actually runs 28 1/2 minutes. Infomercial lengths stop short of 30 minutes or 5 minutes to allow for short commercials to be broadcast before and after the infomercial on cable T.V. stations.

The 10-second commercials identify a product to support another longer commercial. Sometimes two different product companies share one commercial—offering two different products.

Mail order advertisers use 2-minute infomercials on T.V. to be convincing, then follow up the campaign on cable T.V. with a longer infomercial to give more complete product demonstration. Cooking shows that demonstrate appliances such as food choppers are popular.

A short T.V. commercial sticks to one main sales point. Only in five to thirty-minute infomercials and in print brochures is there the time to cover all the points. So the only reason a person watches an infomercial or reads a lengthy sales brochure is to consider the most important points you want to emphasize.

The video script format for infomercials uses the two-column format. Video (visuals) is typed on the left. Audio (sound, music, speech, and special effects) is typed on the right.

The video directors are given in upper and lower case letters. The audio or speaking part is typed in capital letters so the narrator or actor can see the speaking parts stand out for easy reading or memorization.

The visuals show the product demonstration. The narration tells the viewers the unique features and benefits of the product. Don't tell how good it is, tell how it will benefit the viewer.

The ending makes the most impact. A play on words can lend humor to the script if it also lends credibility to the product and emphasizes how the customer will save money and get superior merchandise.

If something is more expensive on T.V. than it is when found in the store, sometimes the customer is persuaded by being told he's worth it. The emotional impact hits home by asking, "Don't you think I'm good enough to deserve this product?" It works particularly well on wives who know their husbands are very tight with money and affection.

The customer's attitude toward infomercials is "When someone starts to make money, someone else will appear to take it away." To combat this psychological attitude, infomercial producers focus on "target marketing." It's the idea of having different promotional videos aimed at various segments of the market.

Software sometimes labeled in artsy language, which simply said is "aiming." In a direct campaign, you target a specific audience of consumers or niche market that includes short news releases explaining the purpose and main pointers in the infomercial. The summary may *aim* an infomercial campaign at doctors by sending video tapes to *hospitals' training departments* and another infomercial campaign aimed at *lawyers*—for the same computer product. You look at what lawyers and doctors have in common—the need for training on software that does *specific tasks* that both lawyers and hospitals' training departments perform.

A writer of infomercial scripts uses numerous testimonials, endorsements, and product claims highlighted by music, hundreds of cuts to the product, to users of the product, to satisfied customers amidst a background of special lighting and entertainment to maintain the viewer's attention for the half-hour commercial.

The average adult's attention span for viewing a non-fiction video is only seven minutes. Cut this to five minutes for children's attention spans. Commercials often are inserted in TV programs after each ten-minute segment.

The quality of an infomercial writer's script can be carefully measured by audience tracking to see how many orders for the product come in at any time. A video demonstration tape or video magazine acts as a company brochure to sell a product requiring non-impulse buying. The customer still has to come into a store or send away for the product, such as real estate.

This is the age of product intelligence for video scriptwriters. Consumers demand real information. Information has turned the word 'sell' into a noun as in information becoming "real sell."

Infomercials on television advertising became popular when the cost of buying time on cable television became low. Advertisers can afford to run five minute to half-hour commercials on cable.

The video scriptwriter of infomercials needs to give complete information and a sales pitch at the same time. Interactive technologies allow viewers at home or corporate viewers at the office or plant to choose which segments of an infomercial they wish to see instead of flipping through a parts catalogue.

Corporate viewers now use their computer keyboards to order products seen on a video tape linked to their computer through desktop video devices. Desktop video enables viewers to interact with a personal computer at home or in the office and with a video cassette tape played on a home or office VCR player and send out orders through a computer modem to anyone's telephone number, usually, with a toll-free 800 number.

Consumers are hungry for information by which they make decisions. A video writer puts in information and leaves out the jingles and other frills seen on short T.V. broadcast commercials that imprint the brain and wring the emotions.

In one survey, 68 percent of viewers said that short commercials don't give any points about a product. They only create an image. An infomercial is designed to give important points. It's similar to a product demonstration tape script or an instructional video.

Information alone is not remembered. The viewer will always take images emotionally. A creative writer's tendency to achieve dramatic results by waiving the rules works in short commercials where style and form evoke more emotions than substance.

For example, a black background with white lettering where the white lettering is printed over or with a photo background imprints the brain. People remember a reversed color advertisement better than white background with black letters.

The success rates of infomercials that break the rules are unpredictable. Video copywriters use what works to obtain consistently high sales results. In any bookstore the how-to books dominate and appeal to the mass audience reader. People come in for straight information when they want to make decisions on what to buy or how to build it.

HOW TO WRITE THE SCRIPTS FOR THE VIDEOS YOU WILL PRODUCE:

Use symbolism and metaphor in your infomercial. A script can visualize the waves of the ocean, flow of a river, or waterfall, or ticking of a clock with the handles speeded up to show the passage of time or evolution of a species. A toy crane truck can recreate an accident to teach decision-making.

Use symbolism and metaphor on camera to re-create the events of your life as they flow, perhaps, by showing the flowing river near a client's hometown. Symbolism creates new meanings in a script. The symbol must be recognizable by the audience and cross-cultural. What works in one culture may be taboo in another. Find out what the taboo colors are for the country the video will go to.

For example, in Saudi Arabia, red is a taboo color. Writing is never shown in red ink. In China certain shades of blue signify death. Exporters who featured blue dishes in China found the products didn't sell because of the shade. Color symbols are important if the tape is headed for export.

In video production, symbolism is used in corporate history videos to show the change of a company's product. It can also show someone age on camera or grow up from childhood. Metaphor compares a person to another object.

In an infomercial (to publicize someone's color consulting franchise whose logo is a rose), show the main character or proprietor to symbolize her logo. She is like a rose and is selling a product that is supposed to remind the viewer of everything a rose symbolizes. The product is like a rose. It's colorful,-sweet-scented, and blooming.

To symbolize this imagery in a video script, cut to the leading character's velvet, black hair and pouting, red lips. Then cut to a bouquet of dark, red rose. Go back to the character walking through her home dressed in the same shade of red to form a certain imagery of the soul of Spain or a wild, Irish rose.

Then a quick cut to her business, a color consulting firm, where she's matching the red shades of a lipstick to a client's best colors. Then cut to your logo stationery, a red rose. A final cut to a bouquet of red roses is placed in her arms as she welcomes her new baby home, named Rose. (The client may want the baby to turn into the business logo on camera.)

HOW DO ALL THESE CONTAINERS FIT TOGETHER TO PRODUCE AN INFOMERCIAL?

A video script's design is composed of all those containers, edited together, fitted side by side. The important points plus the container adds up to (or equals) the springboard.

A creative springboard is the sum total of each container and each point combined, edited together, fitted so that the whole video or film flows like one piece of cloth with no seams or hanging threads. Is the script sound-oriented for radio, or audio-text? A visually-oriented script with fewer words is filled with symbolism and metaphor instead of straight points. Which creative springboard does the producer define?

Time is budget. A sound-oriented or verbal script's purpose is to <u>persuade</u>, to inform, to warn, to close a sale, to obtain feedback, or to be remembered. A visually-oriented script is there to entertain, evoke emotions, and imprint the imagery on a viewer's brain which will be recalled later without thinking. It's subliminal.

Verbal-oriented video scripts offer information that enable viewers to make intelligent decisions about a product or service. Subliminals imbedded in an infomercial are never revealed verbally. Infomercials and information videos work on the left-hemisphere of the brain, the logical, analytical, decision-making side that seeks verbal information.

Visual-oriental scripts work on the right hemisphere of the brain that controls emotions and imagery. That's where subliminals are imbedded, and art forms evoke feelings.

One day a viewer daydreams about that candy bar shown on television next to the image of a beautiful woman in flowing chiffon making romantic gestures. Who can forget the decade-plus Nestle's chocolate bar lyric in the background that begins, "Dreams like this…"?

TARGET MARKET:

Writers who specialize in writing direct mail copy for print mail order and video infomercials headed for cable, Internet, or Satellite television can create thriving writing and production businesses catering to telemarketing and mail order corporate clients and copywriters. Another career track is to write in-house for firms who manage telemarketing.

For those who enjoy the music business, contact musicians, and open a business that sells their music to the movie industry. Another venue is medical marketing.

Video and audio tapes are sent by mail order along with print advertising copy and information to customers. Video newsletters may also be included. Direct mail order copywriters for video or print write advertisements, sales letters, and demonstration video scripts to obtain orders for products such as magazine subscriptions and insurance.

A company purchases computer-sorted mailing lists of people in certain geographical, income, professional, ethnic, or age groups. The demonstration tapes or video newsletters are sent to potential customers to motivate viewers to buy a product by direct mail order. An audience-tracking study is followed up to measure the effectiveness of the written copy or the video script. If many products sold through mail order, the writer is judged excellent. The writer's income goes up. The freelancer is now in demand by infomercial producers and direct mail order copy publishers.

Anyone watching an infomercial is an information seeker. A sales video, like a feature film, informs as well as sells escape. The reason to write a nonfiction video script is to create grounds for a decision from the viewer's end. A decision is made not only about a product or service, but about those who identify with the product or feel repelled by the tape.

The infomercial producers set their own guidelines to battle poor public perception of the long-form commercials. The National Infomercial Marketing Association (NIMA) requires members to produce programs based on truthful information in compliance with laws and regulations.

Guidelines cover crucial issues such as sponsorship identification, program production, product claim substantiation, testimonials and endorsements. See the former National Infomercial Marketing Association's guidelines for members. The former National Infomercial Marketing Association is now called the Electronic Retailing Association. The group's Web site is at: http://www.retailing.org/new_site/default.asp

Writers need to work into the script the ways in which customers can order and pay for the product. What prices are fair? Can the customer buy it cheaper in a discount chain? Then why would he order from cable T.V. and pay more? Is it sold in the stores? Are similar and competing products sold in stores, but this product is sold only on T.V.?

The writer must write copy to sell at the client's prices, sometimes knowing in advance that the customer can get it cheaper in the store than by ordering from T.V. Also, what warranties are on the product? What guarantees do the claims make on T.V.? What are the guidelines for refunds?

THE NATIONAL INFOMERCIAL MARKETING ASSOCIATION
(Now called the Electronic Retailing Association)

In the early 1990s, as a condition of the National Infomercial Marketing Association (NIMA) membership, guidelines on refunds, guarantees, warranties, and prices in their information publications for members stated that refunds, guarantees, warranties, and prices are required. Not all infomercial producers are or were members of NIMA. Not all clients of infomercial producers are or were members either.

Today, as a potential video pod caster, you'd look for a client with a product if you do not produce your own product or service that you want to promote through your video pod cast. It's the client who makes the product, then hires an infomercial producer as an independent contractor or freelancer. The infomercial producer either hires a freelance infomercial video scriptwriter for the project or has staff writers working in-house. Some video producers specialize only in making infomercials and nothing else in a local area. As a video pod caster, you can make your own product and promote it in your pod cast. An example would be an inspirational or motivational speech or sermon, news, or a course offered online.

Back in the early nineties, membership guidelines stated that among NIMA members, if a guideline is violated, a complaint is presented to a review board—two NIMA members and three consultants. If the board finds a violation, the program must be removed from the airwaves within 10 days.

Members in good standing can certify TV station and cable networks that each infomercial complies with the guidelines. NIMA provides telecasters with a list of members in good standing every six months. By codifying the conduct of infomercial producers, the infomercial industry can be lead out of a difficult period when many viewers' attitudes toward infomercials were low.

Regulations set by NIMA state in part that each video will be preceded and followed with a clear announcement that it's a paid advertisement. There must be sufficient product to meet the demand within 30 days. There must be reliable evidence for all claims. Testimonials from consumers have to be voluntary and from bona fide users of the product. The stated price of the product must disclose all additional costs, postage, and handling.

RELATED OPPORTUNITIES:

You can produce and/or write direct mail copy for advertising agencies, direct mail firms, and manufacturers. Also, sales videos or pod casting compressed video files, MP4, or audio MP3 files can be made ready on a Web site for downloading. You can produce video pod casts for realtors, marketing research firms, distributors, and any company wishing to create video or slide-show advertisements as video pod casts. Anything you produce as a pod cast also can be recorded on DVDs to mail out to customers and saved in your hard disk drive for updating.

ADDITIONAL INFORMATION:

Associations of Interest

> **American Medical Writers Association**
> **40 West Gude Drive, Suite 101**
> **Rockville, MD 20850-1192**
> **http://www.amwa.org/default.asp?ID=1**

> **National Association of Science Writers, Inc.**
> **P.O. Box 890, Hedgesville, WV 25427**
> **http://www.nasw.org/**

> **American Society of Journalists and Authors**
> **1501 Broadway, Suite 302**
> **New York, NY 10036**
> **http://www.asja.org**

> **Society for Technical Communication**
> **http://www.stc.org/**

> **Association of Professional Writing Consultants**
> **http://www.consultingsuccess.org/index.htm**

> **Council of the Advancement of Science Writing**
> **P.O. Box 910**
> **Hedgesville, WV 25427**
> **http://www.casw.org/**

> **Careers in Science Writing:**
> **http://www.casw.org/careers.htm**

> **World Association of Medical Editors**
> **http://www.wame.org/**
> **http://www.wame.org/index.htm**

> **Text and Academic Authors Association**
> **TAA**

P.O. Box 76477
St. Petersburg, FL
http://www.taaonline.net/

Education Writers Association
2122 P Street, NW Suite 201
Washington, DC 20037
http://www.ewa.org/

Council of Biology Editors
http://www.monroecc.edu/depts/library/cbe.htm

American Society of Indexers (for indexing careers)
10200 West 44th Avenue, Suite 304,
Wheat Ridge, CO 80033
http://www.asindexing.org/site/index.html

Society of Professional Journalists
Eugene S. Pulliam National Journalism Center,
3909 N. Meridian St., Indianapolis, IN 46208
http://www.spj.org/

Diversified Media Associations

American Business Press
http://www.americanbusinesspress.com/

American Society of Business Press Editors
http://www.asbpe.org/

Associated Business Writers of America
http://www.poewar.com/articles/associations.htm

Associazioni ed Enti Professionali—America
http://www.alice.it/writers/grp.wri/wgrpame.htm
Contains a list of South American, Canadian, and US writers' organizations, including language translation firms.

American Marketing Association
http://www.marketingpower.com/content1539.php

Association of Professional Communications Consultants
http://www.consultingsuccess.org/index.htm

Writer's Encyclopedia A-Z List
WritersMarket.com
http://www.writersmarket.com/encyc/azlist.asp

Editorial Freelancers Association
http://www.the-efa.org/

Editor's Guild
http://www.edsguild.org/become.htm
The current online Yellow Pages, published annually since 1997 includes listings by skills as well as a specialties index. This association published the hardcopy, Yellow Pages, a listing of Association members who wished to advertise their skills and specialties, between 1989 and 1999.
http://www.tiac.net/users/freelanc/YP.html

International Women's Writing Guild
http://www.iwwg.com/index.php Or: http://www.iwwg.com
The International Women's Writing Guild, headquartered in New York and founded in 1976, is a network for the personal and professional empowerment of women through writing.

Video Software Dealers Association

http://www.vsda.org/Resource.phx/vsda/index.htx

Public Relations Society of America

http://www.prsa.org/

Deep Dish TV

http://www.deepdishtv.org/pages/catalogue13.htm

Video History Project

http://www.experimentaltvcenter.org/history/groups/gtext.php3?id=37

Advertising Research Foundation

http://www.arfsite.org/

The Mail Preference Service

http://www.dmaconsumers.org/offmailinglist.html

Advertising Associations Directory

http://paintedcows.com/associations.html

Mailing Fulfillment Service Association

http://www.mfsanet.org/pages/index.cfm?pageid=1

Television Bureau of Advertising

http://www.tvb.org/nav/build_frameset.asp?url=/docs/homepage.asp

Home Improvement Research Institute

http://www.hiri.org/abouthiri.htm

Writers-Editors Network

http://www.writers-editors.com/

Professional and Technical Consultants Association

http://www.patca.org/html/articles/ratesurvey/ratesurvey1.htm

Association of Independent Commercial Producers

http://www.aicp.com/splash-noswf.html

National Cable & Telecommunications Association

http://www.ncta.com/

International Association of Women in Radio and Television

http://www.iawrt.org/

National Communication Association

http://www.natcom.org/nca/Template2.asp

The Association for Women in Communications

http://www.womcom.org/

Society of Telecommunications Consultants

http://www.stcconsultants.org/

European Training Media Association

http://www.etma.org/

Advertising Research Foundation

641 Lexington Avenue • New York, NY 10022

http://www.arfsite.org/

International Women's Media Foundation

http://www.iwmf.org/training/womensmedia.php

Videotex Industry Association

http://www.iit.edu/departments/csep/codes/coe/
Videotex_Industry_Association.html

Independent Publishers Group

http://www.ipgbook.com/index.cfm?userid=36155756

American Society of Media Photographers

150 North Second Street, Philadelphia, PA 19106

(Electronic imaging and digital technology)

http://www.asmp.org/

International Interactive Communications Society

http://users.rcn.com/sfiics/

International Multimedia Association

http://www.emmac.org/

National Cable Television Association

http://www.museum.
tv/archives/etv/N/htmlN/nationalcabl/nationalcabl.htm

Information Technology Association of America

http://www.itaa.org/eweb/StartPage.aspx

Electronic Retailing Association (Formerly, the National Infomercial Marketing Association)

http://www.retailing.org/new_site/default.asp

Association of Independent Commercial Producers

http://www.aicp.com/

Directory of PR Consultancies and Press Release Writers

http://www.pro-talk.com/pr-directory/
public_relations_consultancies_list.html

4

Who Are the Audiences for Book Publicity Video Pod casts, and How Do You Produce Book, CD, or DVD Publicity Video Pod casts?

Write columns for Web sites that include print content and audio or video links. What consumers of video pod casts want are "killer applications" so anyone easily can produce a video pod cast from a traveling van, spare room, factory, trade-show, school, or office now that the devices such as video iPods and its competition are available. Video pod casts can be viewed in transit, at school, work, or at home.

Extreme telecommuting for many jobs also is open to video pod casting producers. Do you want to be the premier resource for video pod casting content? Apple currently is the premier Pod cast content and hardware resource, but the competition is growing. Each week about a thousand pod casts are added to Apple's iTunes music store. In 2005, the music store featured more than 15,000 pod casts. As an entrepreneur, you can use the popularity of the growing number of video pod casts to direct your own production emphasis.

The biggest corporations are getting into the video pod casting act. When iPod recorded a second filing seeking a trademark on the term iPodcsat, it included not only the usual "hardware devices and apparatus for recording, transmission, and reproduction of sounds, images, data, and magnetic data carriers," but also "telecommunications services such as telephone services and leasing of communications apparatus."

It's first filing seeking a trademark for the term iPod cast included images, sounds, and other data such as electronic bulletin board services," according to the September 4, 2005 *Apple files for Pod casting Trademark* article. There's a vast RSS community online that has opinions on what Apple should be offering or 'trademarking.'

Branding is a big issue in the video pod cast revolution. When video iPod and iPod-like devices are widespread in the student and young adult community, there will have to be content with variety to meet the needs of the types of viewers most likely to use video pod casting content. The gerontology community also has a wide intergeneration community emphasizing expression of creativity for memory enhancement in the golden years. Life stories and lifelong learning content has vast potential with both the older community of retirees seeking information, leisure, hobbies, life story recording for family, and learning, travel, and fun material for mental stimulation.

There's a video pod casting publicity audience for books and videos among home-schoolers, children, and teenagers, and a potential for tutoring and learning new skills or for armchair travel and family auto travel. Research the trends in job-training, corporate seminars, trade shows, and professional associations. Human resource personnel can use the video conferencing and branding aspect of video pod casting. Besides music TV or entertainment, there are virtual museum tours, and libraries offering a video version of narrated audio books, live plays, and entertainment for fun or learning.

Distance learning is another aspect of teaching online through the video pod cast. If you want to open a business, find a job, or have a career in the video pod casting revolution, you need to partner with those who can help you optimize video pod casts and/or produce them for a targeted audience.

Branding and infomercials at trade shows are only one aspect of networking, learning, or relaxing with video content in a pod cast format. Software support is where the jobs will be. Who's creating software to optimize and produce video pod casts? Microsoft? Apple? iLife?

How many other companies are making the software that makes it possible for anyone without technical background to make a video with a Web camera or camcorder, save it in a computer, publish it online, and save it to a DVD for mailing? In the direction of the corporations that are making video pod casting simple to produce for most anyone online is where you follow the money. What affordable software is there that is supported by Windows?

Video pod casting support has been around for a decade, but on May 13, 2005, the Wall Street Journal had only spotlighted audio pod casting, but not the potential of video pod casting at that time. See the May 13, 2005 article titled, *Papers Turn to 'Pod casting.'* It's cached on the Web.

The article reported that the Denver Post, Seattle Post-Intelligencer, Philadelphia Daily News, Washington Post and Forbes have started pod casts. Most people would rather look at video pod casts than listen to audio, unless they're operating machinery or driving while listening. Listening to audio pod casts while driving is as distracting as listening to music with lyrics, or lectures and news. However, listening to music without lyrics is less distracting unless the music is hypnotic or promotes sleep.

The low-tech, low-budget 'pod casted' audio files are on each newspaper's Web site. The Wall Street Journal article noted that pod casts can be automated and that numerous university journalism students recorded audio pod casts as volunteers but were negotiating for pay. But major newspapers have been producing their own *video* pod casts since the Internet went public. The video pod casts of news reach younger audiences raised in front of TVs and Web sites.

All you need to start an audio pod cast are one or more professional microphones, a beginner's level audio mixer, and recording software. However, video is the media of the present and near future, if it can be sufficiently compressed. The Daily News pod cast features advertising. It has a sponsor. To open an advertising agency offering video pod cast production, you need a sponsor.

You could open up a business that only offers creative advertising to clients in the form of video and audio pod casts, much like you'd sell TV and radio advertising time. Depending upon what type of advertising you'd specialize in, you'd need to find yourself a sponsor who specializes in that the type of business that supplies the news industry, such as a computer retailer. The problem you'd need to solve for your clients is how to drive traffic to your video pod casting site and once there, how to persuade the traffic to buy what's advertised. You'd make your money by selling ads.

Have you listened to the sound on most amateur pod casts? Does the pod cast take too long to download? If you do interviews, keep them about 15 minutes in length. Attention span for pod casts is short. Interviews are the way to go if you're a beginner with video pod casting. There is always someone interested in being interviewed.

Start with print-on-demand book authors who have to publicize and promote their own books because it's difficult to get reporters to review books that may or may not be copyedited by experienced copyeditors. The greatest fear of those who buy print-on-demand books is that the books aren't organized by people experienced in organizing books. That's why interviews are easy to find among authors promoting books. You could also interview retailers with a product to sell who want customers, teachers, clergy, psychologists, or tutors and teachers who have a lecture or how-to instruction in a niche area.

C/Net's "News.com" (News of Change) posted an article online on October 14, 2005, titled, *"Pod casters Prepare to Launch Video Era."* One of the biggest fears stated in the article emphasized the video revolution in pod casting attracting a flood of pornographers. Not only the sex trade, but religious sermons are expected along with comments from the almost anyone.

It seems as if Apple's portable media player and the competition from Microsoft and other manufacturers of similar devices will let anyone download free video segments. Sure, students already know anyone can download audio MP3 files to an iPod or similar device. Ever since MP3 players of all sizes have been on the market for several years, students, parents, and senior citizens have been downloading a medley of favorite radio programs from business to alternative health.

The video revolution is termed that way in most major newspapers. Although it's the 'amateurs' most often referred to in newspaper articles around the world, most of these 'amateurs' are interested in how to make money from their creative expressions in the way of video pod cast productions.

In mid-October of 2005, Apple announced its first video-enabled iPod models. Local talent and local broadcasters, people of all ages that dream of having their own radio talk show, entertainment, or teaching with video pod casting on the Web are the probable consumers of the video-enabled iPods and other similar devices made by any company that can and will make video devices.

What entrepreneurs ripe for producing video content for these iPod and related devices want is to be able to combine technologies and software to produce content that draw in larger numbers of viewers. What's most popular currently is opinionated programs and sex. Anyone with a Web camera or camcorder who longs to be an opinionated, perhaps controversial or volatile radio or TV talk show personality now can have his or her own Internet-based 'video' or 'radio' reality program with pod casting.

Video pod casting technology can be used to train employees, home school, teach courses, or lead seminars in subjects that draw niche audiences. The how-to audience is in demand. People want to see free video on how to make money from a hobby, travel, stay healthy, build, craft, or sew an item, find a job, or how to make a business presentation using a certain type of software.

One of the most useful ways to sell a book is by presenting school librarians with the title before the book is written and asking whether the librarian might buy such a title. Video pod casting can be fine-tuned to cater to the needs of certain groups such as high-school and college librarians, if the entrepreneurs knew where they could get a list of the email addresses of librarians from their professional associations.

Major publishers that sell books to these types of customers have such lists. The question is can video pod cast producers find out how to reach their intended market without spamming and annoying anyone in a position of buying the video pod casting content or advertising?

The way to get around this is to set up interviews with authors whose books are targeted to audiences that include school and public librarians, teachers, students, and parents. Then, without spamming, let the customers view freely the authors discussing their book titles and content that appeal to a specialized audience that might be interested in the information.

Clergy—preachers and other religious speakers were among the first to show an interest in video pod casting. Fundraisers also find a niche audience when they ask for donations to charities by pod casting video segments of their charity work around the world. When it comes to religious audio pod casts, check out iTunes' listings. According to the article, *Pod casters Prepare to Launch Video Era,* there are about "1,400 religious offerings available on iTunes."

The type of entrepreneurial person most likely to start a video pod cast from home is a journalist interested in economics. This can be consumer economics communications or finance. Journalists who also are media analysts would be interested. If an average retailer opens a video pod cast, the individual may not have the necessary funding or may not know where to start or what to post on the Web in the way of quality video that already has a built-in audience.

If you're already a video content producer and can do fundraising to get the money, such as a professor of documentary production, you can become a Web-based documentarian offering specialized video, such as personal history, life-story reality pod casts, business advice, or consulting/counseling. Since a huge number of first-time businesses fail before going online, you have a lot to overcome to stay afloat. It's not for someone who hasn't researched the intended audience's preferences and needs. Video is so much more involved than audio MP3 broadcasts. You need to start by learning from documentary video producers before you learn about putting the content online.

You can start by looking at the materials published by the International Documentary Association (IDA). See the IDA Web site at: http://www.documentary.org/. Or you can start your own national association for video pod casting. Who is going to fund your video production projects? Do you have an industrial-quality camcorder? Are your documentaries short enough? Can you use software to compress your documentaries?

What software is best? Who will judge the quality of your video objectively? Can you ask a video professor in a university to help you judge the quality or someone in the video profession? Get at least three opinions as they may differ as to the quality of your editing. Who will edit your work, or will you use software and edit on your own computer? Are you experienced in editing videos for pod casting on the Web? Who is around who is that you can hire—or learn from?

Find out who your audience will be. Young people look at video iPods when they are waiting in restaurants, malls, sports centers, food courts, or traveling in public transportation. Young people view videos during lunch breaks at school or while shopping and waiting for others to try on clothing. They also view while hanging around the malls. Can people view your content in public?

For those who want to put pornography on video pod casts, they have a magazine all their own for this industry. There's the Adult Video News, a trade magazine of the industry. Those entrepreneurs will probably gear content to be watched by couples at home, parked in cars which would bring back the 'private' drive in, or otherwise view the content where the public isn't watching what they're seeing—certainly not in libraries or schools. On the other hand, educational content can be viewed in libraries or schools.

Entrepreneurs might want to create online virtual worlds that residents of a community can offer ideas on 3-D models of prototypes of parks. These virtual worlds are in some ways similar in theory to the interactive learning materials, simulators, avatars, role-playing games, hypertext interactive fiction, and video worlds that existed in the early 1990s.

For example, Democracy Island is a three-dimensional testing ground inside an online virtual world called Second Life. The virtual world is funded by the $50,000 grant from the International Center for Automated Information Research that went to the New York Law School's Institute for Information Law and Policy. See the November 8, 2004 Internet Week article titled, *Online Virtual World is Part Fantasy, Part Civics Experiment* by Christopher T. Heun at: http://internetweek.cmp.com/173600540. The idea of a Web site is now not merely a Web site but a place and state of mind known as "your island" or "your virtual world." The idea isn't really new. Before the Internet became public, people played virtual world role-playing games with interactive computer software, most often in virtual reality video arcades at shopping malls.

Business Presentations with Book Publicity Video Pod casting

If you're making a presentation for yourself or any of your clients, make a video pod cast using Powerpoint or Keynote. Your intended audience can save your video in their video iPods and similar devices and play your presentation when they get back to the office or home on their own computers.

The video also can be saved to a DVD and mailed. For videoconferencing globally, your business can be built and based on synchronizing MP3 audio files with video or changes your MP3 files into MP4 files. You'd need video compression software. If you have Powerpoint slides, you can import each slide individually as an image. Check out Keynote software.

Another software to try out is iMovie, which lets you import each image as a separate clip. After all your clips are imported into the software called iMovie, you'd have to record your audio track. The only problem left to solve then would be to adjust the amount of time for each still image. The time adjustment is done in order to synchronize your video with your audio. But if it's a slide show you want to turn into a video pod cast, your job would be to make sure the video slides "lined up" in time with the correct audio tracks. Also, iTunes lets you import audio files for each of your slides.

The video pod cast revolution happened because people were not comfortable sitting in front of a computer staring at a bright screen while trying to listen to audio. There's enough unread blogs out there to fatigue the eyes. What consumers want is mobility—the listening or viewing while in a setting such as the beach, hiking, out in nature, or viewing anywhere outside or in bed, but not sitting with aching shoulders in front of an eye-fatiguing computer screen.

Children riding in the back seat of a car on a long vacation automobile trip enjoy watching DVDs on a DVD player. Teenagers and college students can afford iPods and similar devices to take on the run or from room to room. The mobility is what video pod casts are about, not the tiny viewing screen. At home, your large-screen TV can play that same file saved on a DVD using a DVD R/RW instead of the old fashioned DVD or CD player.

Games are a big market for video pod casts that don't necessarily have to be played on a video iPod or its competition. Video pod cast games also can be played on game video players. Try Sony PSPs, GameBoy Micros, PlayYans, Series 60 smart phones, and ZVue movie players. No doubt hand-held size computers will soon feature video pod casts. Some MP3 players could be enhanced for video in the future.

Consumers buying video iPods already loaded with videos usually don't have time to download videos from computer sites. You also could walk in a used game store and buy UMDs (interactive videos).

Another alternative is to look at the DVD-to-PSP Web site at: http://www.gamerbots.com/DVD2PSP/index.htm. With this software, you can convert your DVDs, and play them on your PsP. The Web site reads, "We are also throwing in with this auction—Directions on how to activate the hidden browser in PSP. Use it to Surf the internet over a wireless network! We'll show you how step by step with pictures." Your system requirements would be Microsoft Windows, Internet Explorer, a USB cable, and a DVD drive on your PC.

If you want to provide video pod casts for customers, you need cost-effective ways to obtain movies already formatted for any video pod cast device you might buy. Companies that create video content include iFilm http://www.ifilm.com/?htv=12, AtomFilms http://www.atomfilms.com/ (watch short films and animation) and JibJab http://www.jibjab.com/Home.aspx (animated cartoons and riddles featuring Nasty Santa, Hoola Boy and the Riddle King).

Videoblogs Promoting Your Books or Talks

To create video content for iPods and other small, portable viewing and listening devices, you need to get an RSS feed. Check out RocketBoom, a three minute daily videoblog based in New York City at: http://www.rocketboom.com/vlog/about.html. According to the RocketBoom Web site, it covers and creates "a wide range of information and commentary from top news stories to quirky internet culture. Agenda includes releasing each new clip at 9am EST, Monday through Friday. With a heavy emphasis on international arts, technology and weblog drama, Rocketboom is presented via online video and widely distributed through RSS."

An RSS feed stands for "Real Simple Syndication". Read an in-depth definition and explanation by Mark Pilgrim at the O'Reilly XML.com Web site at: http://www.xml.com/pub/a/2002/12/18/dive-into-xml.html. Also, an excellent book on RSS feeds is titled, Developing Feeds with RSS and Atom *By Ben Hammersley. April 2005. ISBN: 0-596-00881-3.*

RSS is actually a format for syndicating content. It's used primarily for news and similar Web sites. Examples of news content online using RSS feeds include Wired and Slashdot. Actually RSS feeds are used for articles, book excerpts, reviews and other personal Web log materials.

To organize your writing for RSS format, you need to divide your material into small enough articles that are able to be syndicated with RSS feeds. Don't put your unpublished novel into an RSS feed. People spend only a few minutes reading each syndicated news story online.

If you edit books online through RSS feeds or do tutoring, break items down into news-size chunks of text. The average attention span looking at video is only seven minutes, and people need breaks from reading on screen material. After you put your writing in an RSS format, a program that syndicates RSS news can keep returning to the feed and pick up your frequent news updates or include your other changes.

RSS technology lets people subscribe to your site. What you put up there in the way of newly published content can be downloaded to any portable player or computer. This means not only text, but also video and audio are considered content for RSS feeds.

Each subscriber (at no cost to them) can view the *free* video you've put up on the RSS feed. Subscribers don't have to download your video and waste time for buffer delays. If you're interested in video blogs, check out MobuzzTV, a video log (vlog) at: http://www.mobuzz.com/. Watch the latest shows.

The old fashioned way is to upload your mpeg videos to your Web site, use up a lot of bandwidth, and keep people waiting until your hour-long video is saved in their hard disks where they can save each video to a DVD.

It takes a long time to download that way, without an RSS feed, and some people are not on faster-loading DSL, cable, or other ways to download material from the Internet. Those who still have slower modems may run out of patience. That's why video blogs using RSS feeds cut the downtime waiting for any video to load.

Mobile phones are getting into the video pod casting arena with video player phones just as they got into the game with video recording and camera phones. Check out Verizon's VCast. See the article from the PC.com Web site titled "*Verizon's VCAST: Video Over EVDO Phones* at: http://www.pcmag.com/article2/0,1759,1749429,00.asp. According to the article by Sascha Segan, on February 1, 2005 the carrier, Verizon began "selling three phones for its high-speed EVDO (Evolution Data Only) network: one from LG, one from UTStarcom (formerly Audiovox) and one from Samsung."

You can open a business charging people a monthly fee to download your videos. With Verizon, the company charges a monthly fee plus what the corporation also charges for existing voice plans. As of February 2005, Verizon's customers in 32 cities could download, if they chose to, video clips: news from CNN and NBC, weather from AccuWeather, and entertainment content from channels like VH1 and Comedy Central.

It looks like the entertainment industry is getting into the production act as well. According to the PC.com's article, *Verizon's VCAST: Video Over EVDO Phones,* "Fox will produce exclusive serials for Verizon's new VCAST video service, too, including one based on the TV show '24'."

Let's suppose you want to produce video content that video pod casting phones would receive. Do you approach the phone companies or the phone manufacturers? You start with the phone companies and at the same time, you approach large production corporations and small, independent producers with your sample video clips. Keep your video pod casts short. Verizon's clips run two to five minutes. Your business might start out with a dozen or a hundred video pod cast clips. Verizon makes available about 300 video clips every day.

What if you're out of cash, but still want to produce video pod casts for the Web that can be downloaded to iPods or video phones and similar gadgets? You could post your videos on iTunes Pod cast Directory where people can download your video clips to their iPods if you have the software called Quick Time 7 Pro. You can buy the software at a very affordable price online at: http://www.apple.com/quicktime/download/win.html.

The Quick Time 7 ProWeb site reads, "The perfect companion for your Windows PC, QuickTime 7 Pro will convert you from a video watcher to a video maker. Harness the power of QuickTime 7 Pro for everything from creating pod casts to transcoding media in more than a dozen formats. Create video using the Web's premier codec: H.264 Record audio for producing pod casts Create movies for iPod New full-screen controls Convert media to more than a dozen formats."

What helps you to become familiar with QuickTime is to first to try out before you upgrade to the Pro version is the free QuickTime 7.03 or later version download. It's at: http://www.apple.com/quicktime/download/win.html. Click on Download the Free Player. Connect your camcorder or digital video Web camera with a Fire Wire 1394 cable to your computer. Shut off any versions of AOL Instant Messenger or iChat AV. If you don't have a camcorder, most digital video cameras are fine. One example would be the iSight. You don't have to use this equipment if you don't have a Mac. Most any digital video Web camera or camcorder will be fine.

If you use the Mac, according to Apple Hardware's Web site at: http://www.apple.com/isight/, iSight is a "state-of-the-art video camera that's the easiest way to video conference with your colleagues, friends and family over broadband. Featuring an autofocusing autoexposure F/2.8 lens which captures high-quality pictures even in low lighting, iSight also includes a dual-element microphone in its stylish compact aluminum body."

You can either open Quick Time 7 Pro and use it according to directions or use QuickTime 7 Pro for Mac OS Video Pod cast: iPod Edition. The software lets you "Create video for iPod" and easily "convert your existing movie collection for playback on iPod." If you have a PC, purchase the Windows version for Windows XP.

5

DESCRIPTION OF BOOK PUBLICITY BUSINESS
Using Free Walking Tours and Travel Groups to Publicize Your Audio Book

Make Use of Tours to Promote Your Informational, Travel, or Historical Audio Books

Have an audio book on the local history, nature, or archaeology of an area? Is your audio book about local cuisine, parks and trees, or what to do, where to go, and what to see in a neighborhood or new city? Arrange talks promoting your book, especially an audio book that may be listened to and saved in MP3 audio files to be listened to on iPods, MP3 players, or similar devices brought along on free walking tours.

Accompany travel groups to any city, anywhere. Instead of you spending energy doing the talking live while walking alongside the tour group, your audio disc or download can do the speaking for you. Also include older adults who take mall walks in groups weekday mornings. Let them listen and walk or shop while you promote your book or offer shopping or other information. They can listen to your information or 'broadcast' while they walk and window-shop those early mornings at the mall.

To promote your books this way, contact fitness groups for older adults that include walking tours, mall walks, and neighborhood walks. Adult and continuing education courses are a good market. To get a foot in the door, offer to teach a course in life-long learning as a volunteer if you don't have a teaching credential for adult education. Work your book into the course or offer information to other teachers.

This works with audio books, but not with videos, unless you are marketing travel videos. People want to listen to audio information as they view sites when they run out of conversation with fellow travelers. Your audio travel guide books fit right in with free walking tours of various cities in any country.

Make use of free tours to promote your audio books. Two types of free tours exist if you're looking for free travel. The first kind is where you visit a city and take advantage of the free tours offered of the city. These usually are walking tours of streets, galleries, government buildings, theaters, or museums on free admission day. Make a list of cities and check the Web at sites such as Chicago Traveler at: http://www.chicagotraveler.com/attractions/chicago-greeter-free-tours.html, or New York City for Visitors at: http://gonyc.about.com/cs/toursbr/a/bigapplegreeter.htm, or The Paramount (free theater tour) at: http://www.theparamount.com/artists/public-tour.asp. When you use your search engine with the key words "free tours," you'll see a list of cities or places that offer free guided walking tours of an area or buildings.

When you visit a city and don't know anyone, don't have a car, don't know the bus, trolley, or train schedule, and don't know where to go, a free tour can help you to meet new people, walk in safety with a group, and learn some historic or contemporary information about a particular area. In New York City, for example, check out the free walking tours by viewing the Web site at: http://www.newyorkmetro.com/urban/guides/nyonthecheap/pleasures/walkingtours.htm.

The advantage of a free walking tour is that you learn details that people who lived there may never have heard. The New York metro.com site contains a headline from an article that explains: "Free walking tours dish the dirt on neighborhoods, landmarks, parks, and celebrities. Rediscover City classics or set out for the road less traveled."

Check out the San Francisco City Guides site at: http://www.sfcityguides.org/ where free walking tours of San Francisco have been offered for the past 25 or more years. If you really love any city, its history, lore and legends, you can volunteer to offer free walking tours. Build experience by volunteering in your area. When you've learned the lore of any city you want to travel too, consider gathering a group of tourists or travelers who will pay to travel with you to a particular city. You go to that part of the world free in exchange for conducting a walking tour of that city.

There are in many cities, people who give walking tours for pay. They usually negotiate with a tour bus or travel service to give a number of tours in an agreed upon time frame for commission or pay.

You can offer walking tours free as a volunteer, or organize a walking tour business of your own. To get paid and still go free on the tour, you'd have to get a certain number of people to pay for the tour and work out a deal with the airlines, cruise ship, hotel, hostel, school, tour bus or travel service whereby you work by giving a certain number of tours in exchange for free travel.

Another way to go free is to run your business from scratch. Tourists pay you a fee. You make all the arrangements, and take them on a walking tour of a certain country or city. Your fee per person would be enough to pay for your lodging and travel expenses.

After you've taken several free walking tours of any city, consider whether you'd like to start a home-based business offering walking tours of any city, anywhere in the world that you'd like to see and where walking tours are relatively safe.

Find out what kind of insurance you need and which travel agencies you want to contact. Promote your walking tours in travel and entertainment publications and Web sites that reach tourists and travelers, including business travelers and those attending conventions.

You could conduct walking tours of any city, anywhere. Often travel agencies have arrangements. Some stipulate that if you find a certain number of paying tourists to go take a tour of a particular area that you can come along free as the tour guide.

Or start your own independent walking tour that specializes in taking people to another part of the world. If you sign up enough paying tourists, you can go free, if those type of arrangements are made with your travel agent, a particular cruise company, hotel, hostel, or as part of your own independent business.

Walking as a Book Promotion Business

You can produce pod casts on the subject of guides to neighborhoods for walkers. The walkers can download your pod casts on their devices, such as iPods and listen to the historic description of a neighborhood as they walk. These audio guides can be developed for any city in the world that walkers can stride or tour.

If you love to walk, contact various offices of any type where the people usually sit all day. Offer to take groups on lunch hour walks in a particular area of the city in which you live. Take the office employees—whether you work there or not—on long walks during the flexible lunch hour.

Start a home-based weekend-only neighborhood walking tour business on a shoestring budget. Give your walking tour business a name such as "Inside Details" or "Images and History." Pick an original name for your business that explains in two words what you offer on your walking tour. Start with sedentary office workers and offer lunchtime walks with a stop so they can sit somewhere and eat or buy lunch, sit down, and eat for 15 minutes before walking back to the office as a group.

During vacation periods from your usual weekday job, take tourists on walking tours all over the most fascinating cities of different countries. Pick a country that's relatively safe for walking. Eventually, your walking tour business can offer international walking tours of foreign cities as well as local, neighborhood, and wilderness sites.

You start local at first, obtain knowledge of where to walk in which countries or cities, and finally, turn your small business, into an international walking business with a new name that explains where you walk. Finally, turn your international walking business into a nonprofit group dedicated to promoting neighborhood walking in urban, suburban, and rural environments throughout the world. As you expand, you'll have to hire people to run the walking tours seven days a week. You also can work with volunteers as well as paid employees. You decide how far you want to go as a nonprofit group with a commitment to promoting safe walking around the world.

You can charge a small fee, such as $3 or walking, or let everyone walk free and operate as a nonprofit business to promote safe walking for health and stress reduction. You can cater to older adults or office workers or all age groups, or specialize in walking for people with special needs.

If you operate as a nonprofit agency, you can offer free walking tours and run on donations to your nonprofit agency. You'll be able to maintain a rented office with a volunteer staff if enough donations come in for your nonprofit safe walking tour group.

Most people would not like to spend a fee for walking. You'll probably find your people dropping because the walks cover the same area repeatedly. So it's best to operate as a nonprofit agency and run on donations with a volunteer staff rather than a paid staff.

To bring in more money, publish a newsletter listing walking times for an annual $10 or $12 subscription. When running your non-profit walking tour service, make a list of categories to which people can contribute money.

Out-of-town trips will generate more income. In addition, the volunteer walking leaders can arrange their own trips and go through your nonprofit safe walking tour service to take walkers on tours of foreign cities or national locations if they can find enough walkers willing to walk through the cities selected at an agreed-upon price. They have to work up a budget.

For the working crowds, keep offering midweek lunch break walks. Some of these office workers will be happy to take your walking tours to other countries when they get vacation time. Your clients would be sedentary office workers.

Other features offered by your free and safe walking tours in addition to offering walking the various neighborhoods of your area could include a once-a week lunch group that visits different ethnic restaurants. You can offer a Saturday walk for older adults or singles so they can walk and chat.

Offer free walks through local parks focusing on older adults or singles groups to meet, walk, and talk. One day of the week offer a walk through various wilderness sites in your area. Schedule different types of walks throughout the week depending upon demand and needs of various age groups and special interest groups.

Besides walking within one city, take a group for a weekend trip to another nearby city to see a show and spend two days overnight for a reasonable price—perhaps for under $200. Contact a reputable bus line and take your group to mountain resorts or other areas where they can walk safely. Make sure you and everyone else has insurance in case something happens to someone on a walk. Keep insured for surprises.

Take walkers to see a play or other event combined with a day of walking. Let them see a show and rest after a walk, and make sure there are places for them to eat, perhaps at different ethnic restaurants or have a take out lunch. Take the walkers to a resort where they can have a wine and cheese party and in the summer, use of a swimming pool (provided the resort, you, and the walkers are insured against accidents or other surprises). Make sure you have liability insurance.

Your walkers would enjoy a Sunday spent with breakfast at a hotel followed by a tram ride and a sightseeing walk. Let them look at lakes. Keep rules, such as never allowing a tourist to pass the leader. If they walk ahead of the leader, don't let them participate again in the walk. You need to follow these rules for safety. No one can walk ahead of the leader or move out of site. You don't want people getting lost in a mountain or wilderness setting or moving out of site and being late or missing for the ride home.

To start your walking regimen, lead a downtown walking group. Specialize in older adults or the group you want. Morning walks starting at about 10 or 11

AM are excellent for older adults. Take your walkers on a golf course walk around dinner time—between 5 and 6 PM.

Another walking group can start with a train ride to the old town of your city followed by an hour and a half walk with a stop for a refreshing snack and water, including breaks for restroom use. Older adults and non-drivers who use public transportation usually prefer morning, afternoon, or early evening walks.

For all ages, Saturday night walks are excellent as free entertainment. In addition, Saturday night walks traditionally draw younger singles and those who still drive. Families with young children in strollers enjoy morning or afternoon walks on weekends.

You also can offer an early Saturday morning hike if you live near a mountain. Volunteers can take this tour with walkers in good condition who like steep and strenuous walks. For persons who need to take it easy, Saturdays could unfold at 8:30 AM, beginning with eating together at the Y or elsewhere, meeting people, and chatting, followed by a volunteer-led mild walking tour of downtown or another area that offers historic and cultural points of interest.

As a nonprofit service, your walks can continue all day with a variety of volunteers focusing on different areas such as a river walk, a beachcomber walk. At 6:00 PM, you could have a volunteer conduct an evening walk. Offer a Sunday breakfast walk at 7:00 or 9:00 AM, followed by a merry-go-round walk at 8:00 AM. By 3:30 PM, you could offer a coffee or high tea walk led by volunteers. Different volunteers would offer the walking tours each day of the week.

Your high tea walk could offer herbal tea followed by walks along your harbor or other point of interest to enjoy sights and sounds. In winter, volunteers could show the walkers the colorful sunset on a 5:00 pm. Spend Sunday evenings at a coffee or tea house for an optional visit after the walk. Offer flat walks for those who can't climb steep sidewalks or hills. Classify your walks into mild and moderate. Offer a large variety of walks and give your walking group a name.

Find fit volunteers to offer family fitness walks at 9:00 AM one day a week when families can walk together. At 10:45, a good time for older adults who don't like getting up early in the morning for 7:00 or 9:00 am walks, offer a mild walk. Award a price for the oldest walker.

Take senior citizens from various senior community centers on a mild one-hour stroll that emphasizes spectacular views, including views from high-rise buildings from the inside as well as outdoors. For example, many seniors like to look at views from the 40th floor or higher of a building to see the panorama of their city. Others like to stroll outdoors. Include wheelchair walks for those who use power chairs and scooters as well. Walk at the pace of the slowest walker and have volunteers trained to work with older adults. Patience is a virtue when people need to walk slowly. The goal is enjoyment of the walk, stress reduction, and relaxation.

Take walkers on tours of high-priced homes or home tours when available. Looking at the outside of expensive homes is free, whereas looking inside a home, usually around the holidays, usually costs money that often is donated to charities to raise funds for various causes. Morning tours are best for viewing expensive homes from the street. Make sure the homes don't have loose dogs running in the street before you take a group on a walk of neighborhood sidewalks.

Your nonprofit walking service needs several vice presidents, a treasurer, secretary, and numerous corresponding secretaries. Have an emphasis for your nonprofit group dedicated to walking—such as family fitness. Make sure special groups are taken on walks, such as those with disabilities. To contribute to causes, do fundraising as a nonprofit group.

Make sure any leaders are trained and certified where fitness is concerned. Conduct several walks as fundraisers. Shoes are important in the walking business. Contact shoe manufacturers. Negotiate with companies that sell walking shoes to help you arrange a shoe fund and annual picnic. Ask the manufacturers and sellers of walking shoes to provide shoes to needy children in your area. Support your shoe fund.

You'll find that there will be some people who like to walk for miles. Others want to stroll around posh areas. Volunteers who are trained, certified, and fit can conduct walks for those who are fit enough to take eight-mile hikes. Schedule the walks around the lovely areas of your town. Include the expensive and beautiful country clubs, the places famous for attracting vacationing movie stars, and resorts or hotels with golf courses that attract the wealthy and world-class golf professionals.

What you need for your nonprofit walking group are high teas and coffee klatches. The best day for these events is on each Fridays morning after the walk or at noon lunches after the walk. It's one of the "Thank God It's Friday" type of events. After a Friday morning walk or at lunch time after the noontime walk, a lot of office workers still have spare time to get back to the office. So make time for lunch. Or offer your high tea at 9:45 instead of the usual 4:00 PM.

Walkers will look forward to stops for scrumptious breakfasts are made after the early morning walks that might typically run from 7:45 to 9:45. Friday morning walks followed by breakfast or lunch are for those with flexible working hours and retirees. Early morning, lunch, and after-work hours draw a crowd of office workers, work-at-home parents, people who work afternoon shifts, and those into family fitness.

Total family fitness walks can be your most popular offering. Schedule at 9:00 AM a toddlers and grandparents walk together around flat areas such as lakes or beach areas that run about a mile in length. Allow families to decide how many laps around a lake, beach, park, or other area they want to walk. They can choose a nature trail or the sidewalk to finish the workout.

Include training and walking, a jaunt with lunch, or a midweek wilderness walk on trails plus lunch. Train and certify your volunteers on how to lead people on walks. Give them awards.

Talk to newspaper reporters about your need to recruit volunteers to lead the walks with free training provided. The training is not only about safe walking. It's also about the sights and events discussed on the walks. Leaders can earn money by taking walkers on their own customized walking tours anywhere.

On one of your walks, include seeing a musical play. For example, an hour's walk can complement taking in a dramatic theater play at a discounted fee. The walkers could meet in front of the theater at matinee or evening time, walk for an hour, and return at 1:45 PM or 6:45 PM to wait for the play performance in the theater.

Focus on walking throughout the world as a fitness recreation. Classify your walkers and volunteer leaders as casual, moderate, moderate/plus, brisk, and very brisk, depending upon the speed at which the group walks. Casual is clocked at 2-3 miles per hour, moderate, 3 miles per hour, moderate/plus, 3 ½ miles per hour, brisk, 4 miles per hour, and very brisk, more than 4 miles per hour.

Start a nonprofit walking group that attracts a certain group of people—for example, families with children, fitness enthusiasts, older adults and retirees, singles, sedentary office workers, persons with special needs, mall walkers, artists, photographers looking for a clearer focus, birdwatchers, dog-walkers, or a job/client-hunting community seeking to net-walk. Your photographers, artists, or birdwatchers may want to stroll with cameras, camcorders, or sketch pads ready for the unexpected in nature.

Don't forget the large number of people, including older adults who enjoy morning or noontime mall walking as exercise. If you want to learn how an actual nonprofit walking group operates, contact the National Organization of Mall Walkers, at PO Box 191, Hermann, MO 65041. Check out Web sites at: http://www.peternielsen.com/walking.htm and at: http://www. chiropractic-software.com/mall_walking.htm. If you want to bring more walkers to malls for walking combined with culture rather than shopping, offer poetry or drama readings in shopping malls, perhaps near food courts and book stores. Reading excerpts from books near a bookstore might also bring in the walkers, and the food courts may look inviting even to rest, after a long mall walk.

Design your own walking program. See the Web site at: http://www. peternielsen.com/walking.htm. For more information, *The Rockport Guide to Lifelong Fitness* tells you more about an easy-to-use test that helps you design your own walking program. Send a self-addressed, 45-cent stamped envelope to Walking Test, The Rockport Walking Institute, 220 Donald Lynch Blvd. PO Box 480, Marlboro, MA 01752.

6

DESCRIPTION OF BOOK PUBLICITY BUSINESS
Branding, Logos, & Business Creativity Video Books
How to Offer Simple Solutions to Promote Your Book

Offer simple solutions to promote your book. Create a brand name and logo for your book. *Branding* is your mark of creativity. The simple solutions to people's questions offer more choices and productive results. Use book publicity video pod casts to create and promote brands for your book (or anyone else's book). Brand your book by offering precise yet simple solutions and results also if you want to sell information about a variety of products and people. Make sure the solutions are easy to follow.

You can promote your book by promoting other people's products. Your clients could be other authors and public speakers or manufacturers and marketers of products or services. Create a book title brand for yourself and your experience. Read the advice of professionals.

Choose an area of expertise to focus on. It can be anything from teaching to cleaning. For example, Linda Cobb is known professionally as The Queen of Clean. She writes excellent, helpful books on how to organize, clean, and remove clutter. And she has her own TV show featuring tips on how to clean and make your own cleaning products from less costly materials such as vinegar, borax, ammonia, water, and unseasoned meat tenderizer for removing stains.

Her books and shows feature an enormous number of helpful tips that save money and work right on the materials they clean or organize. For example, there are tips such as when sitting at the dinner table, as soon as something spills on your clothing or carpet, putting salt on stains from gravy or food takes out the stains in an emergency.

Club soda removes red wine, coffee, tea, and even red pop soda if you put it on the stain right away. What all these tips show is practical creativity. You can live on less and make a living at it by sharing creativity about your helpful, practical applications that show people how to improve and simplify their lives through step-by-step useful how-to information.

Become aware of a community need. Work with inspiration and motivation. Research niche areas not yet covered to create your own original video pod cast.

Find out through research what people want most in the way of a video pod cast. Help people solve problems such as getting rid of clutter, organizing a home-based office, cleaning, repairing, or planning creative home schooling experiences. What else do people need answers or solutions to in your area?

INCOME POTENTIAL

Charge a flat fee or by the hour to create branding logos and themes for other businesses. Use the current rate for other people who design logos and branding themes as well as publicity. About $100 an hour for creating a logo works in areas where other designers make that sum. Charging $25-$35 an hour works in other areas. It all depends on your reputation and how well you are known in the business community. Competition exists with graphic designers who design logos, book covers, brochures, and press kits.

BEST LOCALE TO OPERATE THE BUSINESS

Work in an area where there is a lot of industry. You need contacts with new businesses and stores.

TRAINING REQUIRED

Anywhere you can find creativity enhancement courses or practice in creating logos and branding themes. This would include courses in advertising, branding, graphic design, and logo design, desktop publishing, and typesetting.

EQUIPMENT NEEDED

You'll need graphic design software and a computer with a color printer/photo printer as well as a text printer. You might want to add a machine that binds books if you are hired to create booklets or small books for corporations.

OPERATING YOUR BOOK PUBLICITY BRANDING BUSINESS

To express creativity about living on less and sharing the experiences, first create your own logo, title, and plan of how you will share useful information. Will you be the next ogre of organization, curmudgeon of clutter, duke of drains, prince of plumbing, or cloisonné of clean?

Will you be the next earl of examples, marques of mothering, sovereign of simplicity, viscount of ventilation, lady of less, sultan of sources, sheik of shopping, or baron of bargains? You get the picture.

Put creativity into the elbow work. Use a term that's familiar to many or a proverb that you expand into *branding.*

If you're going to show people how to use branding as a business that teaches people how to cut expenses, instead of showing them how do you live on less, show people how to get higher quality for less money. Show them how they can have more, and get what they pay for. Start with the hidden markets like the wholesalers, shelf-pulls, and overstocked items or the imports and exports.

Teaching branding is about emphasizing simplicity and commitment. That's what you market in your buzz appeal campaign to the media and to the public as your customers and clients.

Your first step would be to use branding to make a 'brand' or trade name or logo and slogan for yourself that represents your basic concept and message. That's a proverb or quotation that in one sentence or less tells the public what you represent, to what you are committed. Keep it simple and short. After you have your branding complete with slogans and proverbs, launch your *get what you pay for* theme in the media.

To select a reporter from the media, find out by reading publications and newspapers who is writing a story similar to your concept or who has recently written a similar article. That reporter may not do another similar story, but can refer you to someone who might. Call the features editor and ask who has written similar articles or will be assigned a similar topic on bargain hunting for quality, getting what you pay for, simplifying your life, or living on less, saving, and enjoying the lifestyle more.

If you emphasize extreme telecommuting, travel, working outdoors, mobile lifestyle, working at home, or any other lifestyle, work style or attitude, focus on publications that emphasize publishing information or advertising those types of products.

If your writing is honest and dramatic, it will appeal to the newspaper reporter who is writing on a subject similar to yours. If that reporter from a national newspaper or other national publication with a very wide circulation writes about your story or interviews you and incorporates passages into the reporter's piece, quoting your story—fiction or biography—you have a great chance of publishers and agents contacting you. Usually, it will be an agent who is willing to bid your story to publishers.

Here's a famous example. Jessie Lee Foveaux, at the age of 98, sold her memoir for a million dollars, and she had never published before. She sold her book and movie rights. Was it luck or buzz appeal? The Life of Jessie Lee Brown from Birth up to 80 years had been written in longhand for an adult education class in writing for senior citizens writing their life stories.

In fact, she wrote the book manuscript 18 years before it found a market. How did she get it auctioned to competing book publishers and movie producers? How did she find her agent? Her life story is all about how she, as a battered wife married to an alcoholic husband, managed to raise eight children alone after leaving her husband and how hard she struggled to put food on the table. It is because she is from Kansas and spent her time knitting cross-shaped bookmarks for her church members that the story had universal appeal to agents?

The message of the book emphasized commitment and simplicity. It's hard to find an agent who would take on a 98-year old great, great grandma and sell her life story for a million dollars. Foveaux wrote her memoir back in 1979 when friends encouraged her to enroll in an adult education writing class. Her writing teacher, who also is a farmer, gave out assignments to the senior citizens in the class to write the story of their lives.

Foveaux even protested to her writing teacher at adult school that she didn't have the time to write. He insisted that she make the time and encouraged her to write. She took his advice and brought in her assignments each week with up to four thousand words of her life story.

When you try to sell simplicity and commitment in any item, whether it's your diary or a gift basket of hand-made products, write down what's different about what you have to offer? Foveaux wrote the details of how she spent her childhood, the characters who inhabited towns in which she lived, and details of her relatives.

Then she started on a narrative and got to the deeper story of her life. That's what you have to do—get to the deeper story of how to get what you pay for. Details and information are what sells—the facts and how to apply them in a practical, yet simple way to improve. Foveaux wrote about commitment using a simple plot with lots of details of her life story. She worked as a grocery clerk and other jobs to support all her children.

What in this story differed from the thousands of memoirs that are written by seniors in adult education classes? It's this story that brought in a million dollars from publishers, plus movie rights. How did this story differ from the others? The visibility or "buzz" appeal began with Foveaux's writing teacher who put her writing in his newsletter that contained the writing of all the students in the senior citizen writing class.

When we analyze how the first step led to the next, we have to look at her writing teacher's credibility adding to her credibility by publishing the writing of all the students in a newsletter. Normally, that would have been the end of the line. Except, by mailing the newsletter to a reporter from The Wall Street Journal, this reporter wrote about the author. That article published in the Wall Street Journal helped to give visibility and credibility to significant highlights of the book. The book soon sold to major publishers for a lot of money.

So you have to have a similar leap from adult education class newsletter of writing to actually being published in a national publication that has national credibility. The most important step of buzz appeal occurred when the Wall Street Journal reporter actually took a step forward to make Foveaux's writings known to the wider world of Wall Street Journal readers.

Your approach and product or attitude needs to be the perfect forum for a particular newspaper or magazine or other media venture. There had to be a reason why the newsletter went to this particular reporter at The Wall Street Journal. After all, most people think of The Wall Street Journal as a financial newspaper full of articles on stocks, investments and mergers. The newspaper's focus is far removed from a senior citizen's memoirs of raising a large family in an unhappy marriage, yet it made the perfect forum because it has universal appeal.

The writing teacher had read a previous article in The Wall Street Journal by that reporter who wrote an in-depth article on senior citizens that attracted the interest of the writing teacher in the Midwest. He sent the article to the reporter because it emphasized the **commitment to family and faith**. To create buzz, your writing, product, or application of your idea **must have some redemptive value to a universal audience.** That's the most important point.

What you need for your idea is **momentum**. You need to have a practical application—details, facts, and step-by-step instruction people can follow in what you present to the public. The Wall Street Journal reporter drew close to the writings of the 98-year old woman. Those writings had such redemptive value to create buzz (universal appeal). The Wall Street Journal reporter developed more buzz (appeal) around the manuscript by writing an article about the author and the manuscript.

Momentum resulted. The momentum moved it along the pipeline so that all the right connections had access by reading the Wall Street Journal. The point is if you want to reach all the right connections for your applications of ideas, you need a pipeline, a publication or other media that is credible enough for the people in power to view.

Make sure the people you want to reach read or view the publication or media to which you send your promotional writings. Do these people you want to reach even read or watch the media that is publishing your work? Before you launch anything in the media, think about who you want to reach.

Do these powerful people actually see that publication daily? Would they be interested in your information on how to get what you pay for or how to live on less and enjoy it more? Would you be better off sharing information not on how to live on less, but on strategies that the wealthy and famous use to get richer and happier at the same time? Think about it. Two very simple values sell to the rich and poor alike. They emphasize commitment. Those two values are *doing the best you can* under the circumstances, and *trusting in your faith*. It's like the old proverb, "You know that I care more than you care what I know."

A front-page story ran in the Wall Street Journal on March 7, 1997. Offers from publishers immediately flooded the writer. A lawyer hired by the writer's relative helped to find a literary agent to look at all the publisher's offers and select the best one. When 20 publishers called and 20 movie producers, offering six-figure movie contracts, the power of buzz—of **credibility** created through **visibility** in the major national press—spun into action.

The point is that without "buzz" (as they say in the publishing world), would that book have gotten the attention it deserved before the author had an agent? If you sent a book manuscript directly to a publisher, it most likely would come back with a note that unsolicited manuscripts are not read.

You'd most likely be told to find a literary agent willing to send your book to publishers. That manuscript might stay on the agent's desk for a year before you finally received it back with a rejection form letter. Who wants to spend that many years trying to find an agent who thinks your book will earn a commission or sell widely?

No matter how great your idea or product is, unless you find someone to buzz you into the national press, you aren't going to be noticed that easily. That's where creativity plays a role. Forget the cliché of thinking outside the box. Instead view the familiar box from a different angle.

To be more creative, find out what's in vogue. What's the current interest? Simplicity and commitment always is in vogue, but you need the next step—time. Look at trends. Research the trends to find out whether what you have to offer is coming at a time when people are trying to hold a family together and put bread on the table at the same time. Now get even more creative. You have buzz appeal.

In any promotion for a video book, audio book, paper book, documentary, pod cast, or online Web log, (or site) offer *simple* solutions using step-by-step instructions people can follow. Solve problems. Emphasize results, benefits, and advantages. Use facts that can be checked for credibility. Make sure claims are scientifically substantiated, and show viewers where and how to check your facts. Focus more narrowly. Are you appealing to American women? Do the trends say that this is the time when American women are working to support families? What practical steps can you offer them to make life and work easier, less costly, and of better quality?

According to a variety of daily newspaper articles, Foveaux's book was auctioned at more than a million dollars, and Warner cast the top bid. Think about how the author's manuscript went through certain steps to get to the person at Warner with the power to make things happen for the author. Think of what happened in between, the lawyer who helped the auction to happen and the publishers who took an interest. What made all these people take an interest?

Look at the value of your writing or information. Is what you have **simple** enough to sell for a million dollars? It has to be really simple to make so much money. Simple means *understandable* by the average viewer, and that's buzz (universal) appeal.

If you want to make a living by living on less, share what's simple and earthy about what you have and what you do. Be yourself. Publishers can spot phoniness in a minute. Can your customers or clients do the same?

If you write, be a real person in your writing. Be true to yourself. What's worth a million? The book emphasized morals, faith, and values. If you analyze what powerful publishers buy for universal appeal, it's a steady focus on values. Publishers look for faith in something greater than our lives. They seek stories of commitment and simplicity of values.

Publishers who buy a book or any other item on its buzz value are buying simplicity. It is simplicity that sells and nothing else but simplicity. This is true for computers, MP3 players, books, or items that have to be assembled by the buyer. Simplicity sells in instructional manuals and in how-to kits. It's good storytelling to say it simply. People want user-friendly gadgets, stories, and information.

Simplicity means what you have to offer gives your customer all the answers everyone looks for in exotic places, but finds close by. What's the great proverb that sells anything to anyone? It's to stand on your own two feet and put bread on your own table for your family.

Living on less and enjoying it more or you get what you pay for are moral points telling you to pull your own weight. And pulling your own weight is a buzz word that sells any product or application of an idea that teaches and reaches through simplicity. The backbone of the media emphasizes the values of simplicity, morals and faith (or trust). These are universal values. Doing the best to take care of your family sells. That's the buzz appeal you need to emphasize.

Consumers and publishers go through fads every two years—angel books, managing techniques books, computer home-based business books, novels about ancient historical characters or tribes, science fiction, children's programming. The genres shift emphasis, but values are consistent in the bestselling books, toys, and any other product.

You need to offer simplicity, values, morals, and commitment in whatever you want to share to make a living. Look at trends. To live on less and have more, find the highways to simplicity. Target those values. Emphasize commitment. Buzz is universal, but you need national press to get publishers bidding. National press gives you credibility in the eyes of major publishers. The world is impressed by front page coverage in The Wall Street Journal because of what it symbolizes—stability, dependability, security, centeredness.

Find a newspaper article that relates to what information you want to share. Write to the reporter covering the feature. Query to see whether there is an interest in your story or feature. Make sure you have a new angle on your project. Does your item emphasize universal values, morals, simplicity, and commitment?

Does it span real history in a way that reads and works well? Quality is the most important trait. Visibility and credibility give your product momentum. Buzz appeal gives momentum to the practical application of your idea. Universal values and simple lifestyles sell each time they solve problems, give results, and offer benefits with balance.

Take drop-ship products from a company at no cost to you. Sell the products online, on eBay, for example. The products are stored in the company's warehouse, not in your home. You could have the company mail the product directly to the customer after you collect the payment, take your share or commission, and notify the company of the sale and customer's shipping address.

ADDITIONAL INFORMATION

Resources: Simplicity, Balance, & Commitment

Living the Simple Life
http://www.cottagesoft.com/~cynthia/nfbkrevw/simplife.htm

Books and Magazines about Balance
http://www.marciaconner.com/fav/balancereading.html

Right on the Money
http://www.rightonthemoney.org/shows/116_simplify/

7

DESCRIPTION OF BOOK PUBLICITY BUSINESS
Promote Your Book with Keepsake Albums: Scrap Booking & Life Story Skits or Plays, Personal History Vignettes, and Genealogy Slide Shows

Plan, write, produce, and syndicate digital scrap booking video pod casting news releases. Scrap booking is so big that news releases emphasize the customer's needs and new products available for the craft of keepsake albums and memorabilia—from photos to time capsules.

Publish scrap books combined with life stories you can read for hours as you thumb through the pictures and the details of the experiences in text as paperback or hardback books. Then slip out a CD or DVD in a book's inside back cover and pop into your DVD player. Suddenly, the life story, wedding, historic site, or other event becomes a 'movie.'

Additionally, turn oral or personal history significant events and life story highlights into video pod casts of 45-minute one-act plays for student audiences. Skits and plays are *time capsules* that can be included with family history and genealogy keepsakes. Record and transcribe the skits, monologues, life stories, oral histories, or plays.

Here are the steps you need to take in order to gather life story highlights to turn into skits, plays, monologues, vignettes, or other time capsules for high-school, college, or junior-high student audiences. Anything recorded needs to have a text transcription in case the technology advances and the recording medium disappears before the material can be transferred to a newer medium.

Digital scrap booking of oral history and photos or videos can be put in a variety of multimedia formats. Examples would be records made for 'Victrolas' or old-time phonographs would not be able to play on current DVD players. If one generation forgets to transfer the time capsule from video tape or DVD to the next technology, at least photos and transcribed text would be viewable.

INCOME POTENTIAL

Charge a flat fee such as $100 for putting an edited one-hour life story oral history on a CD or DVD. Or charge less for an unedited oral history on disc or tape. You can charge $75 or more to put the life story on the Web at a Web site where space is bought, or make time capsules—containers of keepsake memorabilia and albums. Another alternative is to charge $100 to transcribe a one-hour oral history tape into a printed out transcription.

The purpose of a transcription of what's on a video or audio recording is to have the words on paper in case the technology evolves so that a disc or tape cannot be played in another generation or in a century or more in the future. Just in case someone forgets to transfer the recording to the newest technology, you have a library file of the printed out text that can be translated and emailed or put in a database.

BEST LOCALE TO OPERATE THE BUSINESS

Scrap booking stores operate in any locality where there is family life. Houses of worship, libraries, online at home, and in suburban, family-type neighborhoods and community centers or schools are good places as are supplies in educational settings. Craft, art, and hobby supply stores also carry scrap booking supplies.

TRAINING REQUIRED

Classes in scrap booking are given in continuing and adult education centers as well as in shops selling supplies for scrap booking, crafts, artists' tools, and hobbies.

EQUIPMENT NEEDED

You'll need scrap booking supplies you can get from suppliers of craft, hobby, art, and scrap booking stores. Some suppliers and vendors also sell kits where you can be trained to teach others how to scrap book.

Digital scrap booking uses software with clip art and photograph album-creating as well as genealogy and pedigree chart software. Contact the suppliers listed under scrap booking supplies. One excellent Web site for scrap booking supplies you also can sell to your students is at: Y

Set up classes of your own and train others. Contact your local church or house of worship and community center to see whether they already have scrap booking classes. You can teach at any adult education, park, or informal craft class and charge fees for a class ranging from $25 to $35 per person (or what your market will bear) for instruction in scrap booking, either paper hard copy with photos or digital with scanned and digital photos.

OPERATING YOUR BUSINESS

Use the following sequence when gathering oral/aural histories:

1. Develop one central issue and divide that issue into a few important questions that highlight or focus on that one central issue.

2. Write out a plan just like a business plan for your oral history project. You may have to use that plan later to ask for a grant for funding, if required. Make a list of all your products that will result from the oral history when it's done.

3. Write out a plan for publicity or public relations and media relations. How are you going to get the message to the public or special audiences?

4. Develop a budget. This is important if you want a grant or to see how much you'll have to spend on creating an oral history project.

5. List the cost of video taping and editing, packaging, publicity, and help with audio or special effects and stock shot photos of required.

6. What kind of equipment will you need? List that and the time slots you give to each part of the project. How much time is available? What are your deadlines?

7. What's your plan for a research? How are you going to approach the people to get the interviews? What questions will you ask?

8. Do the interviews. Arrive prepared with a list of questions. It's okay to ask the people the kind of questions they would like to be asked. Know what dates the interviews will cover in terms of time. Are you covering

the economic depression of the thirties? World Wars? Fifties? Sixties? Pick the time parameters.

9. Edit the interviews so you get the highlights of experiences and events, the important parts. Make sure what's important to you also is important to the person you interviewed.

10. Find out what the interviewee wants to emphasize perhaps to highlight events in a life story. Create a video-biography of the highlights of one person's life or an oral history of an event or series of events.

11. Process audio as well as video, and make sure you have written transcripts of anything on audio and/or video in case the technology changes or the tapes go bad.

12. Save the tapes to compact disks, DVDs, a computer hard disk and several other ways to preserve your oral history time capsule. Donate any tapes or CDs to appropriate archives, museums, relatives of the interviewee, and one or more oral history libraries. They are usually found at universities that have an oral history department and library such as UC Berkeley and others.

13. Check the Web for oral history libraries at universities in various states and abroad.

14. Evaluate what you have edited. Make sure the central issue and central questions have been covered in the interview. Find out whether newspapers or magazines want summarized transcripts of the audio and/or video with photos.

15. Contact libraries, archives, university oral history departments and relevant associations and various ethnic genealogy societies that focus on the subject matter of your central topic.

16. Keep organizing what you have until you have long and short versions of your oral history for various archives and publications. Contact magazines and newspapers to see whether editors would assign reporters to do a story on the oral history project.

17. Create a scrapbook with photos and summarized oral histories. Write a synopsis of each oral history on a central topic or issue. Have speakers give public presentations of what you have for each person interviewed and/or for the entire project using highlights of several interviews with

the media for publicity. Be sure your project is archived properly and stored in a place devoted to oral history archives and available to researchers and authors.

Using Oral History Interviewing/Recording Techniques to Promote Your Book

1. Begin with easy to answer questions that don't require you explore and probe deeply in your first question. Focus on one central issue when asking questions. Don't use abstract questions. A plain question would be "What's your purpose?" An abstract question with connotations would be "What's your crusade?" Use questions with denotations instead of connotations. Keep questions short and plain—easy to understand. Examples would be, "What did you want to accomplish? How did you solve those problems? How did you find closure?" Ask the familiar "what, when, who, where, how, and why."

2. First research written or visual resources before you begin to seek an oral history of a central issue, experience, or event.

3. Who is your intended audience?

4. What kind of population niche or sample will you target?

5. What means will you select to choose who you will interview? What group of people will be central to your interview?

6. Write down how you'll explain your project. Have a script ready so you don't digress or forget what to say on your feet.

7. Consult oral history professionals if you need more information. Make sure what you write in your script will be clear to understand by your intended audience.

8. Have all the equipment you need ready and keep a list of what you'll use and the cost. Work up your budget.

9. Choose what kind of recording device is best—video, audio, multimedia, photos, and text transcript. Make sure your video is broadcast quality. I use a Sony Digital eight (high eight) camera.

10. Make sure from cable TV stations or news stations that what type of video and audio you choose ahead of time is broadcast quality.

11. Make sure you have an external microphone and also a second microphone as a second person also tapes the interview in case the quality of your camera breaks down. You can also keep a tape recorder going to capture the audio in case your battery dies.

12. Make sure your battery is fully charged right before the interview. Many batteries die down after a day or two of nonuse.

13. Test all equipment before the interview and before you leave your office or home. I've had batteries go down unexpectedly and happy there was another person ready with another video camera waiting and also an audio tape version going.

14. Make sure the equipment works if it's raining, hot, cold, or other weather variations. Test it before the interview. Practice interviewing someone on your equipment several times to get the hang of it before you show up at the interview.

15. Make up your mind how long the interview will go before a break and use tape of that length, so you have one tape for each segment of the interview. Make several copies of your interview questions.

16. Be sure the interviewee has a copy of the questions long before the interview so the person can practice answering the questions and think of what to say or even take notes. Keep checking your list of what you need to do.

17. Let the interviewee make up his own questions if he wants. Perhaps your questions miss the point. Present your questions first. Then let him embellish the questions or change them as he wants to fit the central issue with his own experiences.

18. Call the person two days and then one day before the interview to make sure the individual will be there on time and understands how to travel to the location. Or if you are going to the person's home, make sure you understand how to get there.

19. Allow yourself one extra hour in case of traffic jams.

20. Choose a quiet place. Turn off cell phones and any ringing noises. Make sure you are away from barking dogs, street noise, and other distractions.

21. Before you interview make sure the person knows he or she is going to be video and audio-taped.

22. If you don't want anyone swearing, make that clear it's for public archives and perhaps broadcast to families.

23. Your interview questions should follow the journalist's information-seeking format of asking, who, what, where, where, how, and why. Oral history is a branch of journalistic research.

24. Let the person talk and don't interrupt. You be the listener and think of oral history as aural history from your perspective.

25. Make sure only one person speaks without being interrupted before someone else takes his turn to speak.

26. Understand silent pauses are for thinking of what to say.

27. Ask one question and let the person gather his thoughts.

28. Finish all your research on one question before jumping to the next question. Keep it organized by not jumping back to the first question after the second is done. Stay in a linear format.

29. Follow up what you can about any one question, finish with it, and move on to the next question without circling back. Focus on listening instead of asking rapid fire questions as they would confuse the speaker.

30. Ask questions that allow the speaker to begin to give a story, anecdote, life experience, or opinion along with facts. Don't ask questions that can be answered only be yes or no. This is not a courtroom. Let the speaker elaborate with facts and feelings or thoughts.

31. Late in the interview, start to ask questions that explore and probe for deeper answers.

32. Wrap up with how the person solved the problem, achieved results, reached a conclusion, or developed an attitude, or found the answer. Keep the wrap-up on a light, uplifting note.

33. Don't leave the individual hanging in emotion after any intensity of. Respect the feelings and opinions of the person. He or she may see the situation from a different point of view than someone else. So respect the person's right to feel as he does. Respect his need to recollect his own experiences.

34. Interview for only one hour at a time. If you have only one chance, interview for an hour. Take a few minutes break. Then interview for the second hour. Don't interview more than two hours at any one meeting.

35. Use prompts such as paintings, photos, music, video, diaries, vintage clothing, crafts, antiques, or memorabilia when appropriate.

36. Carry the photos in labeled files or envelopes to show at appropriate times in order to prime the memory of the interviewee. For example, you may show a childhood photo and ask "What was it like in that orphanage where these pictures were taken?" Or travel photos might suggest a trip to America as a child, or whatever the photo suggests. For example, "Do you remember when this ice cream parlor inside the ABC movie house stood at the corner of X and Y Street? Did you go there as a teenager?

37. What was your funniest memory of this movie theater or the ice cream store inside back in the fifties?"

38. As soon as the interview is over, label all the tapes and put the numbers in order.

39. A signed release form is required before you can broadcast anything. So have the interviewee sign a release form before the interview.

40. Make sure the interviewee gets a copy of the tape and a transcript of what he or she said on tape. If the person insists on making corrections, send the paper transcript of the tape for correction to the interviewee. Edit the tape as best you can or have it edited professionally.

41. Make sure you comply with all the corrections the interviewee wants changed. He or she may have given inaccurate facts that need to be corrected on the paper transcript.

42. Have the tape edited with the corrections, even if you have to make a tape at the end of the interviewee putting in the corrections that couldn't be edited out or changed.

43. As a last resort, have the interviewee redo the part of the tape that needs correction and have it edited in the tape at the correct place marked on the tape. Keep the paper transcript accurate and up to date, signed with a release form by the interviewee.

44. Oral historians write a journal of field notes about each interview. Make sure these get saved and archived so they can be read with the transcript.

45. Have the field notes go into a computer where someone can read them along with the transcript of the oral history tape or CD.

46. Thank the interviewee in writing for taking the time to do an interview for broadcast and transcript.

47. Put a label on everything you do from the interview to the field notes. Make a file and sub file folders and have everything stored in a computer, in archived storage, and in paper transcript.

48. Make copies and digital copies of all photos and put into the records in a computer. Return originals to owners.

49. Make sure you keep your fingerprints off the photos by wearing white cotton gloves. Use cardboard when sending the photos back and pack securely. Also photocopy the photos and scan the photos into your computer.

50. Treat photos as antique art history in preservation.

51. Make copies for yourself of all photos, tapes, and transcripts.

52. Use your duplicates, and store the original as the master tape in a place that won't be used often, such as a time capsule or safe, or return to a library or museum where the original belongs.

53. Return all original photos to the owners. An oral history archive library or museum also is suitable for original tapes. Use copies only to work from, copy, or distribute.

54. Index your tapes and transcripts. To use oral history library and museum terminology, recordings and transcripts are given "accession numbers."

55. Phone a librarian in an oral history library of a university for directions on how to assign accession numbers to your tapes and transcripts if the materials are going to be stored at that particular library.

56. Store copies in separate places in case of loss or damage.

57. If you don't know where the materials will be stored, use generic accession numbers to label your tapes and transcripts.

58. Always keep copies available for yourself in case you have to duplicate the tapes to send to an institution, museum, or library, or to a broadcast company.

59. Make synopses available to public broadcasting radio and TV stations.

60. Check your facts.

61. Are you missing anything you want to include?

62. Is there some place you want to send these tapes and transcripts such as an ethnic museum, radio show, or TV satellite station specializing in the topics on the tapes, such as public TV stations?

63. Would it be suitable for a world music station? A documentary station?

64. If you need more interviews, arrange them if possible.

65. Give the interviewee a copy of the finished product with the corrections. Make sure the interviewee signs a release form that he or she is satisfied with the corrections and is releasing the tape to you and your project.

66. Store the tapes and transcripts in a library or museum or at a university or other public place where it will be maintained and preserved for many generations and restored when necessary.

67. You can also send copies to a film repository or film library that takes video tapes, an archive for radio or audio tapes for radio broadcast or cable TV.

68. Copies may be sent to various archives for storage that lasts for many generations. Always ask whether there are facilities for restoring the tape. A museum would most likely have these provisions as would a large library that has an oral history library project or section.

69. Make sure the master copy is well protected and set up for long-term storage in a place where it will be protected and preserved.

70. If the oral history is about events in history, various network news TV stations might be interested. Film stock companies may be interested in copies of old photos.

71. Find out from the subject matter what type of archives, repository, or storage museums and libraries would be interested in receiving copies of the oral history tapes and transcripts.

72. Print media libraries would be interested in the hard paper copy transcripts and photos as would various ethnic associations and historical preservation societies. Find out whether the materials will go to microfiche, film, or be digitized and put on CDs and DVDs, or on the World Wide Web.

73. If you want to create a time capsule for the Web, you can ask the interviewee whether he or she wants the materials or selected materials to be put online or on CD as multimedia or other. Then you would get a signed release from the interviewee authorizing you to put the materials or excerpts online.

74. Also find out in whose name the materials are copyrighted and whether you have print and electronic rights to the material or do the owners-authors-interviewees—or you, the videographer-producer?

75. Get it all in writing, signed by those who have given you any interviews, even if you have to call your local intellectual property rights attorney.

How Accurate Are Autobiographies, Biographies, Personal Histories, Plays and Monologues Based on Life Stories?

Autobiographies, biographies, personal histories, plays, and monologues present a point of view. Are all sides given equal emphasis? Will the audience choose favorite characters? Cameras give fragments, points of view, and bits and pieces. Viewers will see what the videographer or photographer intends to be seen. The interviewee will also be trying to put his point of view across and tell the story from his perspective.

Will the photographer or videographer be in agreement with the interviewee? Or if you are recording for print transcript, will your point of view agree with the interviewee's perspective and experience if your basic 'premise,' where you two are coming from, are not in agreement? Think this over as you write your list of questions. Do both of you agree on your central issue on which you'll focus for the interview?

How are you going to turn spoken words into text for your paper hard copy transcript? Will you transcribe verbatim, correct the grammar, or quote as you hear the spoken words? Oral historians really need to transcribe the exact spoken word. You can leave out the 'ahs' and 'oms' or loud pauses, as the interviewee thinks what to say next. You don't want to sound like a court reporter, but you do want to have an accurate record transcribed of what was spoken.

You're also not editing for a movie, unless you have permission to turn the oral history into a TV broadcast, where a lot gets cut out of the interview for time constraints. For that, you'd need written permission so words won't be taken out of context and strung together in the editing room to say something different from what the interviewee intended to say.

Someone talking could put in wrong names, forget what they wanted to say, or repeat themselves. They could mumble, ramble, or do almost anything. So you would have to sit down and weed out redundancy when you can or decide on presenting exactly what you've heard as transcript.

When someone reads the transcript in text, they won't have what you had in front of you, and they didn't see and hear the live presentation or the videotape. It's possible to misinterpret gestures or how something is spoken, the mood or tone, when reading a text transcript. Examine all your sources. Use an ice-breaker to get someone talking.

If a woman is talking about female-interest issues, she may feel more comfortable talking to another woman. Find out whether the interviewee is more comfortable speaking to someone of his or her own age. Some older persons feel they can relate better to someone close to their own age than someone in high school, but it varies. Sometimes older people can speak more freely to a teenager.

The interviewee must be able to feel comfortable with the interviewer and know he or she will not be judged. Sometimes it helps if the interviewer is the same ethnic group or there is someone present of the same group or if new to the language, a translator is present.

Read some books on oral history field techniques. Read the National Genealogical Society Quarterly (NGSQ). Also look at The American Genealogist (TAG), The Genealogist, and The New England Historical and Genealogical Register (The Register). If you don't know the maiden name of say, your grandmother's mother, and no relative knows either because it wasn't on her death certificate, try to reconstruct the lives of the males who had ever met the woman whose maiden name is unknown.

Maybe she did business with someone before marriage or went to school or court. Someone may have recorded the person's maiden name before her marriage. Try medical records if any were kept. There was no way to find my mother's grandmother's maiden name until I started searching to see whether she had any brothers in this country. She had to have come as a passenger on a ship around 1880 as she bought a farm. Did her husband come with her?

Was the farm in his name? How many brothers did she have in this country with her maiden surname? If the brothers were not in this country, what countries did they come from and what cities did they live in before they bought the farm in Albany? If I could find out what my great grandmother's maiden name was through any brothers living at the time, I could contact their descendants perhaps and see whether any male or female lines are still in this country or where else on the globe.

Perhaps a list of midwives in the village at the time is recorded in a church or training school for midwives. Fix the person in time and place. Find out whom she might have done business with and whether any records of that business exist. What businesses did she patronize? Look for divorce or court records, change of name records, and other legal documents.

Look at local sources. Did anyone save records from bills of sale for weddings, purchases of homes, furniture, debutante parties, infant supplies, or even medical records? Look at nurses' licenses, midwives' registers, employment contracts, and teachers' contracts, alumni associations for various schools, passports, passenger lists, alien registration cards, naturalization records, immigrant aid societies, city directories, and cross-references.

Try religious and women's clubs, lineage and village societies, girl scouts and similar groups, orphanages, sanatoriums, hospitals, police records. Years ago there was even a Eugenics Record Office. What about the women's prisons? The first one opened in 1839—Mount Pleasant Female Prison, NY.

Research voters' lists. If your relative is from another country, try records in those villages or cities abroad. Who kept the person's diaries? Have you checked the Orphan Train records? Try ethnic and religious societies and genealogy associations for that country. Most ethnic genealogy societies have a special interest group for even the smallest villages in various countries.

You can start one and put up a Web site for people who also come from there in past centuries. Check alimony, divorce, and court records, widow's pensions of veterans, adoptions, orphanages, foster homes, medical records, birth, marriage, and death certificates, social security, immigration, pet license owners' files, prisons, alumni groups from schools, passenger lists, military, and other legal records.

When all historical records are being tied together, you can add the DNA testing to link all those cousins. Check military pensions on microfilms in the National Archives.

ADDITIONAL INFORMATION

The Digital Scrapbook Place

http://www.digitalscrapbookplace.com/

Accents 2 (Scrapbooking Shopping Director)

http://www.accents2scrapbooking.com/scrapbooking_links.htm

Scrapbooking Press Releases

http://www.topix.net/hobbies/scrapbooking/pr

8

DESCRIPTION OF BUSINESS
Promote Your Book with Free Entertainment Directories

Help other authors promote their books and guides along with your book by publishing electronically or in print directories showing people how to find free or low-cost entertainment in any city of the world or locally. Most university campuses offer free concerts where graduate or advanced music students present rehearsals or master's thesis concerts and similar free performances, plays, or lectures open to the public.

With a library card, you can view free educational, business, scientific and literary videos, attend the free days for museums and galleries, and enjoy free concerts given in places such as shopping malls, museums, or library galleries. On the Web, you'll find The FreeBay.com site at: http://www.thefreebay.com/.

There is a Freebie site also at: http://www.eversave.com/eversave/consumers/CampaignReg.jsp?sourceid=7632&cid=163. You can find free coupons and other free offers. Discover ideas about what people buy from sites such as Shop.com at: http://www.shop.com/.

INCOME POTENTIAL

Sell advertising for the directories and leave them at various stores and hotels, convention centers, and chambers of commerce meeting rooms. The directories of free entertainment also can be free which dramatically increases circulation, a positive selling point when trying to sell display or classified advertising in the directories from companies that provide free entertainment.

Use current rates for free newspapers and other publications to sell advertising. For example, you can charge $25 or $50 for a small display advertisement or as high as $100 depending on what type of businesses advertise.

Good targets are restaurants, theme parks, museums, zoos, and any other establishment that has a free day or offers free entertainment or walking tours on any particular day of the year, perhaps as a sideline to some other product being sold. Free lectures and seminars offered at convention centers or meeting rooms are an excellent source of advertising. Also try mall walking clubs, food courts, and shopping malls as well as park and recreation district offerings, free classes, adult education or continuing education, writers' clubs, craft and hobby clubs, library lectures, concerts, and folk dancing classes.

BEST LOCALE TO OPERATE THE BUSINESS

Look for free entertainment by various music bands that come to malls on certain days of the week at certain times, such as a noon lunch hour. Some churches offer free concerts at noon or evenings for downtown works to spend their lunch hour.

Check out FreebieDot.com at the Web site: http://www.freebiedot.com/ 3p1.htm. Look at FreeMovieMayhem.com at http://www. freemoviemayhem.com/index.cgi?src=WC-31275aaa:33320:

Look at sites such as Memolink.com or FreeDVDs.com at: http://www. freedvds.com/Default.aspx?N=1&P=168. In short, there are freebie sites on the Web. Check them out as to what the conditions are. Free entertainment is available without having to go online. Find out what free entertainment such as music exists at your local college campuses, high schools, churches, public libraries, art galleries, concert halls, museums, and community centers or shopping malls. Public places often have days of the year offering free entertainment or admission.

OPERATING YOUR BUSINESS

Publish a directory online and/or in print of free entertainment at parks, museums, church picnics, church concerts, brown-bag luncheon concerts downtown for workers, poetry readings, recreational presentations, street entertainment, art walks and art shows, student concerts, campus lectures open to the public, free film presentations at campuses and other public places, club meetings open to guests, community centers, galleries and libraries, targeting days with free admissions.

Explore the possibilities for video pod casting on various media players. Demonstrate your pod casts at exhibits, conventions and city information offices, local visitors' bureaus, chambers of commerce, hotels and convention centers, tourist industries, museums. Pod cast videos of historic homes open to the public, galleries, and professional association meetings.

Video pod casts may be shown on various media players at expos, public lectures, and national association meetings. Trade shows and events related to a wide variety of industries and educational programs are shown. Look at listings of free offerings from professional associations and their meetings announced in newsletters and trade journals.

Sell advertising to make income from your directory. It's logical and easier to sell the advertising and give the publication away free than by trying to persuade any consumer to pay for a directory of free entertainment.

If the zoo or museum cost too much to bring your family to frequently, buy a year membership at a discount or volunteer to work there as a docent a few days a year in exchange for a free pass for you and a guest.

Zoos also have one day a year with free admission. To cut expenses, show up early. If there's a particular museum, gallery, or exhibit you want to attend, offer to volunteer there a few days a year in exchange for a free admittance to the exhibit.

Conventions, conferences, meetings, and theatrical presentations also offer free attendance in exchange for volunteer work as an usher or registrar, people-greeter, ticket-taker or other helpful work.

When various theaters present plays and music concerts, they usually need volunteer ushers who get to attend the play or concert free. Call a few weeks in advance and offer to be a volunteer usher, people greeter, helper, or ticket-taker in exchange for getting to attend the particular function.

If you like to attend a lot of plays or, offer to volunteer for university or even high school plays. If you're an older adult, contact various senior centers and theaters and volunteer to give information or help people when the plays or concerts open. You'll get a free admittance in exchange. The same works for art galleries and museums.

If you enjoy hanging around radio or TV stations, call in advance and ask to be put on their volunteer list. Most duties involve answering questions for people who call. Galleries and museums use volunteers as docents. You can do fund-raising work for public TV and radio stations in exchange for free tickets to various functions, such as theatrical or musical productions or live shows.

If you want to work in public relations roles, volunteer to help out at conferences, conventions, or concerts. If you want to become more involved as an event planner, join professional associations for event planners and offer to help find speakers for a panel.

By volunteering, you can learn more about how event planners put together an event or how artists or musicians are promoted.

Another field in the entertainment business is selling the music of professional musicians to the movie industry. You'd be the middle person or go-between finding the right musicians and placing their work with various movie producers and directors.

For those who only want free entertainment without much complexity or involvement in the industry, by volunteering a few days a year in any media, you can ask for free tickets to an event in exchange for being a helper when help is needed. Helpers in the entertainment industry answer phone calls at a radio station or greet and register people at a convention. It's a form of bartering a few hours a year of volunteering in exchange for tickets for you and a guest to attend specific entertainment events.

Not everyone wants an actual career in the entertainment industry You may only want free tickets to see a show or look around in a museum, zoo, or at a convention. Another form of free entertainment is to become an independent tour guide.

You find a required number of persons to pay for a cruise or tour, and you go free on the tour or cruise. Check out the cruise lines and various tours and travel businesses that allow you to go free if you find a required number of paid guests.

Take advantage of free walking tours of various cities. For example at the Web site: http://www.newyorkmetro.com/urban/guides/nyonthecheap/pleasures/walkingtours.htm, you'll find New York metro.com. The site explains that the free walking tours give specific details and history of a neighborhood.

Almost every city offers free walking tours. That's another type of free entertainment. To find free walking tours for other cities, just use your Internet's Web search engine and put in the key word "free walking tours." What pops up, for example, at http://www.google.com is a list of Web sites from various cities offering free walking tours.

Look for docent organizations, and consider giving a free walking tour yourself of your city to meet a lot of new people. Become a docent, a volunteer who offers a tour of a place, city, neighborhood, museum or gallery. Join docent groups and receive free training to be a docent. Or just take advantage of the free walking tours of any city. You'll see online free walking tours of various European cities. It's your choice of where you want to take your free walking tour or offer one in your neighborhood.

If you're looking for free entertainment, the walking tour will give you some exercise and outdoors experience. You can choose where you'd like to walk.

RELATED OPPORTUNITIES:

Live Docents, Promotional Docents, and Video Pod cast Docents

Talk to docents from various museums and outdoor events programs or groups to list free entertainment. An example of docent training and free walking tours would include Las Angelitas in California. If you attend their docent training when it's offered, you can learn about early California and Los Angeles history and how to give small group tours.

After completion, requirements are to give tours 2 weekday mornings per month or 1 Saturday morning. Las Angelitas is a diverse group of people from all over Southern California who also go on historical tours and have social gatherings.

With free entertainment such as walking tours, they are useful if you're interested in history. Most docent groups include social gatherings. It's a good way to make new friends with similar interests and experience the free entertainment.

Historical walking tours can be started in almost any place where people are willing to take walks and discuss the historical events of that community.

Every spot in the world has its own history. And history is as much entertainment as walking. For persons with disabilities, for example, wheelchair historical tours or tours for the deaf community also are resources to help others learn the history of a neighborhood, institution or city. Also try campus walking tours. For example, the University of California, Berkeley has walking tours of the campus where there also are nearby museums. Cultural tours are forms of entertainment where you learn where your values direct you.

Join professional or trade associations and offer to find people to give presentations or speakers for their panels. Whenever an expo, trade show, conference, convention or meeting is scheduled, the professional association or society needs volunteers to help run the show. You get to attend the expo or show free, listen to speakers or enjoy the entertainment.

To find speakers for panels, you contact speakers' bureaus and members of the association with expertise in an area and experience in public speaking. Bring the speaker to the convention and get rewarded with free entertainment. You work through either event planners or the trade association/professional group, or volunteer to work on the group's newsletter.

Another way to work the conventions is to greet people and register newcomers. You can be a ticket-taker or help the event planner. If you're looking for a career as a party-planner, working with event planners is one way to learn the ropes.

Entertainment is a broad area to define. Looking for free entertainment can be found at libraries or theme parks, hotels, casinos, and at performances of musicians or artists at college campuses. A quick way to find out what's free is to call talent agents and promotional companies in advance and ask what you can do to help in exchange for free tickets. Of course, the easiest way is to check with convention and visitor's bureaus and information bureaus for any city and ask what the free admission days are for the local events such as zoos, museums, galleries, theaters, concert halls, and theme parks.

Free university lectures are given almost daily. Check the particular college's newspaper for dates of free lectures. Also check each department's list of events. My field of interest is listening to anthropology lectures. I'd call the department of anthropology at several universities nearby as well as the museums and ask what days free lectures are given that are open to the public.

You'd be surprised at how many people are speaking at university ballrooms and auditoriums, for which most of these lectures are free and open to the public interested in that particular subject. Some people giving an oral presentation for a graduate thesis welcome strangers to quietly sit in the room or auditorium and listen to their presentation to their faculty advisers.

Entertainment that's free can come in the form of seminars. For example, the Federal Technology Center presented a free seminar on negotiation. Business information is a form of entertainment. Contact your local small business and economic development center. Free seminars are frequently offered.

Newspapers that emphasize niche markets such as job listings and information often present career fairs. Attend a free career fair. It usually offers free lectures, seminars, and sometimes entertainment. Attend the free franchise expo circuit. These franchise expos at hotels offer seminars, exhibits, or entertainment, and sometimes free giveaway items such as pens, note pads, samples of products, mugs, book marks, or paperweights.

Make the rounds of exhibits and trade shows. The vendors' rooms are often free to attend. You can also ask a local weekly paper for an assignment to write up the highlights of the convention in exchange for a letter asking for a free press badge.

With a press pass or free press badge, you can attend the lectures and entertainment of the convention or trade show. When you're done, turn in a one-page media release of any important facts you've learned from attending the conference.

Interview the vendors and emphasize what's the upcoming trend and what's most popular on the agenda. Then turn in to the publication your typed two-page story. Or email it.

Ask the editor of any professional association's newsletter if you could review the convention in exchange for a free press pass to the convention. You wouldn't get paid for the article, but you'd get a press pass to attend the convention free. Trade publications, professional associations' newsletters, niche market magazines, such as local computer publications, popular Web sites, and weekly business publications are most likely to be interested.

Attend the job fairs at your local convention center. Usually, there's some form of free entertainment. If you have young children, volunteer at various children's theater projects. Most cities have a children's theater or drama group. If you want to attend expensive business awards banquets, ask whether you can be a volunteer.

Besides the general chamber of commerce groups, there's also the various ethnic chamber of commerce associations that present annual business awards at banquets. Although tickets to these affairs cost upwards of $100, there may be a spot for someone who volunteers to be of help where needed for the event, if you call well in advance.

Most ethnic chambers of commerce include the name of a city followed by the ethnic group such as "Hispanic chamber of commerce" or "African-American Women's chamber of commerce" or "Asian chamber of commerce." How many different ethnic chambers of commerce can you locate?

The smaller the niche, the more opportunity you have to get to work with people in exchange for a free ticket to entertainment offered or a chance to help promote projects, causes, or raise money for the group. You can work with church groups also that offer entertainment in connection with a project.

Look in your area. Call your local college's ethnic studies department. Find out how many different ethnic or other category chambers of commerce in your area are giving business awards and recognition banquets.

ADDITIONAL INFORMATION

Other forms of video pod cast entertainment can occur in your home. Free CDs or DVDs can be obtained if you volunteer or perform paid work part time as an audio book reviewer. Check out the various audio publishers' associations.

Then contact magazines that publish short reviews, usually about 100 to 110 words per review. Offer your reviewing services, and you'll be placed on the publisher's or the publication's list to receive several audio books each month.

In exchange for reviewing the audio book for a publication, you'll receive the books free which you can keep or sell on eBay or other online sales sites or sell at garage sales. Or you can just enjoy the free entertainment and eventually donate your audio CDs or cassettes to libraries, libraries for the blind, or schools where they are needed.

Some publications pay writers to review audio books. You can contact the publishers of the audio books directly or go through magazines that publish reviews. When you've made yourself known as an audio book reviewer, video or DVD reviewer, or print book reviewer, publishers and publications will contact you.

Also, your Web site can be used to practice writing reviews. Keep them one paragraph in length and about 110 words. Emphasize the audio presentation, not the literary review, unless you're reviewing a print book.

Contact authors for "author interviews" in addition to reviews, and offer the interviews to magazines with the approval of the author for a taped interview. Ask the magazine in advance for a go-ahead before you contact the author.

Give the author the chance to change anything he or she said before you send out a transcribed and edited tape interview. Keep the number of words to what the publication wants as space is very limited.

9

DESCRIPTION OF BOOK PUBLICITY BUSINESS
Inspirational Markets: Video and Audio Combined with Print Publishing
How to Motivate the Mind-Body-Spirit Markets

Promote your book in the inspirational, self-help, fitness, health, nutrition, motivational, new age, ethnic, or religious "mind-body-spirit" markets by answering questions, solving problems, and offering results that increase positive outcomes. Focus on audio books that people can listen to in the gym or while traveling. Video pod casts are distracting outside homes, planes, trains, buses, schools, hospitals, hospices, and nursing facilities. They're great for home schooling.

The markets range from fundamentalist and conservative religious to new age light workers, self-help, alternative medicine, ethnobotany, health and nutrition research publications to actual text books used at different grade levels in home schooling.

Included in this category also are the parenting, leisure lifestyle, and behavior modification books for different demographic groups. There's also a need for problem-solving informational books among various support groups.

Don't watch videos while driving. When riding for hours in trains, planes, and busses, you may want to be motivated, distracted, and inspired by sermons, alternative healing, and all types of inspirational talks or dramatizations.

One example would be books aimed at students who need to write term papers and research a particular subject such as teenage pregnancy. There are also markets for books and video pod casts on nutrition and special diets, on behavior modification, or exercises for fitness or correction of problems with biofeedback.

Another example of book and video combination markets would be for self-paced courses. Documentaries, games, and entertainment are suited for video. History, reality, and travel are thriving markets for documentaries.

Inspirational and motivational video segments emphasize human experience with solutions to problems. Some fall under the mind-body-spirit or self-help classifications. Your inspirational pod cast shows others how to solve problems, learn from and transcend prior mistakes, end bad habits by replacing them with healthier habits, or cut expenses and obtain higher quality products and services. Your video pod cast can explore your previous writing for the inspirational markets by producing inspirational materials.

Videos of significant events, turning points, or highlights of life stories can show that by sharing people can learn alternatives and possibilities for healthier and happier choices. Help people make more informed decisions. You can focus either on religious video pod casts or self-help and inspirational solutions and turning points that reveal positive results.

It makes no difference what religion or spirituality essence you select, but writing a life story for the religious or inspirational markets is in demand and expanding its need for sharing life story experience in the form of books, stories, or featured articles and columns.

What many religious, self-help, or inspirational markets are looking for are steps that others can follow showing the viewer how to arrive at a decision or choice by growth and transformation. Your message of self-help could be about how you or someone gained wisdom that everyone can share. Inspirational video pod casts are about how you searched for answers in exotic or complex places but found close to home, usually right in front of you. And the answer (growth) wasn't complex at all, but simple as commitment to family, faith, and universal values.

By sharing your experiences and life story, readers will learn how you made decisions and why, what wisdom you gained from your growth or transformation, and what made it possible for you to grow and change and become a stronger and better person. The stories you'd write about would be those universal messages we all go through, such as rites of passage, dealing with the stages of life in new ways, finding alternatives, and how you handled the challenges.

The pod cast's theme could be on how you found the answer close to home that helped you make a choice, what caused your transformation, how and why you changed or grew, and what you learned from your prior mistakes. Include step-by-step guidelines that achieved results.

INCOME POTENTIAL

After you produce your video pod cast, write a short article of about 1,500-1,800 words, and submit a query letter, and then the article to magazines interested in inspirational, religious, self-help, health, mind-body-spirit, or new age markets. Each magazine may offer a different payment based on the number of words published after editing. Some publications pay a nickel a word or ten cents a word and others pay a dollar a word or more. Income depends on whether you write articles for magazines, newspaper columns, books, or go on public speaking tours on a specific inspirational subject.

Try the religious, new age, holistic health, and inspirational markets, and the book publishers under the title Mind-Body-Spirit or "inspirational books." You can earn from making your own CDs or DVDs with inspirational messages, lectures, or humor. Or create audio books with inspirational and life story themes.

Join various small publishers' groups such as Publishers' Marketing Association (PMA) at: http://www.pma-online.org/ or Small Publishers Association of North America at: http://www.spannet.org/ for instruction and information in operating an inspirational publishing business if you want to publish your own material.

BEST LOCALE TO OPERATE THE BUSINESS

Working at home online is the cheapest way to get started in publishing or writing inspirational material. You can work from small offices in the libraries of churches or church offices, any office in a house of worship or inspirational organization.

The Bible belt location also is helpful if you're writing or publishing religious books. Being close to a center of inspirational, new age, trendy, or alternative healing conventions works best if you need foot traffic.

If your business comes from selling at trade show or convention booths, locate to where most of the alternative health and healing conventions take place, where the foot traffic is high if you want to take a booth at conventions. Otherwise, work online or by catalogue. Otherwise, working at home and online can be done from most locations.

TRAINING REQUIRED

Read inspirational books and articles and study what the publications want most, especially in new trends in publishing. Every two years there's a new fashion in publishing such as angel books or published diaries. Familiarize yourself with what the inspirational market needs by talking to booksellers, publishers, and those who buy inspirational books. Ask them what sells more each year.

The religious and spiritual or inspirational markets want stories that offer pictures and choices and show how you solved your problems. The reason people read your story is to find out how to solve their own problems and make decisions. Give them information they can use to make decisions, even if you write fiction. Have some authority and truth in the fiction, particularly about facts and historical information.

People buy your story to make choices, including choices in the later stages of life or choices in growing up and making transitions. As people move from one career to another or from one stage of life to the next, they want to read about how you made that passage in time and space, and what choices you made.

Life story writing should be more preventive than reactive. Biography writing is reactive because it responds only when people are in need, in transition, or in turmoil. What sells is preventive story writing.

Give transformation, growth, and problem solving information so people will be able to prevent making your past mistakes. Show readers, viewers, or listeners how you've learned from your mistakes and pass on your wisdom, growth, and change. Readers want to share your understanding.

OPERATING YOUR BUSINESS

Put rewards and possibilities for personal growth into your life story. Don't merely dump your pain and prior abuse on readers or your history of how you were tortured. That's not going to solve their problems.

What will is writing about how you've worked at understanding challenges. Look at your readers as your future selves.

Approach life story writing as you would approach writing song lyrics. Pick an industry and focus on the industry as you develop a life story built around an industry or event. If you write about your own life story, do interviews. Gather many different views.

You'll discover blind spots you would never have noticed about yourself. Treat your life story not only as a diary with a one-sided view, but as a biography. Interview many people who have had contact with you as you grew up or during the experience you're targeting.

Writing the Forward

If you write a biography of another person as a book, story or article, or as fiction in a novel, you'll need a foreword. This is what you're doing as you first meet the person you're interviewing. Have two tape recorders going at the same time in case one isn't working properly. Get permission to record. Write what you're doing as you first meet the person you're interviewing. It should be about 16 double-spaced pages or 8 printed pages, or less.

Writing the Preface

What is the person most conscious of? What is the individual whose biography you're writing doing right now as you first interview that person? What's the biography going to zoom in on? Describe the body language.

In Andrew Morton's Monica's Story, Monica stifles a yawn and pulls on black leggings as the preface opens with the title "Betrayal at Pentagon City." The preface summarizes the most important event in the entire biography.

It should be about 10 double-spaced pages or 5 printed pages. Is your character going to be the right person at the right time in the wrong place? Or the wrong person at the wrong time in the right place?

Writing your First Chapter

Begin with the person immediately becoming involved in the action if he is not well-known. If your person is in the news and a known celebrity or royalty, start with the date and season.

It's all right to begin with the birth of your biographical character if the child-hood has some relationship to the biography. You can describe the parents of the character if their relationship has a bearing on the life of the main character you're portraying.

The less famous or news-worthy your character, the more you need to start with the character involved in the middle of the action or crisis, the most important event. Avoid any scenes where the book or story opens and the character is in transit flying to some destination. Start after the arrival, when the action pace is fast and eventful.

Characters

You can make a great career writing true story books about people in the news, celebrities, and the famous. If these are the type of books you want to write, focus on the character's difficult childhood if it's important to the story and the character is famous or in the news frequently. To create the tension, get into any betrayals by the third chapter. Show how your character's trusting nature snared the individual in a treacherous web, if that's in your story. If not, highlight your main crisis here in the third chapter.

By the fourth chapter, show the gauntlet or inquiry your character is going through. How did it affect your character and the person's family? How will it haunt your character? Where will your character go from here? What are the person's plans?

Focus on an industry or career, whether it be the world of modern art or computers to get the inside story of the people and the industry and how they react and interact. What is your character's dream? How does your character realize his or her dream?

How does the person achieve goals in the wake of the event, scandal, or other true story happening? Take your reader beyond the headlines and sound bits. Discover your character in your story and show how readers also can understand the person whose life story you're writing.

It makes no difference if it's your own or another's. You may want to bring out your story's texture more by adding a pet character and focusing also on the pet's reactions to your characters. For further information, below is a list of several book publishers and magazines in the field of religious and inspirational markets. Contact the various inspirational or religious booksellers associations, publishers associations, and religious or ethnic publishers associations.

Some Religious and Spiritual Book Publishers

Abingdon Press
Augsburg Fortress Publishing
Baker Book House
Behrman House
Bethany House Publishers
ChariotVictor Publishing
Dharma Publishing
Discipleship Resources
Feldheim Books

Gefen Publishing House Ltd.
Gospel Advocate Company
Hachai Publishing
Hazelden Publishing Group
Herald Press
Hope Publishing House
InterVarsity Press
Jason Aronson Inc. Publishers
Jewish Lights Publishing
Jewish Publication Society
Jonathan David Co., Inc. Publishers Joy Publishing
Judson Press
Kar-Ben Copies
Ktav Publishing House
Liguori Publications
The Littman Library of Jewish Civilization
Llewellyn Publications
Moody Press
Numata Center
Paraclete Press
Paulist Press
Pilgrim Press
Pitspopany Press
Red Heifer Press
St. Anthony Messenger Press
Targum Press
Thomas Nelson
Tyndale House Publishers
United Methodist Publishing House
Urim Publications
Vendanta Press
Westminster John Knox
Zondervan Publishing House

Magazines

Alive Now
Angels on Earth
Bible Advocate

Campus Life Magazine
Catholic Digest
Celebrations
Christian Families Online
Christian Home & School
Christian Science Monitor
ChristianWeek
Catholic Peace Voice
Catholic Rural Life
Children's Ministry
Church Herald and Holiness Banner,
Companion Magazine
Expression Christian NewspaperGreen
Cross Magazine
Guideposts for Kids
Indian Life
Moody Magazine
New Writing Magazine

Our Little Friend (Weekly take-home paper for 1-6 yr olds)
Presbyterian Record
Spiritual Life
Teens Mission Launch Pad
The Upper Room
The Quiet Hour Echoes

Alphabetical Listing of Periodical Publishers
http://www.colc.com/pubbook/periodical.htm

Association of Jewish Book Publishers
http://www.avotaynu.com/ajbp.html

Christian Book Publishers
http://www.colc.com/Publish.htm

Secular Newspapers with Religion Editors
http://www.colc.com/pubbook/reli-ed.htm

Pod casting News: Religion and Spirituality Directory
http://www.pod castingnews.com/forum/links.php?id=73

10

DESCRIPTION OF BOOK PUBLICITY BUSINESS
Make Smaller Booklets, Pamphlets and Health Videos or Audios to Promote Your Book

Write and publish booklets that promote your fuller-sized book. Then help recruit speakers for panels at conventions, conferences, and meetings. After some experience with a professional or trade association, volunteer to be on a panel yourself. Answer questions related to the subject and purpose of your book.

You can offer this question and answer service on radio as well or on a TV panel with other guests or alone, with experience. It's also helpful online if you want to answer questions without payment to help you accumulate questions and answers from a wide audience, including feedback.

Your book promotional audio and video pod casts can cover seminars, lectures, and conventions. Show people at seminars and in other situations finding higher quality and/or alternative nutrition and health care. If you don't have insurance or need to save money on your health, make sure you take advantage of free health screenings offered at health fairs. Senior centers, shopping malls, health departments, and other health agencies or businesses have frequent health fairs. Some items you can get for free include blood pressure and bone density screenings, cholesterol and blood glucose readings, weight, and other measures.

Flu shots usually are given free or at very low cost to certain age groups such as older adults. Call each health fair and ask the requirements.

Many screenings don't have age requirements. Ask that copies of the reports be sent to you as well as your doctor. Keep a record of your numbers and measurements. Different health fairs emphasize screening for different health issues such as bone density, blood sugar, blood pressure, or other research. Your health department and the sponsors of the health fair will have the schedules.

Study the health Web sites for factual material that you can research in magazines and journals. Health food stores have free booklets and pamphlets on various supplements and health food products.

INCOME POTENTIAL

There's income in referring people to various health establishments ranging from clinical trials that pay people or give them free examinations to spas, rehabilitation centers, home health care services, senior services, assisted living apartments, anti-aging conventions, alternative medicine and health treatments, nutrition retreats, free plastic surgery from physicians who donate their time free and travel around the world on hospital ships, to reducing farms.

Usually, you would earn a commission much like a travel agent from the health care establishment you refer people to by educating them with facts about the establishment or the research as in clinical trials of various new treatments. Ask the establishment what percentage of a commission for referrals you'd be paid.

You can also publish material or reports about the health service or offer marketing communications services and information dissemination. You're acting as "an observer" reporting information about the health care establishment, procedure, clinical trial, or other service. Or you're making referrals by finding new clients for the establishment for a commission or flat fee.

Use your public library to read about what foods and nutrients work best. Make use of any offers for paid-for DNA testing for ancestry. Some genealogy surname groups on the Web offer to pay for DNA tests for ancestry.

Find out whether your surname fits the projects being researched. These tests usually are for males, and the Y chromosome is tested for ancestry research connected to some surname groups. Ask the various DNA testing companies that emphasize testing for ancestry whether there is a surname group offering to pay for DNA Y chromosome ancestry tests for males with the same surname, if there's a project researching the ancestry of that particular surname.

Besides attending conventions or expos and trade shows, referring people for clinical trials, or traveling to give lectures as a medical journalist or health referral agent, you could write and/or publish alternative health booklets. Here's how to publish these types of pamphlets.

OPERATING YOUR BUSINESS

Produce video pod casts of the highlights and significant points of your own or with permission, other authors' 72-page or 98-page pamphlets and booklets on alternative health, clinical trials, nutrition, spas, procedures, or contemporary issues, pet training, animal behavior, parenting, or school-related subjects such as biographies of historical characters, ethnic studies, or any other subject of interest to a wide or niche audience. You can publish the pamphlets, write them yourself or use with permission other writers' pamphlets, and then produce video segments dramatizing, reviewing, or discussing the materials. Also, you could narrate the video pod casts.

Before you produce pod casts based on booklets or pamphlets on controversial issues in the news or controversies in health, nutrition, or other issues, you'd have to write and publish those pamphlets. Your video pod cast can publicize what you write and publish yourself.

Pamphlets can be of the general consumer type found at supermarket checkout counters or specialty pamphlets on how-to subjects. Or they can be genre fiction such as children's stories, romances, or biography. Another form of pamphlet is the one-act 45 minute play suitable for high-school drama classes.

Here's how to write and sell a fast-selling paperback 98-page (when published) pamphlet or booklet, the kind you see on supermarket impulse racks at the check stand. They can sell quite a number of copies, or you can sell them by mail order or online from your Web site.

Start by writing about twice the number of pages that will be published. For a 98-page booklet, about 196 double spaced typed pages produces, usually a single-spaced booklet with double spaces and headlines between the sections. You may come out with having to write less than 196 pages, it depends upon the font and size of the booklet. However, here are the dimensions you'll need.

The size of the booklet may either be six inches wide by nine inches in length or five and a half inches wide by 8 inches or 8 1/2 inches in length. Take your choice. The difference is that trade paperbacks of 6 by 9 inches fit on supermarket impulse racks at checkout counters, whereas the mass market paperbacks you see in supermarkets and book stores in the back areas on special 5 by 8 book-size racks are standard for novels in the mass paperback market.

Let's say you choose the 6 by 9 size, which is the best fit for the impulse check out stand supermarket size. It will also fit into gift shops and specialty store racks. You'll have a soft, glossy cover with your price, usually $2.99 printed on the upper right hand corner of the book cover. The title will be placed in the middle of the book cover toward the upper half. It will be centered and have a two-word to five-word title that speaks volumes about what's in your little paper book.

In the middle of the cover, explain in one short sentence in smaller font, about 24 point what your book shows people how to do. It must be a how-to book such as how to find and keep a soul-mate, or some other how-to theme.

Below the explanation is the author's name: By: Joe John, or whatever name you want on the cover. Inside the cover on the left hand side you print the name of your publishing company. Assuming you're publishing the booklet yourself, put an intelligent-sounding two-word name for your publishing company such as Behavioral Digests and trade mark your publishing firm, even if it's only you at home.

Then under than you can put a longer publishing company name, just in case you want to publish other items besides these little paperback booklets. Put something light Published by International Palm-sized Books, Inc., and your address. You can incorporate your publishing company. Use an office address or a PO Box number, not your home address. You don't want people showing up on the front steps.

Under your mailing address, write: "Copyright, the year, by, your publishing company, address and e-mail address." Leave out your home phone.

You can add a disclaimer in small font at the bottom that "Reproduction in whole or part of any (your publishing company's name) without written authorization is prohibited. Then add at the bottom, "printed in the USA" or wherever you send the booklet to be printed. I understand printing prices in Singapore are great, so I hear from greeting card publishers nowadays.

On your first page's right hand side, print the name of the book centered up close to the top of the page, leaving a 2 inch margin from the top. Put in a small clip art illustration or your own art, and then a line and a by (author's name) at the bottom, leaving another 2 inch margin from the bottom.

The left hand side of the first page can have an illustration centered. On the right hand side put your table of contents. Label it Contents. Divide your booklet into six small chapters and list them. Let's say your book is on how to find a rich mate. Label it with a title, such as why am I single? Then have a second chapter on your cure-all for loneliness.

A third chapter on raising your feeling of importance, a fourth chapter on how to appreciate being by yourself in various settings, a fifth chapter on how to find your soul mate and where to look, and a last or sixth chapter on how to keep your mate once you found him or her. Mostly women will buy this book on impulse, but if the book is labeled, how to pick up girls, of course it will attract guys or anyone who wants to meet girls.

The left hand side of your table of contents page should have artwork on it centered. Then on page 7, a right-hand side page, your first chapter begins with the title, self-explanatory and short, usually asking a question which you will answer in your first chapter. Define your question and answer it. Keep each chapter four printed pages, which is eight double spaced type written pages. When made single-spaced, each chapter runs to about four printed pages each.

Then start your second chapter on page eleven. Break your booklet up into segments or chunks. The printing will be singled spaced with double spaces between each section heading. Show the reader how to solve a problem or fill a need. The problem could be technical or personal, business-oriented or relationship-oriented, health-directed, or about healing and nutrition, parenting, or any subject likely to land on a supermarket check out counter's impulse rack.

After every 14 or 14 chapters, usually 13 to 15 chapters, you'll need a segment or section break with a new title, perhaps outline your case histories, success stories, anecdotes, interviews, or using someone as an example. Don't use real names unless you have signed permission letters and can footnote that at the end of each chapter in a list of references that's numbered. For brevity, use a first name only and an initial, usually a fake false name approved by whomever you interview with an asterisk saying the name was changed to preserve privacy.

Use more than one example, usually two or three case histories. You can also use celebrity examples if you can get permission for success stories that run about 13 paragraphs each.

Have sections divided if you can around page 19, 21, 23, and start another chapter heading around page 28. Every two pages should have section breaks with new headings. You might write and publish a booklet on journaling and describe how it's related to a feeling of self-importance or of accepting oneself as "good," or write a technical or business how-to if you're not an expert on relationships.

More women will buy these booklets if they're about relationships. You can focus on instructional booklets on any topic from needlepoint and crafts to how to paint furniture and offer it to do-it-yourself stores, such as the big chain stores that customers frequent to buy do-it yourself materials for home repair and building. Another fast-selling area is travel writing.

This would focus on where to go and how to find specifics from antiques to restaurants and entertainment for various ages, education, visual anthropology, or special needs, such as traveling with multiple disabilities or traveling with one's dog or cat. One person trains his cat to use any toilet so he can take it into motel rooms without a litter box.

Your main focus is on how to do something, build something, solve a problem, make choices, or fill various needs, from quilting to relationships. Most people buy booklets with general titles such as how to keep a mate from leaving or how to save a troubled marriage.

Your six-chapter booklet should take up about 98 pages when printed, so don't make it longer or it won't fit into the small books rack in supermarkets and gift shops. It's easier to mail that way. Break your six chapters into three sections that run about two pages each per section with each chapter about four to six pages in length, but vary the length throughout the booklet.

Distribute it yourself or find a distributor who handles the supermarket impulse checkout counter rack. Or you can use gift shops or mail order. Another way to go is to offer your booklet to the tabloids as they have publishing divisions for these types of little books. They'll take a lot of your profit, so my advice is do everything yourself from writing to selling.

A print run of 1,500 copies would test your markets, but do your market research first to make sure someone would buy your book in large numbers. You might try a test run in a supermarket to see if the booklet moves and whether it competes with the tabloid-published booklets of similar size and length.

Will the tabloids let you compete with them in their supermarket client's racks? If not, you have the small gift shops and the malls. If you want to move the booklet, also offer it on tape or online for the e-publishing download market or on a CD ROM or DVD disk. Look at all the marketing alternatives and give your booklet visibility in place where people gather. Career booklets belong in community college and high school career counseling libraries.

Non-Fiction Booklets and Pamphlet on Controversial or Contemporary Issues

Write and publish sixty-six-page pamphlets or booklets that are about 4 inches wide and about 6 inches in length. These booklets fill up quickly with your articles. Don't forget to reduce the number of pages you write that first start out as double-spaced typed pages.

You can also provide marketing research for corporations or information for advertising and public relations agencies, employment agencies, or college career centers in this format or mystery shopper news if updates aren't required more frequently than annually.

If you're printing up an 8 1/2 by 11 inch page, usually it takes up to twice as much writing to reduce the size in half when you print up single spaced content with a double space between paragraphs and allow for a 16 point type size font for each heading or larger fonts for chapter headings.

Make Small Booklets with Fresh Information

When you print up small booklets, you'll need much less writing to fill up a whole little booklet. These small booklets are bought by school libraries to fill research folders on a variety of topics that are current issues in the news. If you are marketing to the general public through supermarket racks on impulse shelves near the checkout counter, usually near the checkout person, you'll want to supply each supermarket with your own racks the size of your tiny booklets.

The subjects that sell best are topics that tell the reader how something affects or changes something else. For example, how different foods affect your moods, and subtitle the booklet how people can change their behavior or their lives by adjusting the foods to their moods or any other topic telling readers how to improve themselves with the specific information.

Price your booklets anywhere from $1 to $2. Usually $1.19 in the US and $1.49 in Canada is fine, keeping the price plus tax adding up to an even amount. Find out what the tax would be on your booklets to one person at a checkout counter for the booklet. Then adjust the price so the reader can pay the tax and your price and have it add up to an easy to come up with amount, like $1.20 or $1.50. Calculate your expenses so you can arrive at a price that looks inviting.

Keep your pages around 66. Use an even number of pages. Your cover would have a title and a subtitle explaining what the title can do for the reader, how changing the behavior can change the person's life. Print your company or publishing name and address on the inside cover in the center.

On the first page, label it "Contents" and list you six or seven chapters and the page numbers. At the bottom of the contents page, about two inches up from the bottom of the page have the authors name in small, but easily readable font, such as 10 point Times New Roman or italics.

The left hand side of the contents page should have a disclaimer saying that your book is intended as a reference volume, not a medical manual so you won't be sued for giving medical advice without a license or credentials. Put in there that your booklet doesn't presume to give medical advice.

You really need this in there. Add a "consult your physician before beginning any therapeutic program," to protect yourself from being sued or accused of giving medical advice. You need this disclaimer on any booklet that gives information based on material provided by actual researchers and experts, even if you are using medical articles with simplified English or anything where people are told what to eat to change their health or behavior.

Always put this disclaimer or a similar one into a booklet you write and publish. This is especially true when you interview doctors or read their articles and report what they wrote, even with their written permission, which you always need to have. You don't need this disclaimer of your booklet is about how to knit costumes for animals or how to fix a leaky faucet or repair and antique furniture, but you need it for special diet, food, and nutrition booklets.

Each chapter can run four to 12 pages in this tiny booklet with the chapter divided every few paragraphs into new headings so you break up your booklet in chunks. Try to balance the size of your chapters. Usually four-page chapters work best in this size booklet totaling about 6 or 7 chapters, and total amount of pages being about 66.

Keep your pages an even number. Don't leave blank pages in this size booklet. Place a one or two-sentence description of the booklet centered about one inch down from the top of your glossy back cover.

Put it in a box if you like, and place or print your bar code below with the price on the back. You'll also have the price on the front cover, your logo in the upper left hand corner of the front cover, the title, subtitle, and any illustration, usually a photo in color of a person working with the items in the book or doing some action that sums up what the book says.

Have the book cover put on with two staples in the spine that are not readily noticeable to the reader. Only the backs of the staples should be seen on the spine, and flat into the crease of the spine of the book so as not to catch on any object. You don't need an ISBN number for this kind of booklet, only a bar code so the scanning machine in the supermarket can scan it. Provide your own racks if ones there belong to other merchants and distributors. Have the price on the front and back cover in addition to the bar code so readers can see the price immediately.

If you write on health topics, keep the English simple, writing at 5th grade level. Keep sentences short and paragraphs short, about two sentences per paragraph. Use Times New Roman 12 point type, nothing smaller, or older people won't want to look unless they have their reading glasses. So keep the font large enough for most people to see at most ages.

You can find distributors who specialize in small pamphlets and booklets. Print your own catalogue listing all your pamphlet/booklet titles. Place a catalogue copy on the Internet's Web to reach people around the world. Specialize in supplying college and high school career counseling offices with booklets on each type of career in a group of related careers. Or focus on foods and health or psychology and behavior for self-help.

Inspirational, religious, New Age, nutritional, and holistic health booklets each have individual, customized, expanding markets associated with conferences, conventions, suppliers, vendors, publications, and members of the various groups with similar interests.

If you want people to pay for your booklets, give readers information that's not easy to find and is not usually found among the free literature available in health food stores, community centers, self-help magazines, or religious organizations. Also try specialty gift stores, home building centers, discount stores, libraries, business, professional, and trade associations, corporations, schools, and employee organizations.

Supermarkets have special display racks with informational booklets and short romances. Some of these publishers are parts of larger publishing companies, such as the tabloids. Try gift shops, museums, libraries, bookstores, schools, churches, hotel lobby shops, sports stores such as golf and tennis shops at hotels and resorts, golf courses, and sports clubs.

Keep trying the supermarkets and smaller convenience stores until you find a store that lets you put in your own display rack for your catalogue of booklets or pamphlets. Sometimes used bookstores will allow you to put in a display case or rack of your short romances or historical fiction. School supply stores may be interested in your pamphlets with biographies of historical characters or vocational biographies.

Writing on contemporary and controversial issues in the news supplies school libraries with information for student research. Pamphlets need a bar code and a price more than they need an ISBN, but you can get one in case you want your booklet to go to libraries and schools or be sold by online booksellers and distributed by national distributors.

Write and publish how-to material relating to family history research. Everyone likes to read about his or her own family. Personal history records owe a lot to the invention of writing. And then there is oral history, but someone needs to transcribe oral history to record and archive them for the future.

ADDITIONAL INFORMATION: Pod cast Feed Urls

Pod casting News: Health and Fitness Pod cast Directory
http://www.pod castingnews.com/forum/link_13.htm

Sanoviv Alternative Health Care Medical Institute
Pod cast Feed URL: http://feeds.feedburner.
com/SanovivMedicalInstituteAchievePerfectHealth

A Better Day (Helping to make everyday a better day)
http://feeds.feedburner.com/ABetterDaysMedia

2Down (Weight Loss) Pod cast News Feed: http://feeds.feedburner.com/
TwoDown
Fitness
Pod cast Feed Url: http://feeds.feedburner.com/ABetterDaysMedia

11

DESCRIPTION OF BOOK PUBLICITY BUSINESS
Promote Your Major Book or Series by Writing and Publishing Short & Sweet Romance Stories as Booklets. Then Produce Video Segments of Romantic Stories or Excerpts

First create a following with romantic fiction dramatized and/or promoted on your video pod casts. Interview a panel of authors of published romance fiction and videos. Then publish your own romantic fiction collection as 72-page booklets consisting of romance stories or novelettes.

Set up a display rack near check-out counters of gift, book, and grocery stores. These are called the impulse racks in supermarkets. Turn your sweet or historical romance stories into a 4 inch by 6 inch small, 72-page booklets of either collected stories or one novelette, and sell your work in supermarkets and gift shops, candy gift stores, or packaged with other products.

Don't forget those wonderful romance novelettes and stories you have that are shorter than book length. Keep producing video pod casts of your short romance novelettes, especially those published in nontraditional formats, such as print-on-demand books or written as dramatized story scripts. These can be dramatizations of the entire story or a collection of excerpts from your publications, or author interviews and reviews.

Promote them on holidays such as St. Valentine's Day. Take your booklets to romance writers' conventions and club meetings. Write and publish pamphlets of holiday stories for Christmas, Easter, or any other religious holiday with appropriate stories or historical research articles. Promote them a month before the holidays. Animal stories are good such as cat or dog stories for Christmas or other holiday themes.

If they are sweet romances, short stories in three parts or "acts," of about 23 pages for each act, totaling around 72 pages or so, you can turn them into 72-page, 4 inch by 6 inch booklets, promote, and sell the little pamphlets at supermarkets. They go in the impulse racks at the checkout counters. Most of these small size mini-racks hold booklets about four inches wide by six inches long. This is the ideal size for romance stories or novelettes.

You'll get about a maximum of 300 words on a page: that's a maximum of 10 or 11 words across a line and about a maximum of 30 lines on a page. For first pages of new sections, and you'll have three sections or "acts," you start about two inches down from the top of the page with the first letter of your beginning sentence capitalized and highlighted in a larger font than the rest of the letters.

Print or place a bar code on the back of each booklet. It's a good idea to get an ISBN. It's a number placed on the back cover of books used as a code to find the book or to locate it in The Library of Congress and in the catalogue of the original publisher.

Publishers, libraries, and book sellers locate books through that number. You don't necessarily need an ISBN unless you want to send your booklets to gift shops, libraries, schools, booksellers, or other publishers.

You'll need or put your own racks up to match your customized size in supermarkets if they have room, but the small size that holds the four by six inch booklet is fine.

How to Get an IBSN for Your Book, Pamphlet, or Booklet

If you plan to sell your booklet by mail order to gift shops in hospitals or to libraries, get the ISBN as well as the bar code. The ISBN is a unique machine-readable identification number, which marks any book.

If you need instructions on how to send away for an ISBN number to print on the back cover of your booklet, contact the national or regional ISBN agency in your own country. Presently, more than 160 countries or territories are official ISBN members. Check out the Web site of ISBN information titled, How to Get an IBSN number at: http://www.isbn-international.org/en/howtoget.html. The site for the USA regional office is at: http://www.isbn-international.

org/en/agencies/usa.html. It's called The ISBN Agency for the United States. And it's in operation since 1968. It is located at the R. R. Bowker Co., LLC. Write to them at the following address:

R.R. Bowker Co., LLC
Att. Ms. Doreen Gravesande
Senior Director ISBN/SAN/PAD
630 Central Ave.
New Providence, NJ 07974

Tel: Toll Free/United States: 877-310-7333
All others: (+1 908) 286-1090
Fax: (+1 908) 219-0188
E-mail: isbn-san@bowker.com
URL: http://www.isbn.org

Decide whether you'd like to put an ISBN on the back cover of your book or only a bar code and the price. A typical booklet that is four inches wide by six inches in length has no ISBN number on the back cover. Instead, it has the price and a bar code at the bottom. In the middle of the back cover would be a title and subtitle and three sentences or two paragraphs explaining the main message of your booklet or pamphlet. The typical number of pages would be about 66 for this type of booklet.

The size is suitable for supermarket racks. One excellent example is a booklet titled *What Do Dogs Dream About?* It is published by Mini Mags in Boca Raton, Florida, copyrighted in 2000. The back cover tells you what the booklet is about. And it has a bar code and price on the back cover. The last page contains a box with the sentence: "We Want Your Cute Dog Stories."

When you publish your booklet, use the bottom of the last page, if space allows, to ask readers for feedback and to collect ideas and stories for your next pamphlet. And always obtain written permission from anyone who sends you anything before you use it in any way. A good way to collect ideas or stories is to run writing contests and publish the winning story. Decide what the prize will be and whether one-time publishing rights would be what the author and you agree on. Or work only with your own stories.

Writing and Publishing Your Own Sweet or Historical Romances or Biographies

Here's how to organize your little book of sweet romances or biographies of historical characters. The cover should be a glossy heavier weight paper that can fold easily enough to fit into a small pocket or purse so people can carry the book easily onto transportation. Your book also can contain an envelope inside the back cover with a DVD or CD of your dramatized romance novelette.

Market your video romances and books at racks in airports, train, and bus stations or at transit centers in vending machines if you buy the empty ones and place them where you can get permission. Hotel lobbies have racks that could fit your book, but usually you supply your own racks to hotels and convention centers.

Resorts and antique malls also are great places for your little book. Tourist attraction shops in the "old town" sections of cities are great. Any establishment that sells tourist souvenirs makes a great place to sell your little romances. People staying in hotels and motels can read the little books, and you can offer the same size booklets with adventure stories or romances related to the particular town or resort history.

On the cover have an illustration in color of the couple featured in the romance story, usually a cameo of the couple featured against a pristine background of countryside, or local resort attractions. On the top you can put a ribbon-like title "Your (logo or name) Romance Library" or "Historical Romances of the resort city___" or whatever you want to feature as your own publishing and writing library.

This represents your collection of booklets. You can publish your own writing or those from other romance or historical fiction writers. Travel booklets, auto travel games for kids, or travel romances also can be published in this format.

Usually sweet romances sell better than other genres in this type and size of booklet. People want a sweet romance to escape to and to read at night, especially people traveling on business at hotels. The books will be bought by women and female students of all ages, with the highest demographic being in the 18 to 44 age range and the next highest, 44 to 54 age range.

INCOME POTENTIAL

Sell your pamphlets or booklets for one or two dollars. Keep the price low and similar to the commercial romances and how-to booklets on sale at the impulse counters or racks of supermarket shelves, right next to the check-out counters.

To help sell your romance against the competition, put in a pet character, usually a cat or kitten or a pair of cats in the story that bring the couple together. Your story can feature a female who works at an animal shelter. In this way you can bring in a real animal shelter and dedicate your booklet to animal rescue volunteers, which helps move the story. You can also donate a percentage of your income from the booklet to help animal rescue shelters of your choice.

Make sure your story is universal and familiar enough to sell anywhere in the country or even overseas. Your booklet also can be translated into languages if you sell to various countries. Keep your pamphlet-sized library focused on sweet romance. These supermarket rack pamphlets appeal to a wider and older audience than the actual full-length romance novels found in bookstores.

TRAINING REQUIRED

Read short romance novels found at supermarket check-out stands. Study the pages, how they are stapled and the quality of paper on the cover. Look at the printing. Take a pamphlet or small novel to a printer and get a price quote for these short novels. Ask the supermarket how to get your novel on their rack. Try small bookstores and gift shops first, including hotel gift shops and airport, bus, and train station impulse racks at the food counters. Ask people who buy these booklets what they are looking for in a story.

EQUIPMENT NEEDED

You'll need a computer and a printer. Also, the kind of printer you go to in order to have a booklet published. Decide what kind of art work or photo you want on the cover and what type and size of lettering. Check rates out of the country to see whether printing is cheaper abroad or locally. Make sure the printer staples the covers to the booklets. Proofread everything several times before giving to the printer as they don't usually read the material or check for typos.

To follow a template, buy several of these little romantic stories at your local supermarket counters and study every detail—not only the story, but the way the book is put together. Look at the cover and the art work. Then make your own original template for the cover and layout. Never use the same template of an existing book because everything always is copyrighted. Just use the work to study for inspiration. Then design your own details.

People want to believe that love, commitment, and faith in your ability to hold a family together while standing on your own two feet and pulling your weight conquers all. People buy these little stories to relax, to be nourished, to feel good and important and to escape the real world. Yet the story must be real enough so that it could believably happen to the reader.

Your little booklet will be a tiny version of a magazine. In the romance story, keep it around 72 pages as the best-size and weight for handling, mailing, and reading in one sitting. Most people will buy these as they leave the supermarket to take with them during that long hour or two wait in doctors and dentists offices or while taking a two-hour train ride or while on vacation on the beach or in a hotel or during anytime when waiting is necessary.

The non-fiction informational booklet can be around 66 pages in length. It's not going to make a difference whether your pages run to 66 or 72 as long as the last page isn't a blank waste of space and the two staples on the spine that binds the glossy front and back covers will easily hold together the booklet.

OPERATING YOUR BUSINESS

How to Format Your Book or Booklet Manuscript

Start your story halfway down page 3 with the title of your little book. You'll find about six paragraphs can fit on one page. In a sweet romance story, don't have chapter headings or a table of contents. Instead of chapter headings, you only have the title page with author's name and dedication "to the_____." Fill in to whomever you dedicate the story.

Use three asterisks (***) at the end of each part or chapter of the story instead of chapter headings. The asterisks represent the breaks in the story when the action changes instead of having chapter headings. Your story can run about an average of 23 to 26 pages before the chapter ends with the three asterisks and new action begins, for example, on page 27. Then run the action on to about page 36 and have three asterisks there.

On page 38 the first sentence starts about two inches down with the first letter of the first sentence in larger and highlighted capital letters than the rest of the text. Your middle chapter ends about on page 62 with page 63 started with new action about two inches in margin from the top of the page and the first letter of the first sentence in highlighted, larger capital letters.

You'll notice that the book or story has three acts or three parts. Each chapter can be of unequal or equal length. It doesn't matter as long as it adds up to a total of about 72 pages. So you see, the sweet romance story has, like a full-length stage play or short cinema film, 72 pages made up of three acts. Each act takes up a third of the booklet or story. You have a beginning, middle, and end. It follows the rules for a romance novel with romantic push-and-pull tension between the characters.

In the story you bring together an unlikely couple that conquer the push and pull tension of first impressions that don't prove true as you flesh out the second and third act where sweet romance proves love conquers all.

Build up your own romance library of titles from your own writing or those of other authors. Some authors might want to start a cooperative where they share the cost of publication and distribution, but this is up to you.

You'd do well with only your own stories and publishing your own work. Distribute to supermarkets and gift stores. Then add other sources such as racks in hotels, waiting rooms, airports, hospitals, senior centers, community centers, bus or train stations, cruise ships' libraries, schools, or doctors' and dentists' offices, lawyers' offices, and any place people travel or wait, including tourist gift stores in resort areas and theme parks.

Book stores and libraries or vending machines in rest rooms or on the street near supermarkets are good bets for little books. Romance novelettes should run around 72 pages. Keep them even numbers. On the back cover place a two paragraph review of each character the starring male and female of the couple and tell something about the person in one sentence for each character. Use only two characters on the back cover.

Your third paragraph, a one-sentence statement tells what the story is about in a 15-word sentence that is centered in the middle of the page. Below this three sentence/three paragraph description, put a short statement about your romance library or book, such as "welcome to a cornucopia of sweet romance, where love brings different people together" or love conquers all (this one has been used on Mini-Mags).

So use your own original statement, "romance unites all." Pick your own logo. The bar code goes at the bottom of your back cover, usually in the lower left hand corner. Your own logo image goes at the lower right hand corner. Put your banner and initials centered beneath your "Welcome to the world of sweet romance" or other statement. Use your own statement, not the one Mini-Mags uses. Use them for inspiration only or marketing research.

On your front cover have your banner and logo, an illustration in the center, and your price at the lower left hand corner. Pick your own prices, but don't go over $2.00 or you won't compete with the $1.59 of the current ones. Have your 72-page romance novelettes or stories bound.

Don't use staples in a fiction booklet. That's only for how to booklets or tiny pamphlets on how to change something or improve one's behavior or booklets on food and nutrition or health. So be sure to have a bound booklet for romance that has no staples. Research the booklets in existence and show your printer.

This is one way to find winning strategies or guerilla tactics to salvage your wonderful stories if they are rejected and you know they are really as good or better than similar stories in print and selling wonderfully.

If you have revised your stories and have logical reasons and concrete research and marketing tests showing the content appeals to all audiences and could sell well if published, then a 72-page romance story printed and promoted would cost you far less than publishing a romance novel with no way to distribute it.

Do your research first. Talk to distributors, and find out how to get your small racks into supermarkets or other sources where you can sell them. Try news stands and vending machines or packaging your romance stories. Other products can be packaged with your booklet and offered as promotions. These might include honeymoon packages, lingerie, and mail order products such as gift baskets for bridal showers or booklets sold at writer's conventions.

You can review audio books and send the 110-word reviews to magazines publishing audio book reviews. Concentrate on the audio presentation and narrator rather than on the literary print format for an audio book review. Pamphlets and booklets can be converted to audio format.

You can narrate your own stories or informational pamphlets on audio CDs and market them alone or as package deals with other products or books. Audio material should run an hour on each CD, MP3 CD, DVD, or other format. Most people need a break after listening for an hour. Some tapes and CDs run about an hour and a half. Keep yours in that parameter, an hour to an hour and a half of listening, similar to a feature film.

Formatting Book Manuscripts for an Editor

Here's how to format a book manuscript. The acquisitions editor will hand your book to a group of readers after spending about 20 seconds getting a first impression. Your book manuscript is read as if it were a resume. They expect white 20 pound 8.5" X 11x" paper without textures. The acquisitions editor will photocopy your outline, proposal, synopsis, cover letter, and sample chapters or if fiction, completed book when requested.

If the paper weighs more than 20 pounds, it will be hard to photocopy, and thin, onion-skin paper will tear in the automatic photocopying machine. If you're in another country, send a clear photocopy of your work on this type of paper, if possible. Your book, again, is your resume and application for a business partnership or employment and needs to reflect that business mood.

The cover page will contain your book title, the division of the publishing house for which your book is intended, and the number of words and pages. You put your name and address on the cover sheet and the date. After your cover page, insert a blank sheet and put another blank sheet after the last page to protect the last page of your book from creasing and tearing.

My favorite romance of this size is author, Kathleen Dreesen's sweet romance story, *Loving Touch*. It runs the standard 72 pages, and the novelette booklet is published by American Media Mini Mags Inc., MicroMags logo. Her booklet is dedicated to the staff and volunteers at We Care Animal Rescue, St. Helena, California. The characters are fiction. Only their love is real, says the statement on the first page. I highly recommend reading this booklet to get an idea of the size and type of story that sells well.

On the inside of your cover, put your name, business address, and email. Put the date of the copyright and where it was printed, in the USA or elsewhere. Your title page would have the title centered, the author's name beneath it, and any dedication. On the back of your title page, print any information regarding your decision to accept or not accept unsolicited manuscripts from other writers.

Otherwise, you may get everyone sending you their romance stories in hopes you'll publish them. You don't want your mail or email blocked, so print a statement that you'll only take one-page queries if you're interested, or whether you don't want anyone sending you their own stories to publish.

Editors want a standard of one inch margins all around each page, on everything. Leave room for the reader's and editor's notes on top of the page. Your header is standardized at one inch from the top page and a half inch higher than where your text starts. Make sure your header is the same width as the text line.

On this page, you put the title of your book, your name, and the page number on the upper right corner. Use your full or last name (last name is preferred by most editors). Use the same font throughout, preferably Times New Roman 12 point.

Don't send books in any other font as editors are required to convert for typesetting departments to Times New Roman 12. So convert it if it's in Courier, Ariel or another font. Make sure the font is as black as you can get it and the paper is really white, not tan. It has to be photocopied without a shadow.

Most books accepted had more white space and paragraphs under ten lines. Rejected books almost always didn't have these appearances. When mailing your book, put it in a clear plastic bag, the kind you get from the supermarket or meat counter, with no printing on the bag.

The green or red printing comes off with moisture and ruins the book with stains. So no print is placed on the bag. After your book is in the clear plastic (transparent) bag, fold it over so it fits well around the book and put a small bit of transparent tape in the middle. Then put two rubber bands around your manuscript. One rubber band will be at the top and the other at the bottom to hold the plastic bag in place better and to keep pages together.

Don't send a manuscript in a loose leaf binder and don't put clips on it. Leave off any file folders. Put the manuscript along with a sturdy self-addressed stamped envelope inside a large envelope with book padding. Make sure the return envelope won't tear in shipping and handling when it's returned. Have the correct number of stamps on the envelope.

Also add to this before sealing, a self-addressed stamped post card the editor can return to let you know your book is received. You'd be surprised at the long way this courtesy goes and the effect it has on readers or editors about your attitude to save them the postage of a receipt reply. Print up some business cards and put this into a small envelope with your return card, so you'll look more like a professional writer with a business card.

Have a query letter or cover letter on top of everything so the editor will know what you want done with the book and what it's about, and perhaps a guide to the synopsis. In one paragraph or preferably one sentence, state or pitch what your book is about: For example, it has been said that "Star Trek is Wagon Train in Space."

Never embarrass an editor by sending a gift or artsy crafty item with a manuscript because everything will be returned after going in the slush pile. Manuscripts must never be faxed. They use up the editor's paper supply and make an awful impression on your attitude and boldness. You want to make an impact of courtesy and business-like manners, an aura of professionalism.

Every time someone faxes a manuscript or synopsis, usually it's rejected and taken as an insult for tying up the fax machine and using up the paper at the other end. So treat your manuscript as if it were your best resume. Show your enthusiasm by a professional, business-like attitude and common courtesy. When finished, produce a video pod cast dramatizing what's in your book—either the whole story, excerpts, or reviews. You can include the CD or DVD of your video pod cast in a sleeve inside the book's back cover. Keep the romance short so you don't have to publish at an expense. Or use print-on-demand software technology to turn out books and videos that dramatize the romantic or historical story.

ADDITIONAL INFORMATION

Place of Pines (The First Australian Novel to be Pod cast)
Romance and Historical Fiction
http://www.pod castdirectory.com/pod casts/index.php?iid=831

Life Matters
http://www.pod castdirectory.com/pod casts/index.php?iid=2289

National Public Radio Romance Novel Cover Stories
http://www.npr.org/templates/story/story.php?storyId=1138053

Pod cast.Net
http://www.pod cast.net/tag/romance

Harlequin to Offer Mobile Romances (Cell Phone-Based Entertainment)
http://www.engadget.com/entry/1234000977043124/

Blogcritics.Org
http://blogcritics.org/archives/2003/04/16/131311.php

Romance Writers of America
http://www.rwanational.org/

12

DESCRIPTION OF BOOK PUBLICITY BUSINESS:
Promote Your Book about Play Behaviors, Laughter, Health, Nutrition, or Leisure on Cruise Ships: Playology and Playography

Show duplications of your videos about your book, experience, or documentary on cruise ships. Or be there in person for one cruise. How would you like to work on cruise ships showing passengers and crew how to play for stress reduction and health benefits or work at home selling your play-for-health videos? Your videos can improve the quality of life for others. Wouldn't it be wonderful to make a video on the healing power and behaviors involved in play (playology) or the geography and description of play behavior (playography) linking research with dolphins and autistic children to show beneficial mutual effects? Your videos help therapists take clients to the next level of recovery. Do you have a book on the history of play or how play influences health?

Promote your book among video therapist technicians and creative expression therapists. The video therapist technician assists a psychologist, interpreter for the deaf, psychiatrist, social worker, counselor, teacher, or psychotherapist by operating a video camera, editing the tape, and monitoring a television set to help children and adults with emotional or behavioral problems. In some videos people and animals interact to show the beneficial or healing results from play between the two.

Scriptwriting is another option. The best market today is producing and distributing exercise, fitness, or healing-through-play videos for target populations and special groups of clients or patients such as preschool, seniors, persons with certain illnesses or disabilities.

Video therapy is done also with schizophrenics to show them how to have emotion, and with the elderly for therapeutic communication. It is a new bio-feedback technique that teaches speech volume and coping mechanisms. It condenses behavior into "well" role models on video tape and shows a person how others see him or her.

Video therapy teaches pro-social behavior in prisons, schools, geriatric homes, on-the-job, in psychologists' offices, and in numerous institutional settings. Experience is telescoped. The video therapist's duties are to film the counseling session and carefully to edit the tape to include only appropriate behavior.

The patient then sees the edited tape and becomes his or her own teaching resource. It's also important to videotape interpreters for the deaf as they do their hand and finger signing in American Sign Language.

These interpreters need to be videotaped so that the speaker in the background of the tape can be hand signed for deaf video viewers. Or you can close-caption video tapes and put in written words on the tape.

INCOME POTENTIAL:

A video therapist technician can create applications and uses for niche markets in video therapy, virtual reality, and fitness. As a video therapist technician you can write and/or produce training materials and multimedia for home-based persons or for people who work with a wide variety of clients in the self-help field. Create your own videos and sell them each in the range of $20 to $40 to helping professionals, allied health workers, and the public.

Place and watch advertisements at online auctions for other people or companies if you had nothing to sell. Your business would be a type of sales assistant who takes care of business for others who have lots of items to sell online and little time to watch when an item is sold or whether questions are asked. Mail packages for people who have sold an item online.

BEST LOCALE TO OPERATE THE BUSINESS:

Institutional centers, childhood development centers, schools, geriatric centers, psychiatrist's offices, marketing and advertising research firms, cable television stations, exercise spas, and educational psychology research programs.

Exercise, acupressure, Yoga, and playography videos appeal to stressed-out salespersons, therapists, teachers, attorneys, public speakers, holistic health workers, nurses, physicians, and other allied health workers, sedentary people, and anyone interested in personal growth, fitness, or nutrition. Involve pets in play behavior or exercise with human companions.

Operate your video business or distribute your tapes in areas where holistic health and alternative fitness instruction is popular—such as large cities, the whole state of California, the entire West coast, New York, large cities, ski resorts, health spas, vacation areas, Colorado, and especially, Arizona.

TRAINING REQUIRED:

Video school courses in camera operation and videotape editing are helpful. By learning how to edit videotape, you can save yourself the cost of hiring a video editor.

Many video production supplies stores offer short courses in how to edit tape and in video production techniques. They can also refer you to low-cost adult education courses in the community.

Community college courses in recreational therapy assisting, gerontology, or nursery school teaching also are helpful.

You can even earn a certificate as a "certified" recreational therapy aide or recreational therapist from a community or two-year college and produce videos on recreation for the institutionalized person or for senior centers and nursing homes. In addition, you can earn a certificate as a health and fitness trainer or health promoter from the extended studies division of many major universities. Extension courses (extended studies departments) are open to adults and usually have no-prerequisites.

GENERAL APTITUDE OR EXPERIENCE:

The ability to relate to all kinds of people under extremes of behavior is essential. An aptitude for editing video in an artistic way following specific directions is necessary.

EQUIPMENT NEEDED:

Purchase a broadcast quality video camera or super digital high 8 camcorder or DVD camcorder, video tape, editing machine, VCR player, computer for desktop video, and equipment to produce titles on your videotape. This can be either standalone title makers or computer software that produces titles on videotape and can be hooked up to your video camera. Call your local video supplies store to outfit you with camera, editing machines, title makers, and tape.

It's important that your video doesn't lose quality the more times it's played. Don't use a VHS home camcorder because the tapes lose quality when reproduced and when played over and over. You'll be making many copies of your tapes for distribution to a wide variety of helping professionals.

OPERATING YOUR BUSINESS:

How would you like to work on cruise ships showing passengers and crew how to play for stress reduction and health benefits? Contact psychotherapists, hypnotherapists, prison wardens, psychiatrists, hospitals, schools for special education, speech pathology centers, rehabilitation centers, psycho-dramatists and schools teaching psychodrama, art therapy, or the expressive and recreational therapies, home healthcare nursing departments of hospitals and home care agencies, nursing homes, senior citizens centers, recreational facilities, hospices, fitness centers, weight loss centers, nutrition companies, holistic health clinics, acupuncture schools, allied health care schools, and crises centers to find a therapist you can apprentice to as a video therapy technician.

You can teach Yoga exercises, acupressure, infant massage, exercises for pregnant women or senior citizens, holistic health, personal growth, preschooler's fitness training, alternative fitness techniques, playography (geographic diversity of types of play and their applications) or playology (the healing power of play) for beginners, seniors, the disabled, children, or any targeted audience.

Put the Yoga or acupressure instruction or other mild, stretching exercises on tape for relaxation or rehabilitation. Asian exercises such as Yoga or Tai Chi Chuan (Chinese slow exercises favored by seniors) are available on tape. Read studies of how Tai Chi for mature adults helps strengthen their ability to balance.

There are health benefits to certain other exercises that you could interview people about to make an instructional video. The type of exercise varies from belly dancing to Yoga and Tai Chi to wheelchair aerobics.

You can become an independent practitioner of exercise technology. Call the local spas, nursing homes, assisted living centers, and gerontology-oriented social and community centers. Ask whether they can hire you to work as a video therapist exercise technician. Or make a video on a DVD and offer the video to these types of establishments. Work with the elderly in homes, spas, and gerontology centers.

A decade later, we find acupressure, playography, Yoga, Tai Chi Chuan (Chinese exercise), infant massage, preschool children's exercise, exercises for pregnant women, and slow Oriental exercises for senior citizens tapes popular and in demand by people seeking alternative ways to physical fitness, personal growth, and relaxation techniques.

For example, infant massage tapes and exercise videos for pregnant women can be sold in maternity clothes stores. Alternative exercise tapes for senior citizens can be sold in stores and community centers older people frequent, and playography videos can be marketed at hospital workshops where patients learn stress release techniques or in classes, that nurses, psychologists, and social workers attend to fulfill continuing education licensing renewal requirements.

Playology videos focus on discovering the healing power of laughter and play, especially for people suffering from the fear of play. Playography videos emphasize the diverse and similar types of play around the world, at different periods of history, or within various ethnic groups. You could make videos using scientific data validating the healing power of play, including problem solving by using the creative process.

Compare play among tribal peoples or in contrasting areas of the world such as India, Scandinavia, Africa, Latin America, the USA, Australia, Oceania, the Middle East, Central Asia and Europe. Your videos could help viewers lighten up and learn to play more, laugh to promote health, and have fun wherever they happen to be at the moment in order to relieve stress.

Ellie Katz, R.N., PhD coined the word "*playology*." Highly recommended is her wonderful 10-minute video, "*Change Your Mind*," on the healing power of laughter and play. Ellie Katz traveled all over the world giving *playology* workshops and seminars on cruise ships.

Her 10-minute video is on the subject of how to play in your office, home, with groups, and how to stay healthy, do what you are and get better. The field of *playology*, (the healing power of play and laughter) or *playography* (defined as the geographic and demographic study of play) are field open for you to make videos, audios or other learning materials, including board games.

Show others how to get over the fear of playing and how to use scientific data validating the healing power of play. Or show others in a video DVD how play is enjoyed in different areas of the world—a visual geography or anthropology of play.

In addition to play therapy, you can view the healing power of oriental exercise on video. If you don't know anything about Yoga or Tai Chi, then join a class at your community center or extended studies for life-long learning group. Rent a video on any of these relaxation and healing-oriented exercises. Study scientific and behavioral studies of play as a combination of relaxation, laughter, and mild exercise.

Work with an instructor to make a video of any new approaches to healing or stress reduction through play or slow exercises. Make a video with the instructor giving beginning instructions on a 30 to 60 minute DVD, or produce a series of instructional video discs for beginners, intermediate, and advanced students.

Find out from the instructor, based on market surveys and the instructor's class numbers which tapes are most likely to sell—usually the beginner's tapes or intermediate. Variety for beginners is more important in the workouts than advanced studies that would appeal to fewer students.

Offer your services to work with the patients or clients in offering fitness or health-related videos for instructional or recreational purposes in the field of health and fitness, recreation, activities training, or creative and expressive arts.

When you find the centers you want to work for or the therapists you want to apprentice with, ask them what their specific needs are in video or videotaping to teach their clients pro-social behavior, such as self-esteem realities. Then produce the tapes to meet their exact requirements to help individual clients or patients. Video therapy is about transformation.

TARGET MARKET:

Find manufacturers of exercise equipment and ask them to include your videos prepackaged with their equipment. You can work out a barter deal with them so you can include your advertising on the back of your video package along with their advertising copy. Also ask specialty shops such as maternity or children's stores for permission to put your video display rack in their window or at their checkout counter for impulse buys as people pay for their merchandise.

Cooking videos frequently are sold along with new convection ovens. Exercise videos and booklets, or videos go well with prepackaged products.
Examples include the following:
Tai Chi Chuan
Infant massage
Pet massage,
Play for various age groups
Special interest organizations,
Exercise for pregnant women
Walking tours for older adults.

You can prepackage your video or instructional material with products related to exercise or relaxation equipment and healing music, memory-enhancing devices, furniture, sandals, clothing, appliances, and related types of devices and musical instruments. Some producers put relaxing sounds and sights, like nature and clouds with music on videotape for stress reduction.

Approach the maternity hospitals, birthing centers, or nurseries. Offer your video to new mothers leaving the hospital with their babies. Capture a niche market by focusing your tape on a subject like infant exercise and massage, exercises for postpartum women, acupressure, playography, tummy flattening tapes, or other health and fitness information on video appealing to a specifically targeted market interested in new possibilities for fitness.

Your videos can also come with booklets on the same subject or any type of exercise equipment, holistic health products, food supplements, etc. You could do demonstrations at holistic health fairs and conventions or rent booths to other videocassette producers at theme conventions.

Therapists, hospitals, prisons, and fitness centers use therapeutic video or interactive video to observe people interacting and to record their behavior for study, research, and therapy. You want to reach all helping professionals, such as the following:

1. interpreters for the deaf who want you to put their sign-language expert on videotape to explain their instructional tapes.

2. prison psychologists, who may want you to make a videotape about pro-social behavior and self worth training for the prison population.

3. speech pathologists who may want you to make videos to train stroke victims to look into mirrors to see their opposite hand and try to move it.

4. acupuncturists, acupressurists, and holistic health practitioners or alternative fitness experts who may ask you to make instructional videos for specific audiences.

5. cruise ships, airlines, hospitals, and nursing homes—who may wish to show your uplifting videos on how to improve the quality of life.

You can specialize in creating videos for children. Target preschools, children's centers, hospitals, and schools of education where preschool teachers are trained. Another specialty is creating exercise, fitness, and eating-the-right foods videos for preschoolers and children in daycare, nursery schools, after-school care, and at children's hospitals. Create a children's or preschooler's gym on video by targeting corporate daycare centers and gyms.

RELATED OPPORTUNITIES:

Recreational video exercise therapist, instructional media technologist, cable television programmer, playographer, cruise seminar and event planner, and holistic health practitioner videographer.

Your exercises could focus on preschoolers or infants. Appeal to family gym classes where parents take their infants for workouts and to learn more about play between parents and children. Provide videos so that the whole family, including grandparents can exercise together and get fit.

ADDITIONAL INFORMATION:

American Kinesiotherapy Association (exercise therapists)
259-08 148th Rd.
Rosedale, NY 11422

American Association for Rehabilitative Therapy, Inc.
PO Box 6412
Gulf Port, Mississippi 39506

National Association of the Deaf
814 Thayer Ave.
Silver Spring, MD 20910

National Therapeutic Recreation Society
3101 Park Center Dr., Suite 1200
Alexandria, VA 22302

National Council for Therapeutic Recreation Certification
49 S. Main St., Suite 005
Spring Valley, NY 10977-5635

American Association of Advertising Agencies (AAAA)
666 Third Avenue, 13th floor
New York, NY 10017

American Yoga Association
3130 Mayfield Rd., W-103
Cleveland Heights, OH 44118

13

DESCRIPTION OF BOOK PUBLICITY BUSINESS
Publicity & Promotion: Making Electronic and Print Media Kits

You could promote your book and make money matching clients with independent direct-mail copywriters who specialize in specific products. Or you could give your book publicity using audio or video pod casts that also are available on CDs or DVDs. Whatever you write and produce or publish, make sure your promotional materials also are age-targeted hubs to launch your creative works in the media before you have pre-sold your creative ideas to publishers.

Another way to promote your book is to offer a service writing direct mail packages for business or educational clients. You can offer a service measuring based on orders coming in how much profit a direct mail package generates. When you show your client how much profit the package that you wrote made for that person, you might be hired. Or you can test other writers' direct mail packages. What you look for is measurable profitability for comparison. The goal here is to pre-sell your writing.

Another way to pre-sell your creative work is with video pod casts. Launch your book in the media before you publish. To persuade the press, create an age-elated hub. This can be a mature adult, parenting, or teen hub. Look at any teen hub from the 1990s, such as Goosehead. There's still room for other shows like Goosehead, and one could feature your unpublished writing, learning, parenting, or merchandising ideas.

Create a similar venture yourself online by first developing the content. You could create content for shows similar to Goosehead or create your own concept. After call, a concept is actually made up of facts built around a foundation or basic message. Think of a concept as a sculpture built step-by-step over a wire frame skeleton.

The idea of a teen hub came about when a 14-year old girl named Ashley Power with her personal Web site caught the attention of Richard Dreyfuss. He made a deal to create content for Goosehead. How did such publicity come to a 14-year olds personal Web site?

Thousands of girls from 11 to 15 daily have personal Web sites and need content. One day actor Richard Dreyfuss's niece appeared in a Goosehead video series. It's quite a leap and rare that the niece of an actor appears in a video series that springs out of a 14-year old girl's Web site. Such rarity is what makes for fame. What part did destiny play? According to media reports, Dreyfuss got in touch with Power and made a deal to create at least two interactive episodes to Goosehead.

What can you do that's interactive? If you're a parent, start with what's familiar to you in parenting. Look at similar sites yourself, and decide what about it made the teen hub or senior citizen life-long learning hubs ripe. How did the concept of a teenage hub move from a 14-year old girl's personal Web site into a video series that caught the eye of a star who writes content for interactive Web?

The episodes, by the way, were called Webisodes. Actually, the technical term is multicasting content as opposed to multimedia that's not always online. Before you test the waters, look at the following sites that use stars to plug products they like. Then think of ways how you can *launch* your unpublished writing in the credible media by *plugging a product* you like and that a star also likes. Look at www.gooshead.com, www.babystyle.com, www.voxxy.com, www. sightsound.com, www.shockwave.com, and www.generationa.com. What did you notice about teen hub sites?

Is there anything similar (based on what you love to do most) that you can do with your sites to produce content or plug a product you like for the age group you want to emphasize? Use your unpublished writing to move your content, be your content, plug your content, or launch someone else's product you use for a fee, and enjoy. That's one other way to launch your unpublished books, booklets, scripts, plays, stories, poems, lyrics, content, or learning material.

INCOME POTENTIAL

Charge a flat free and/or a retainer for publicity and promotion, such as getting authors on radio and TV programs. You might acquire space on a radio program and ask authors or other people with trendy occupations and interests to be interviewed by you on your own radio show.

Try pod-casting on the Internet as a way to interview people with audio file-based 'radio' shows that people can download to their iPods or other audio devices. What's the current fee? Charge anything from $25 up to have a four to ten-minute radio interview or whatever the market will bear. For half-hour radio interviews, charge double. Don't overcharge authors.

It's better to have a higher volume of clients paying less than be talked about on chat groups as overcharging. You can upload an MP3 audio file and 'pod-cast' the audio on the Internet for less than it costs to buy time on a radio station and charge people to interview them on the air to publicize their books or other items.

In promotion of someone's product, never make the language seem as if the author or inventor is talking down to the consumer. You want to make people feel important and positive about their choices. The selling point is to put value on people's decisions and to emphasize commitment to what works well and is healthy in the long run. Help make people feel good about their choices.

Scripts, books, and stories that are unpublished can still find a market on the Web if they are customized to the tastes of those who produce such works. If you have ambition and drive, you could aim to producing your own unpublished direct-to-Web material, called entertainment content.

Your creativity doesn't have to be fiction. It could be learning materials or documentaries. If you don't want to compete with the entertainment industry, there are audiences who want how-to films or videos that were never videos in the first place, but produced direct-to-Web with good multimedia authoring software such as Macromedia's *Director* and other software.

Let your unpublished writing plug, launch, or promote any product you like or a star likes and do it online and on TV. Or package your material with someone else's product. If you're into performing arts, start a Web site for teenagers or any other age group.

GENERAL APTITUDE OR EXPERIENCE

You can make yourself or anyone else, even a star, spokesperson. The trick is to produce and star in 12-26 half-hour shows aimed at a specific audience, such as teenagers, where you can use your unpublished book to plug the products advertised on the teen magazine Web and/or cable TV show.

You get visibility, publicity, and market your work all at once. If you go for the teen market, produce shows for a Web site, where you'll get to talk honestly with teens about issues they're interested in. Shows can focus in on niche audiences that need Web sites or cable TV teen magazine shows only for them, such as girls from 11-17.

There's one site www.voxxy.com that did that in new ways. If you have a lot of unpublished writing, you want to sell your work in by these two methods: 1. Use a Web site to draw in the stars of TV looking for shows to produce or be spokesperson for. 2. Ask those starts to endorse your writing as they endorse products they enjoy.

Find out what they want. Then provide that niche of content, branding, or redemptive value. Keep your idea simple to understand and explain everything clearly in a short paragraph or in one sentence.

TRAINING REQUIRED

Join public relations trade associations and attend seminars to learn the techniques of promotion. Read books on public relations strategies and buzz appeal.

The idea of plugging products you like by using your unpublished books and scripts is a form of packaging your books or booklets with products going to be bought. Before the Internet, you'd approach a warehouse or manufacturer and ask that your book be packaged with the products being shipped as a way to give customers a free instructional manual on a product or a sideline, like a cookbook on how to cook with wines or sauces being shipped with packaged wines or sauces.

Now, you do similarly on a Web site, called a Web venture. If you write about baby care, target a Web site for this subject and for your video pod cast. Observe sites such as www.babystyle.com if you're writing books or booklets about baby wear and care, focus your Web site or content on everything about style and babies. Compare text and image-based Web sites to video segments on the Web.

Start your own site focusing on baby style, elder style, teen style, or any other age or other group of interest to parents, women, men, teenage girls, or wherever there is a high demand for information, content, and products. Video pod casts appeal to young people and to life-long learning groups of all ages. Parents and adolescents alike use video pod casts. Primarily, though, high-school and university students download pod casts for lectures, language-learning, and entertainment. Expand the use of video pod casting for travel planning.

Women and senior citizens are increasingly on the Web. So you might want to study new *trends* to get a handle on the latest women's interests. Before you get too narrow, pick the audience for the widest possible number of visits to your site. You need to research your markets. Where do people in different targeted groups really want to spend their valuable time visiting?

EQUIPMENT NEEDED

A spinoff of the 1990s-style 'Docu-tech' machine helps, but you really need access to a printing company. Your computer and laser printer can generate brochures and press kits. A four-color printer helps as well as a scanner that can produce photos scanned at 300 DPI in CMYK color. Check out the CMYK Color Space: The Colors of Printing Web site at: http://www.techcolor.com/help/cmyk.html. You need Adobe Photoshop software or the equivalent to put photos or graphics in your publicity brochures or press kits.

Find a way to endorse a product or keep asking powerful and popular people to endorse a product that will include your unpublished book along with a product being endorsed as a gift or giveaway. Your content and a manufacturer's product must offer specific benefits and advantages to the buyer.

OPERATING YOUR BUSINESS

Use your writing or research to plug someone else's products. If you have an unpublished romance novel, personalize it with the name of the happy couple and package it along with the wedding gifts ordered. Or leave a personalized novel you wrote in guest rooms of hotels with the name of the guests, *if they order it.* Honeymooners might, or it might be of interest to those planning bridal or baby showers, anniversary cruises, or office parties. Always ask the buyer first and show in advance what the product will contain before having anything printed with someone's name.

The quickest way to launch your book is to stage an around the world online launch and media party. Pick a time when most media people are available. Invite the specialty and general press, publishers, agents, entertainment attorneys, producers, directors, book talent managers, book packagers, famous writers, newspaper reporters and columnists. Also invite the members of various public relations and press clubs from your local area chapters.

Include the print media, small press publishers, book sellers, event planners for booksellers events overseas and nationally, and those who come to book sales parties in people's homes. Invite software, book and video distributors to meet you for a conference online where you'll have a chat and put up a presentation with sound, text, and video clips or visuals all about your unpublished book or script.

Did you see the pre release publicity the Harry Potter books received, even coverage on the cover of Newsweek several years ago? What can you do for your unpublished book to create spin that will add to your credibility as well as visibility in the media all over the world?

It all starts with a story board and a press kit that reveals your main character's measured change, transformation, or growth, or if your book's nonfiction, how much everyone needs to know the information you're about to tell. It's not whom you know, but whom you tell—and how you tell it that brings people together. If you want to earn income and cut expenses, you need to be a catalyst.

How Do You Make A Storyboard?

Storyboards can help launch your unpublished book if you use them as a kind of mind map that uses the right hemisphere of the brain to express visually with thumbnail sketches and dialogue bubbles what goes into a novel or script. If you write your story as a play first and flesh out the dialogue into a novel, it will flow easier when based on a storyboard.

You can move to a springboard, where you can bounce the story off of the springboard's role as a summary or synopses of significant events and turning points in your book or script. A springboard runs up to 15 pages long.

A story board can go the length of the book summarizing the highlights in half that number of pages. A synopsis runs about one or two pages, and a high concept pitch is one sentence that tells your whole story such as Star Trek is Wagon Train in space.

What's a storyboard? Storyboards are pages of panel cartoon-like visual images of how a chapter or scene looks visually before the dialogue is spoken. Draw in thumbnail sketches your storyboard for each scene of your novel, autobiography, or script as you write it or adapt it from a novel, news clipping, or story.

To pre sell your unpublished book to the media or publishers, write the significant events, turning points, or highlights of your confrontation where the hero and the opponent come into conflict for the last time. The battle scene is the major test that results in a major change both inside the hero morally and externally so he/she can reach the goal and end the story. This is what you hand to the press and to publishers, agents, or producers. You're highlighting and summarizing the significant events of your book.

1. Hold a mid-night launch party for your life story or other book.

2. Hold a noon launch party for readers who can't drive or go out at night, and have the location near a bus line.

3. Hold a weekend launch party at a department or discount store such as Wal-Mart or any similar store. Or combine with any store's grand opening party.

4. Hold a launch party in a school cafeteria, library, gym, yard, or auditorium for the appropriate age group. Combine launch party with a lecture to elementary or high school classes. Or if more appropriate, to special interest groups and clubs, professional associations, or women's clubs and organizations or related societies.

5. Hold a launch party at a college campus or rent a room or auditorium or space on the lawn.

6. Hold a launch party in a senior citizens apartment complex, recreational center, adult education center, hospital gift shop, or nursing home.

7. Hold a launch party in a place where you can set up an international or national day so that everyone, especially children, if your book is appropriate, can read your book on the same day, in case they do order it. Have all the children across the nation experience *Your Life Story* or *Your Book* on the same day.

8. Hold a launch party in a church recreation hall, park, museum, library, art gallery, zoo, space theater, or social center.

9. Hold a launch party in a mall or on the lawn of a public park or skating rink on a Sunday or at a sports center or field.

10. Hold a launch party on a cruise ship before it sails or in a bus or train station or airport.

Put up a temporary kiosk for your launch party. Or get permission and a permit to launch your book near or in front of a supermarket or convention center or a hotel lobby. Use cruises and travel situations to launch your party. Or charter a flight and launch it in transit to help passengers pass the time. Cruise ships are you best bet.

Ask newspaper reporters from national press associations and public relations associations to cover your book or life story in their articles on lifestyle or business subjects or whatever the subject of your book covers. Societies of professional journalists have monthly meetings. Ask to have your launch party at one of their meetings or invite the whole organization to your meeting.

Gather other writers of similar books and life stories into a pool of vendors and sell booths or tables in a large hall, Masonic center, or other meeting place, like an association of Realtor's Hall, or building you can rent. Have all the writers self-publish their books or photocopy with cardstock cover and illustration or photo and comb binding. Print on demand.

Have numerous copies of books on tables. A group of 10 or 20 writers can have a group launch party and invite the press or sponsor a press club meeting, perhaps on board a docked yacht that's rented for the day or in a hotel or university rented room or meeting hall. Books can be printed on demand and given as press copies to reporters.

Invite entertainment and copyright attorneys, agents, publishers, editors, the media, and writers, also the potential readers of your book such as children and parents or business people. Have your launch party at a convention or conference on a related theme, such as a conference of small press publishers or a book buyer's convention or annual meeting in the US or abroad. Or take a group of writers on a cruise and present books to the press.

You can go free if you gather enough paying people to take the tour with you. Have stationery printed with a logo or slogan. Print the letterhead with enlarged slogan or logo onto a supply of two-pocket folders. Print a scriptwriting logo onto adhesive labels. Stick the labels onto the cover of the folders. The multi-colored two-pocket folders are available in any office supply outlet.

Create a brochure, preferably in color. Include the brochure in the press kit. Make an electronic media kit as well as a print press kit. The brochure could list a writer's services and credentials or credits. If there are no past credits, print all the services provided such as the following:

1. Quality circles for writers

2. Individual instruction

3. Seminars, event planning for communications professionals

4. Freelance technical writing, manual writing, corporate scriptwriting, desktop publishing, word processing, editing, tutoring, instructional courseware design, children's writing instruction, corporate scriptwriting

5. English as a second language writing instruction

6. Fiction written for adults with 2nd grade reading ability

7. Science journalism

8. Writer's speakers bureau

9. Art

10. Publicity writing, or any other type of writing services offered.

Nourishment is a Fountain

What's your most powerful resource you can call on when you need it? It is not only the source within, but the source without also. How do you write about this source? How can you use this source to both cut expenses and bring in income while expanding your creative abilities? Nourishment is all about offering the public and the media positive magnets. Decades ago these magnets or catalysts were called positive hooks because they hooked the readers or viewers. You had a captured audience.

The idea behind nourishment or positive incentives is that people don't want a steady diet of pain, fear, and horror—all the time. If they did, then books such as the *Chicken Soup* series would come in second place to gladiatorial blood sport movies. Nourishment sells. There is a market for joy. Don't dump pain on readers all the way through your writing—not if you are writing for a large audience.

People buy audio books, videos, learning materials, and information books to learn more about health, mind, spirit, investments, or contemporary culture issues. Which sells more books or videos—works about poverty or the habits of billionaires?

The habits of billionaires and efficient people are of more interest than documentaries and books on poverty. Why don't enough people buy books surveying the plight of those in poverty or pain? The media will help you launch your work if you provide solutions to problems and results. Offer easy and quick solutions backed up by detailed step-by-step information people can follow.

Large audiences want to hear about the secrets of healing, love, wealth, and happiness. Nourishment sells along with commitment and inspiration. People also want to improve their memory, enhance creativity, and be happy. Instruction is in high demand. People want instructions that they can easily understand. They want to know how to build, make, or repair an object. Most people have little time or money to spend on luxuries.

Look at the success of home improvement centers. Those with time to "build it at home" want to create a device better in quality, safer, and at lower cost than can be bought commercially. An example would be instructions on how to make your own shampoo from scratch. With home-made shampoo, you could customize a non-toxic formula for your own hair's needs using natural flower essences, oils, moisturizes, scents, or spices. People are looking for safer hair tints, depilatories, and other products that are absorbed by the pores. That's why you need a professional-looking electronic and portfolio-type print media kit.

Whatever your creative project entails, include a press kit when giving presentations, seminars, interviews, radio or T.V. appearances or querying editors, producers, publishers, agents, and entertainment attorneys. Send the press kit to newspaper and magazine editors, television producers, and radio talk show hosts seeking guests from the writing community. Even mystery and suspense novels or true crime accounts have to offer more than violence and justice.

The purpose of a press kit is to inform people that scriptwriting is being done on a full-time basis and assignments are wanted either re-writing other writer's scripts or created fiction or non-fiction video and film scripts for production. Industrial video and the trade magazines are constant users of video scripts for training.

Media kits, also called press kits are included in presentations, pitching, written proposals, sales packets, query letters, and in general correspondence. Marketing and sales for home-based scriptwriters are fields worth writing about in print and in training video script format.

How Do You Create A Powerful Media Magnet?

Every scriptwriter needs an online press kit to pre-sell a script to the video or film market. Most print press kits are discarded by the media without being opened, unless you're well-known. The only way the media will pay attention to a press kit is if it contains a powerful hook. Have one sentence or question that will repeat at the beginning, middle, and end of the press kit. Bring the media to your Web site before you mail out expensive printed material to someone who doesn't contact you and ask for a review copy or press kit of your work.

Use a question hook that makes a busy editor stop and think. Make the question personal and universal. Put on the press kit's cover a hook question that makes the media do some introverted thinking. In large type letters have the question make an impact. You can ask the reader to name his or her strongest source. In the past, media kits used words like "powerful resource" or "strongest magnet."

Notice that that question that holds the reader's attention is the same as the one you ask of your hero when creating a screenplay, novel, or short story. Another powerful hook question that has been used in media press kits and in presentations to the press in the past is, "How many times have you sold out on your plans and settled for something less?" However, today, this type of question might get a response like, "None of your business." So use something that makes your content more *approachable* such as "You don't have to settle for reality anymore. Your dreams just woke up your imagination."

You want the reader in the media to feel important and good about himself while reading your press kit. You want to nourish the press. You don't want to frighten, shock, or remind the reader of human mortality or frailty. Media kits are there to make you likeable.

Use a statement instead of a question to draw the reader in. Questions often bring knee-jerk hostility responses. Soothe the reader. Put the statement on the cover of your press kit folder and also inside the press release.

If you want to launch anything in the media, you need to show commitment and credibility. You're a media strategist, an architect and designer of 'models' on paper that create visibility in the media for your unsold, pre-sold, or in-development content or product.

In the middle of the press release, exert power. Write about how the reader can do something to increase his or her power. You could show the reader what one act he or she could perform to become more powerful. Don't ask a question in the middle of your press release.

A question wastes the limited time available, usually 20 seconds spent to read a one-page media release. Instead, illustrate in words how to solve a problem, obtain a result, or get more powerful by performing one act. That one act would directly relate to your product, premise, or content. In one sentence, tell the reader exactly what he or she has to do to become more powerful. That's the selling point of your item.

Professional-looking press kits publicize any item inexpensively. Paid advertising would cost hundreds of dollars for a two-inch display ad in daily newspaper or high-circulation trade journal.

A press kit is an open invitation for the writer to be hired by colleges of extended studies at $50 an hour or 50% of the gross of student's fees to give a one-day seminar on writing. Experience is more important than a degree at such adult education seminars in private schools. Exposure, such as giving seminars for producers and directors on script analysis and consulting, leads to better chances to have personal screenplays seen by producers.

Stop using fear as an advertisement to draw in people. There are enough ads on TV that start with a screeching ambulance or loud, fast heartbeats, screams, or a man shouting how he's dying or crying. These ads often are broadcast after midnight or late at night, when most frail seniors are up watching TV and just dozing off. It shocks people out of sleep, particularly the frail elderly or people with disabilities who are not able to sleep easily.

So if you fell asleep in front of your TV set, these types of ads may shock you out of your sweet dream with fearful possible reality scenarios that remind you of your mortality, pain, or diseases. The shock ads are there to get you to buy safety products. Older people feel anxiety when such ads come on. It reminds them of what's ahead. Instead of making them think about preparing for possible events or their final expenses, people sometimes are shocked awake into a panic attack or worse by the sudden noise of screaming sirens and shouting or loud rapidly beating sounds. Shock ads are unwelcome by those with panic disorder or sensitized nervous systems.

What ads do seniors like? Serenity is one. You can sell serenity to the media. Instead of wondering how many people get sick watching other people getting sick, use the opposite to attract attention. Offer gently bubbling fountains, quiet rivers and sunsets, beaches, mountains, pine trees, gardens, and anything that brings joy and contentment in TV ads that appear in the wee hours of the night.

To promote a product, use "two word" titles. Or use the word "Why" in your title if you're giving information. For nonfiction, use an insightful, popular, and commercial short two-word title such as "Robot Cowboys" Or a trendy title that tells the whole story of the nonfiction book: "Why Writers Want More Monies and Publishers Want More Funnies." Or "Why Women Want More_(drama)____and Men Want More_(sports)____"

What Do Media Professionals Expect To See in a Media Kit?

Newspaper and magazine editors, radio and T.V. producers, agents, publicists, entertainment attorneys, directors, actors, film, and video creative directors are used to receiving professionally printed press kits. They only read material sent in an "acceptable format."

An acceptable press kit consists of a double-pocketed file folder, the question hook printed on the cover (not typed on a regular typewriter, but typeset with desktop publishing fonts). Inside the flap pocket is another question hook presented on the inside cover. In the flap-pocket is a black and white glossy photo of the writer (matte for television producers).

On top of the photo is a four-page press release about what the writer has to offer that needs visibility—and how the information will help the community or readers. A short, one-page press release goes on top of the four-page release. The short press release gives the writer's biography, credits, credentials, and anything else important the writer has done in relation to what the longer press release covers.

News clippings about the writer or the script are put over the short press release. The clippings are cut out, dated, titled, and pasted on a sheet of paper and then photocopied onto a slick, camera-ready white sheet. Include in the second flap pocket a copy of any article, booklet, book, sample, or tape for media review. This press kit goes to agents as well as media editors and producers. Make sure you have an electric press kit on a Web site and also sent to the media as well as print folders. Too many paper print media kit folders are thrown away or recycled without being read. No one is paying anyone to read media kits sent unsolicited, and there's very little time to read them. The exception would be those on a newspaper staff paid to write book reviews or producers that book radio and TV authors as guests on programs.

*Start a reporting service. Create **press kits** containing DNA-driven ancestry reports. Create folder-type press kits as well as electronic media kits. Mail the paper press kits with reports to clients who have had their DNA tested for ancestry. Or make time capsules on genealogy, ancestry, family history, and DNA testing reports for ancestry.*

With very little capital, you can write a business plan to start *a reporting* service that brings business and client together. One of the easiest enterprises to start with only your computer, printer, and Internet connection is a DNA-driven genealogy reporting service.

You wouldn't have to spend money on equipment such as gifts for gift baskets or fabric, cameras, or other investments. With only your computer, printer, paper, press kit folders, DVD/CD recorder, DVDs and CDs, and email, you can offer information packaged in unique ways. Instead only offering administrative assistant services, typing, or editing and proofreading, you can offer DNA reporting presented in a media kit or package-type folder.

What does a press kit pitch? Place a two-page pitch release on top of all the other information in the kit tells the media why the script is so extraordinary, so unique and different and who can benefit by seeing it. Include a marketability study of who would be buying the script, book, or tape. The new age video market is on the rise.

On top of every release, place the final cover letter as a courtesy, telling why you want the media to print selected press releases and the photo inside. The cover letter is one page or less in length. The first paragraph of the cover letter contains a premise—of the release. What's important is summarized in one sentence.

Use concrete credentials that can be checked. If the press kit is going to a publisher to sell a book/script package deal, include a chapter breakdown. The titles of the chapters sell the book just as the title of a video script determines its commercial appeal.

Book chapter summaries vary from three paragraphs to under a page for highlights. Tell the media exactly what viewers will be told when they view the script. For script/booklet combinations such as book and audio tape combinations, or video and instructional manual packages, write down the components of the book in a press kit, and send a sample. This technique holds true for self-published and self-produced video/book packages used for instruction or motivation.

The first chapter of a book is like the first scene of a video script. It's the selling chapter. In a media kit designed to sell and outline a book and video package, tell the reader why she needs to read the book and view the video. Include photos or a mock-up copy of the video or book combination.

The fastest way to impress a reader about a video is to have an advertisement or poster with a black background and white print. The print is superimposed over a photo in the background. Viewers will remember that video above one on a white background with black lettering and design.

It's possible to create an infomercial to mail out to potential buyers who might be interested in purchasing a produced video or a published book, but it's expensive. A press kit creating visibility for a video, a script, or a book is more direct. Use one sentence to summarize your book, pamphlet, article, or script's premise.

Marketing researchers often report that readers will respond faster to an article written by a reporter about a person, business, or product than to a paid advertisement placed by the entrepreneur. An article I wrote for a high-circulation paper brought in 600 requests for information when I included my post office box number.

The tiny, classified ad I placed in the back of the paper (which was expensive for me) brought no responses. Visibility influences marketing.

Contacts with video software distributors lead to contacts with producers. A commercial title can pre-sell a script. Free publicity and press coverage pulls more weight than small, paid display ads announcing "script for sale." Press coverage is free, and can be obtained by a phone call and a news angle or a press kit.

ADDITIONAL INFORMATION

Press Kit (The Author's Guide to Self Promotion)
http://www.writing-world.com/columns/promotion/press12.shtml

American Library Association (Professional Tools)
http://www.ala.org/ala/proftools/professional.htm
Press Kits (American Library Association)
http://www.ala.org/ala/pio/piopresskits/alanationalconference2004/
acma2004.htm

14

DESCRIPTION OF BOOK PUBLICITY BUSINESS:
Expose Hoaxes and Cover Hidden News

Cover the news that didn't make the news, exposing corporate, institutional, or government corruption through your investigative video reporting. Your video could carry the news that didn't make the newspapers because of censors.

Make a video of underground news. Be an investigative video reporter and expose corruption. Be a video muckraker and raise hell. To understand muckraking video, you need to know a little about what it's like in print.

Read Jessica Mitford's introduction to Poison Penmanship: The Gentle Art of Muckraking. Mitford's investigative writing led to social change by inspiring and motivating the public. In 1963, she exposed the funeral industry in her book, The American Way of Death. Beneficial changes resulted. Therefore, your video surely can find subjects to explore, muckrake, and expose.

INCOME POTENTIAL:

Since fewer than 20 corporations now control most of the United State's mass media, your income potential as an independent is unlimited as long as you cover the subject of information control and how it exploits our minds. Any video on mind manipulation is sure to earn an income for you depending on repetition.

To make a successful video, you must use continuous and lasting propaganda. You must not leave any gaps. If your video lasts a long time, you can expect to gross between $20 and $40 on each video.

Expensive videos usually sell through direct mail order for $39.95. Popular mail order DVDs are priced around $19.95 to $29.95. There are low-cost documentaries and DVD movies for sale online for less—for $5 or $7, plus shipping. You can offer a video mail order distributor a commission to sell your video at their own prices. Make sure that whatever you price your video at that you make a profit and at the same time the video is cheap enough to attract enough customers who think it's a fair price and affordable.

Do a test mailing first to find out your viewer's opinion of the price in relation to the content. Is it really affordable by the majority of your potential market?

The rule is the lower priced the tape, the more copies it will sell. Video stores will only take it if it's priced low enough to have high turnover, and if they can get their cut of your profit.

You could be better off with your own mail order flyer going to a list of club members interested in the subject of your video. If you charge anywhere from $19.95 to $30 to the public by direct mail order, you can expect some income from clubs, workshops, seminars, and association meetings, as well as video-of-the-month clubs. Sell your tapes at a discount during meetings and conventions.

Getting your video into stores usually means it would have to air first—either in front of a national convention of video software dealers, or on the local or public broadcast news—or run as a documentary on one of the news magazine shows on television or on cable television. Create visibility by airing your video at conventions of people interested in the subject matter of your tape.

The tape can make the national meeting rounds. Usually every month there's a convention or conference in different cities of local chapters of various associations, clubs, or organizations interested in the subject matter of your tape. Call public speakers who travel around the country giving presentations at conventions and ask them to show your tape during the meeting or pass flyers out to the captured convention audience.

BEST LOCALE TO OPERATE THE BUSINESS:

You can run your muckraking video production company from any location where there is censored news to be exposed to the public. It's not necessary to live in any special city, but you'll need to have rapport with the underground video and alternate media/broadcast industry as well as the standard media old boys' network.

Being in Washington, DC will help if it is a government or a military service you plan to expose in your videos. It's better to be near the large broadcast media firms in New York, but you have to be on the road all over to tape your investigative reports.

TRAINING REQUIRED:

If you already know how to run your industrial quality camcorder, the next subject to learn is investigative reporting. You can get in touch with the Investigative Journalism Project (Fund for Constitutional Government), 122 Maryland Ave NE, Suite 300, Washington, DC 20002 (202) 546-3732, or join IRE (Investigative Reporters and Editors), 100 Neff Hall, University of Missouri, School of Journalism, Columbia, MO 65211. This organization puts out enough publications to train you at home to be a great investigative reporter if only from reading what they publish—journals, newsletters, books, etc.

Read about Media Watch, Media Alliance, or the Media Institute (addresses are in the appendices at the back of this book). There are enough publications published by the media organizations (listed in the back of this book) to help make you an investigative reporter using video as your medium of expression. You also can connect to the Internet on your personal computer and exchange information with people all over the country and abroad.

GENERAL APTITUDE OR EXPERIENCE:

Good interviewing skills are essential. You need to be a bit of a private investigator, have a willingness to expose corruption, and have an interest in finding out what's happening that affects most people's lives in a universal way. A journalism writing aptitude helps, or a partner who does the writing while you do the technical video work.

Muckraking videos really do dig up the dirt and expose it to the public in order to have beneficial changes made. Generally, you should really want to save the world in a small way with your video camera and have a nose for news.

EQUIPMENT NEEDED:

You'll need your broadcast quality field camera, tape, batteries, sound, lighting, and editing equipment, mobility, and a readiness to travel anywhere to videotape the news or expose corruption. Some taping will be in the homes of people you'll be interviewing.

OPERATING YOUR BUSINESS:

Making underground videos out of news that usually is censored each year has to be one of the most exciting ways to earn money with your video camera. To begin, first you spot important, but overlooked news in the back pages of your local newspaper—or the newspaper in some small town.

Perhaps it's news of ecological disaster. Or you want to make a video on why 12 million children go hungry in this country each day because you saw an alarming report issued by the United Nations Children's Fund.

Perhaps you consulted the Tyndall Report, which monitors evening network news, and wondered why some reports don't make the top ten list of news subjects on the networks during any month. Maybe you disagree and feel that your video is an important way of making sure the censored news gets to the public. Subscribing to a news clipping service or keeping news clippings on your own personal computer database helps to find subjects video worthy.

Perhaps you choose to monitor what's happening in the sparsely-populated desert areas, finding that the military has quietly resumed biowarfare testing. For example on January 27, 1973, the Salt Lake Tribune reported such headlines as: "Army Resumes Biological Agent Test ad Dugway (Utah) After 10-Year Cessation;" and "Dugway to test disease-causing agents at remote lab" (Author: Jim Woolf).

There were the headlines of September 21, 1993, *"Dugway Base Cited for 22 Waste Violations,"* (author: Laurie Sullivan). In the High Country News, the title appeared on September 8, 1993, *"Biowarfare is Back,"* (author Jon Christensen). On September 15, 1993, the High Desert Advocate ran an article with the title, *"Utah Biowarfare Oversight Group Wants To Do Its Work Behind Closed Doors."*

If you kept news clippings of what was happening then in Dugway, Utah, you could have found funds from one of the video investigative reporting support groups, perhaps, or used your own low-budget to travel to the high desert area of Dugway, Utah with your video camera and talked to the people interested or involved in the matter.

Your investigative news angle would be: the U.S. Army has brought biological warfare testing back to the Dugway Proving Ground in the same western Utah location that ten years ago it claimed was not safe. The news angle is that military scientists are testing "the Biological Integrated Detection System" at the same facility the military says is now renovated. Is it? Your video would tell the news from an investigative reporting point of view, designed to expose corruption, if any exists, by interviewing experts and scientists.

The defensive weapon is supposed to detect the presence of biological agents. Your video would be about whether it works—whether it gives soldiers enough time to put on biohazard suits. The tests involved anthrax, botulism, and the plague.

To make your video, for an example, you'd have to interview Dugway representatives who would let you know in what liquid the germs were carried because the people of the town were afraid of the germs getting into the air. Doing some local history, you'd find out that the Dugway facility first closed in 1983 because of a fear that if there was an air leak in the sealed chamber, deadly germs would get into the air.

As your video progressed, you'd be able to show the viewers in exactly what ways the facility was renovated, and whether the safety precautions that exist now are enough to prevent a leak. Only experts and scientists interviewed on the video, and an up-close shot on the safety measure, could convince the public that safety was really that secure. Or is it? Would the military let you tape the renovation changes?

This is how you make your investigative videos of the news that normally doesn't get into the big city papers. An excellent resource of the stories that could make great videos can be found in the book, Censored, The News That Didn't Make the News and Why, Carl Jensen & Project Censored, published in 1994 by Four Walls Eight Windows, 39 West 14th St., #503, New York, NY 10011.

This excellent book contains chapters on raking muck and raising hell, U.S. censorship, and a lot of censored news that never made the news but should have. These include the biohazard story, and other news that would make excellent muckraking videos.

You even can send Project Censored interesting news you spot hidden in the back pages of your newspaper. Send your clippings to: Nomination, Project Censored, Sonoma State University, Rohnert Park, CA 94928. Their annual deadline is October 15th.

To make muckraking videos, you'll have to look in small-circulation magazines and or small-town rural newspapers as well as in your local big-city news, if you live in the big town. What you're looking for are stories you think should have received more coverage. Your video's purpose is to give those stories the coverage they deserve.

The video you make will be designed to show the public what's happening and why. The story should be timely and of national or global importance. If the story is significant, it's worthy of being made into a videocassette that you can offer to a variety of audiences, including the big-time media as well as the locals.

Stories you put on tape need not have appeared in the news. It could have appeared in a trade journal. Or it could have come from a local paper, or even a tabloid—if it's factual. It could have briefly been covered on television or over-heard in a radio talk show interview.

Once you have written permission from where ever you saw it first to dig deeper into the story, find out whether it received any follow-up. If the lack of exposure is bothering the people in the news, offer to interview them on tape. Then dig deeper and interview others.

Get shots of where it happened, and ask the usual, what, who, when, where, how, and why questions. Show rather than tell on the tape. Avoid "talking head" shots that go on for minutes. Instead, cut to other scenes and do voice-overs to show movement and action.

What you're selling in this kind of video is simply the censored news, the news that most newspapers and magazines refuse to print. You're satisfying the public's right to know and make beneficial changes.

TARGET MARKET:

Muckraking videos that emphasize the news stories that the media usually censors primarily appeal to mail-order catalog customers. You can offer your video, if it fits the 23 or 53 minute news slots, to half-hour or full-hour news programs, or to producers of specials on network television.

Your advertising usually will be in specialty magazines that appeal to readers interested in a particular subject related to your expose video. You can offer your video to nonprofit organizations related to the subject of your tape, to the gov-ernment, and to schools. Or you can give seminars on the subject of your expose and sell your tape at conventions or through bookstores, club meetings, and cor-respondence courses.

RELATED VIDEO OPPORTUNITIES:

Expose hoaxes on video. Making videos that expose corruption is related to alter-native media public relations. Any government can hire a videographer to make a propaganda film or video. The question is on whose side are you on? Pick an industry you want to expose. Medicine? Meat packing? The funeral industry? Ecological disasters related to environmental terrorists? Cover-ups?

Related video opportunities exist with the alternative broadcast media produc-ers and organizations. Look at the variety of video direct mail order catalogs.

You can make a social issues expose video of the self-enhancement industry. Find out what corruption hasn't been exposed yet.

Your goal is to empower the public. Show your readers or viewers why experts can be trusted. Have these experts offer solutions to common ground problems.

Expose government cover-ups with air-tight cases that even the tightest skeptics can't disprove. Have facts that can be checked and validated by experts and scientists who have reputations for being credible. Viewers will pay what they can afford to see information they can use to make important decisions—information that may never air on the network news.

ADDITIONAL INFORMATION:

Associations of Interest to Consumer Economics Communications Experts, Nutrition Journalists, Nutritionists, Dieticians, and Health Care Professionals:

> **American Dietetic Association**
> http://www.eatright.org
>
> **American Obesity Association**
> http://www.obesity.org
>
> **American Society for Nutritional Sciences**
> http://www.asns.org/
>
> **American Society for Clinical Nutrition**
> http://www.ascn.org/
>
> **The Annapolis Center for Science-Based Public Policy**
> http://www.annapoliscenter.org
>
> **Association of Food & Drug Officials**
> http://www.afdo.org
>
> **American Diabetes Association**
> http://www.diabetes.org
>
> **American Farm Bureau Federation**
> http://www.fb.com
>
> **American Heart Association**
> http://www.americanheart.org
>
> **Botanical Center for Age-Related Diseases**
> http://nccam.nih.gov/news/2005/040705.htm

Calorie Control Council
http://www.caloriecontrol.org

Center for Health Promotion
http://pan.ilsi.org

Consumer Healthcare Products Association
http://www.caloriecontrol.org

CropLife America
http://www.croplifeamerica.org

Egg Nutrition Center
http://www.enc-online.org

Food Marketing Institute
http://www.fmi.org

Food Allergy Research and Resource Program
http://www.farrp.org

Grocery Manufacturers of America
http://www.gmabrands.com

International Association for Food Protection
http://www.foodprotection.org

National Dairy Council/Dairy Management
http://www.dairyinfo.com

National Policy and Resource Center on Nutrition and Aging
http://www.fiu.edu/~nutreldr

North American Agricultural Journalists
http://naaj.tamu.edu/

Society for Nutrition Education
http://www.sne.org

World Sugar Research Organization
http://www.wsro.org

Government-Related Agencies

Centers for Disease Control and Prevention
http://www.cdc.gov

Center for Food Safety and Applied Nutrition
http://www.crfsan.fda.gov

Fight BAC ™
http://www.fightbck.org

Food and Drug Administration: Consumer Inquiries
http://www.fda.gov

Joint Institute for Food Safety and Applied Nutrition
http://www.jifsan.umd.edu

National Cancer Institute: Press Office
http://www.nci.nih.gov

National Digestive Disease Information Clearinghouse
http://www.niddk.nih.gov

National Diabetes Information Clearinghouse
http://www.niddk.ninh.gov

National Health Information Center
http://health.gov/NHIC

National Institutes of Health
http://www.nih.gov

National Marine Fisheries Service
http://www.nmfs.noaa.gov

President's Council on Physical Fitness and Sports
http://fitness.gov

US Dept. of Agriculture
http://www.usda.gov

USDA/Food, Nutrition, and Consumer Services
http://www.fns.usda.gov/fncs

USDA/Food Safety and Inspection Service Information
http://www.fsis.usda.gov

USDA/Meat and Poultry Hotline
Phone 1-800-535-4555

USDA/Animal and Plant Health Inspection Service
http://www.aphis.usda.gov

USDA/Foreign Agricultural Service
http://www.fas.usda.gov

USDA/National Agricultural Library
http://www.nalusda.gov

USDA/National Agriculture Statistics Service
http://www.fas.usda.gov

US Department of Health and Human Services
http://www.hhs.gov

Foodborne Illness Education Information Center
http://www.nalusda.gov/foodborne/index.html

US Department of Health and Human Services
http://www.hhs.gov

US Environmental Protection Agency
http://www.epa.gov

US Federal Trade Commission
http://www.ftc.gov

◆   ◆   ◆

Associations of Interest to Medical or Science Journalists

American Medical Writers Association
40 West Gude Drive, Suite 101
Rockville, MD 20850-1192
http://www.amwa.org/default.asp?ID=1

American Society of Indexers (for indexing careers)
10200 West 44th Avenue, Suite 304,
Wheat Ridge, CO 80033
http://www.asindexing.org/site/index.html

American Society of Journalists and Authors
1501 Broadway, Suite 302

New York, NY 10036
http://www.asja.org

Association of Health Care Journalists (AHCJ)
Center for Excellence in Health Care Journalism
Missouri School of Journalism
10 Neff Hall
Columbia, MO 62511
http://www.ahcj.umn.edu/

Association of Professional Writing Consultants
http://www.consultingsuccess.org/index.htm

Council of Biology Editors
http://www.monroecc.edu/depts/library/cbe.htm

Council of the Advancement of Science Writing
P.O. Box 910
Hedgesville, WV 25427
http://www.casw.org/
Careers in Science Writing:
http://www.casw.org/careers.htm

Education Writers Association
2122 P Street, NW Suite 201
Washington, DC 20037
http://www.ewa.org/

International Food, Wine & Travel Writers Association (IFW&TWA)
1142 South Diamond Bar Boulevard #177
Diamond Bar, CA 91765-2203
http://www.ifwtwa.org/index.html

Journalism.org—Researches, Resources & Ideas to Improve Journalism
http://www.journalism.org/

National Association of
Science Writers, Inc.
P.O. Box 890, Hedgesville, WV 25427
http://www.nasw.org/

North American Agricultural Journalists
http://naaj.tamu.edu/

Society of Professional Journalists
Eugene S. Pulliam National Journalism Center
3909 N. Meridian St., Indianapolis, IN 46208
http://www.spj.org/

Society for Technical Communication
http://www.stc.org/

Text and Academic Authors Association
TAA
P.O. Box 76477
St. Petersburg, FL
http://www.taaonline.net/

World Association of Medical Editors
http://www.wame.org/
http://www.wame.org/index.htm

Diversified Media Associations of Interest to all Communicators

American Business Press
http://www.americanbusinesspress.com/

American Society of Business Press Editors
http://www.asbpe.org/

Associated Business Writers of America
http://www.poewar.com/articles/associations.htm

Associazioni ed Enti Professionali—America
http://www.alice.it/writers/grp.wri/wgrpame.htm
Contains a list of South American, Canadian, and US writers' organizations, including language translation firms.

American Marketing Association
http://www.marketingpower.com/content1539.php

Association of Professional Communications Consultants
http://www.consultingsuccess.org/index.htm

Writer's Encyclopedia A-Z List
WritersMarket.com
http://www.writersmarket.com/encyc/azlist.asp

Editorial Freelancers Association
http://www.the-efa.org/

Editor's Guild
http://www.edsguild.org/become.htm
The current online Yellow Pages, published annually since 1997 includes listings by skills as well as a specialties index. This association published the hardcopy, Yellow Pages, a listing of Association members who wished to advertise their skills and specialties, between 1989 and 1999.
http://www.tiac.net/users/freelanc/YP.html

International Women's Writing Guild
http://www.iwwg.com/index.php, Or: http://www.iwwg.com
The International Women's Writing Guild, headquartered in New York and founded in 1976, is a network for the personal and professional empowerment of women through writing.

Video Software Dealers Association
http://www.vsda.org/Resource.phx/vsda/index.htx

Public Relations Society of America
http://www.prsa.org/

Deep Dish TV
http://www.deepdishtv.org/pages/catalogue13.htm

Video History Project
http://www.experimentaltvcenter.org/history/groups/gtext.php3?id=37

Advertising Research Foundation
http://www.arfsite.org/

The Mail Preference Service
http://www.dmaconsumers.org/offmailinglist.html

Advertising Associations Directory
http://paintedcows.com/associations.html

Mailing Fulfillment Service Association
http://www.mfsanet.org/pages/index.cfm?pageid=1

Television Bureau of Advertising
http://www.tvb.org/nav/build_frameset.asp?url=/docs/homepage.asp

Home Improvement Research Institute
http://www.hiri.org/abouthiri.htm

Writers-Editors Network
http://www.writers-editors.com/

Professional and Technical Consultants Association
http://www.patca.org/html/articles/ratesurvey/ratesurvey1.htm
Association of Independent Commercial Producers
http://www.aicp.com/splash-noswf.html
National Cable & Telecommunications Association
http://www.ncta.com/
International Association of Women in Radio and Television
http://www.iawrt.org/
National Communication Association
http://www.natcom.org/nca/Template2.asp
The Association for Women in Communications
http://www.womcom.org/
Society of Telecommunications Consultants
http://www.stcconsultants.org/
European Training Media Association
http://www.etma.org/
Advertising Research Foundation
641 Lexington Avenue • New York, NY 10022
http://www.arfsite.org/
International Women's Media Foundation
http://www.iwmf.org/training/womensmedia.php
Independent Publishers Group
http://www.ipgbook.com/index.cfm?userid=36155756
American Society of Media Photographers
150 North Second Street, Philadelphia, PA 19106
(Electronic imaging and digital technology)
http://www.asmp.org/
International Interactive Communications Society
http://users.rcn.com/sfiics/
International Multimedia Association
http://www.emmac.org/
National Cable Television Association
http://www.museum.
tv/archives/etv/N/htmlN/nationalcabl/nationalcabl.htm
Information Technology Association of America
http://www.itaa.org/eweb/StartPage.aspx

Personal and Oral History Associations

Association of Personal Historians
http://www.personalhistorians.org/index.html

Oral History Association
http://omega.dickinson.edu/organizations/oha/about.html

International Oral History Association
http://www.ioha.fgv.br/ioha/english/index.html

Texas Oral History Association
http://www.baylor.edu/TOHA/

Southwest Oral History Association
http://soha.fullerton.edu/

New England Association for Oral History
http://www.ucc.uconn.edu/~cohadm01/neaoh.html

Michigan Oral History Association
http://www.umich.edu/pres/history/oral.html

UCLA Oral History Program
http://www.library.ucla.edu/libraries/special/ohp/ohpindex.htm

"California As I Saw It," First Person Narratives of California's Early Years:
1849-1900. The Library of Congress.
http://memory.loc.gov/ammem/cbhtml/cbhome.html

Nutrition and Health-Related Associations, Research Institutes, Corporations, Academies, and University Programs

American Academy of Family Physicians: http://www.aafp.org/
American Association of Family and Consumer Sciences: http://www.aafcs.org/
American Dietetic Association: http://www.eatright.org/
American Heart Association: http://www.americanheart.org/
American Institute for Cancer Research: http://www.aicr.org/
American Public Health Association: http://www.apha.org/
American Society of Clinical Nutrition: http:// www.ascn.org/
Center for Science in the Public Interest: http://www.cspinet.org/
Chocolate Manufacturers Association: http://www.chocolateusa.org/
Consumer Federation of America: http://www.consumerfed.org/

Consumer Healthcare Products Association: http://www.chpa-info.org/
Council for Responsible Nutrition: http://www.crnusa.org/
Egg Nutrition Center: http://www.enc-online.org/
Federal Trade Commission: http://www.ftc.gov/
Food and Nutrition Board, Institute of Medicine: http://www.iom.edu/board.asp?id=3788
Foundation for American Communications: http://www.facsnet.org/
Asian Food Information Center: http://www.afic.org/Press%20Centre.htm
Institute of Food Technologists: http://www.ift.org/cms/
International Dairy Foods Association: http://www.idfa.org/
International Life Sciences Institute: http://www.ilsi.org/
Kleinfeld Kaplan & Becker: http://www.fda.gov/ohrms/dockets/dailys/00/Aug00/082400/cp0001.pdf
Lehigh University, Department of Journalism and Communication: http://www.lehigh.edu/~injrl/sciwrit/
National Cancer Institute, US National Institutes of Health: http://www.cancer.gov/
National Cooperative Business Association: http://www.ncba.coop/
National Food Processors Association: http://www.worldfooddayusa.org/CMS/2951/8939.aspx
National Potato Promotion Board:
http://www.uspotatoes.com/
Office of Dietary Supplements, National Institutes of Health: http://ods.od.nih.gov/
The Popcorn Board: http://www.popcorn.org/index.cfm
Purdue University, National Institutes of Health Botanicals Center for Age-Related Diseases: http://www.purdue.edu/UNS/html4ever/000920.Weaver.nihcenter.html
Purdue University, Department of Foods and Nutrition: http://www.cfs.purdue.edu/
Rutgers University, Nutraceuticals Institute: http://foodsci.rutgers.edu/nci/
Soyfoods Association of North America: http://www.soyfoods.org/
Saint Joseph's University, Erivan K. Haub School of Business: http://www.sju.edu/
Tufts School of Medicine and Nutrition: http://www.tufts.edu/med/nutrition-infection/
Tufts University Health and Nutrition Letter: http://healthletter.tufts.edu/
United Soybean Board: http://www.unitedsoybean.org/

United States Department of Agriculture, Agricultural Research Service: http://www.ars.usda.gov/main/main.htm

United States Food and Drug Administration, Center for Food Safety and Applied Nutrition: http://www.cfsan.fda.gov/list.html

University of California, Davis: http://www.ucdavis.edu/index.html

University of California, Davis, California Institute of Food and Agricultural Research: http://aic.ucdavis.edu/

University of California, Davis, Robert Mondavi Institute for Wine and Food Science: http://www.news.ucdavis.edu/mondavi/iwfs_facts.html

University of Illinois, Department of Food Science and Human Nutrition: http://www.fshn.uiuc.edu/

University of Illinois, Functional Foods for Health Program: http://www.ag.uiuc.edu/~ffh/ffh.html

University of Massachusetts, Department of Food Science: http://www.umass.edu/foodsci/

University of Missouri, Columbia, Department of Food Science and Human Nutrition: http://outreach.missouri.edu/hes/food.htm

University of Missouri, Columbia, Missouri School of Journalism: http://journalism.missouri.edu/

University of Southern California, School of Pharmacy: http://www.usc.edu/schools/pharmacy/

Virginia Tech Center for Food and Nutrition Policy: http://www.vt.edu/

Food Safety Research Information Office: http://www.nal.usda.gov/fsrio/acad.htm

15

DESCRIPTION OF BOOK PUBLICITY BUSINESS:
Personal History, Memoirs, Life Stories & Biographies

Promote Your Book as Part of a Panel of Biographical Author Interviews

Videobiographers interview people who want to put a variety of life stories, events, or corporate histories on videotape. Your non-corporate client may make a videobiography to clarify life purposes or values, record family history, or document events for historical preservation. Your corporate client may wish to make a video record of the history of a family business or company, documenting several generations of business history, including annual and financial reports, mergers and acquisitions, or expansion starting with the founding family members.

Videobiographies also may contain an oral history, documentation of events affecting a person's life, a legal deposition, local history, autobiography, life events and rites of passage, corporate history, poetry, love letters, messages to children and future descendants, fiction, Reader's Theatre, war stories, holocaust survival documentation, life validation, confessions to family members, apologies, psychohistory, or biographies of celebrities on video tape for collectors, museums, libraries, genealogy archives, and family records.

Other people who may wish to make a videobiography to give to friends are those in hospices whose time is short. Religious leaders may want sermons combined with slices of life experience stories or anecdotes put on tape.

Videobiographies may contain images of persons reading their love letters and poetry to loved ones. Prisoners may want to make a videobiography saved on a DVD or CD to send to their relatives or their victims. Prisoners on death row may want a video and/or audio record to send to relatives who live too far away to visit regularly, and the relatives may wish to chip in to have such a tape produced as a form of family reunion. Some prisoners use such a video recording to make confessions, to apologize to their victims or relatives, or to get onto broadcast television to appeal their cases.

Videobiographies are requested by the elderly home based, the disabled, psychotherapists, hypnotists, and counselors, people with confessions to make on video to send to someone, entertainers, or entrepreneurs seeking the one-on-one personal approach with customers. There is a popular market for hypnosis tapes, and some hypnotherapists may hire a video producer to make tapes for special clients or to sell to the public. Authors can promote books, ideas, and other materials through personal history interviews. Teachers can offer courses in personal history documentation and offer copies to be archived in oral history libraries at many universities.

Why stop at video? Put your videos and still images on virtual reality CD compact disk, read only memory on your computer to be played with a CD or DVD player. Create interactive photo shoots and combine them with biographical videos. Make an impact by combining high quality video images with regular video on DVD that can be played on most DVD players or a personal computer. Keep a text copy as technology evolves to a time when DVDs no longer can be played because the players become obsolete like Victrolas, phonographs, certain tape recorders, and some old VHS video cameras.

Snap your favorite pictures and save them to your computer's hard disk. Then transfer them to video tape. Use your computer controls to direct the people or items in your photos to a variety of poses. Pick your own multiple camera angles or close-ups.

Practice your video and photography skills on your personal computer and edit your best shots back onto your videotape. Create a CD-ROM game using your videos and still shots. Your videotapes can be transferred onto computer disks to create virtual reality imagery or video. Or work exclusively in video to produce exquisite videobiographies.

INCOME POTENTIAL:

Charge $100 to $175 an hour to individuals for taping, directing, editing, and producing a videobiography, genealogy, or autobiography on tape and a $200 per minute fee to corporations to record and edit a corporate history. You can charge a discount to other family members for separate tapes that include clips of a relative's tape.

Decide whether you will charge special rates for ministers and officials of religious organizations. Video pod casts can document the life stories of members of their congregations. They may be able to give you a continuing list of referrals. Most videographers who monitor people in the news charge approximately $175 an hour for monitoring events on tape. Updates can be made and edited to an original tape, or older tape can be edited to new tape to preserve it.

You can videotape profiles and portfolios of actors, performers, or speakers. Interview people at their homes and social centers or in your home or studio. What types of personal history projects would you like to emphasize? If you interview people on camera for other journalists, charge $175-$200 an hour for a taping using the journalist's questions rather than your own. You can interview people for television stations and news programs for a fee to save the studio money or when the person interviewed can't come out to the studio.

You can also travel on cruise ships or in flight and interview people on vacation to make vacation videobiographies for them to document their vacations. Charge $100 to $175 per hour to videotape vacationers, travelers, or people on cruise ships. Keep a copy of the tape for your library and get a letter of permission from them in writing if you plan to use clips of your clients in your own future videos.

Many people who travel for business or tourism would love to have a professionally edited 60-minute tape of their vacation or honeymoon. For a flat fee, usually $200 if you're traveling along with them, plus expenses, you can go anywhere in the world to capture honeymooners, vacationers, business travelers, or business deals being made on tape.

Edit special life events onto videobiogaphies, like documented surgical operations or daring sports events, musical performances, or a client's photographs and illustrations. You can charge a special fee to tape parachute or bungee jumps, car races, ski jumps, ice skating, tennis matches, or any other sports event. If the client wants you to go up in a plane and videotape them sky diving, then charge expenses plus your usual fee.

Although video monitoring fees range around $175-$200 an hour plus expenses, producing a 10 or 20-minute corporate history or training film has a different fee scale at $200 PER MINUTE for scriptwriting it, plus $200 an hour for taping it—only for the videography or camera work. Editing is extra, especially if you send the video out to a post production editing studio. Learn to edit the tape yourself and make extra money.

You can add expenses to that for props, lighting, studio rental, hiring the narrator, and other expenses when you make up your first budget. A straight taping of someone telling his or her life story runs about $175 an hour, plus editing expenses.

BEST LOCALE TO OPERATE THE BUSINESS:

Videobiographies may be produced from any location. Or you could travel around the world or work on cruise ships. Corporate histories are videotaped from office locations (or even the golf course) anywhere in the world and may be edited for global videoconferences by satellite. Approach businesses or community centers where people want to put their experiences on tape.

Compile video books by asking many people one provocative question. Then put their response on tape as well as in an accompanying booklet. Choose universal questions that apply to all people's lives. Or ask controversial questions. Another approach is to make unauthorized celebrity biographies by talking to friends and acquaintances of the person in the biography.

Ask the children of famous parents or parents with extremist views to talk about how they feel. Most of your videobiography business will be from older people who want to preserve their memories, confessions, messages, love letters, and life experiences on tape for their grandchildren to pass on to future generations.

Design a workbook and audio tapes to accompany the videobiography, especially if it's going to schools, libraries, and museums or is to be used for instructional or historical research purposes.

TRAINING REQUIRED:

The best way to learn about creating biographies is to read brief biographies and view as many videobiographies as you can—the 30 and 60 minute tapes. Visit your museum libraries and view oral histories on videotape, including the libraries and archives of the videobiographies of war, disaster, and holocaust survivors of the past half century. Look at biographies on film as well as on videocassette.

In addition to studying the technique of creating a videobiography, learn to use your video camera to create interviews. Read a few books (you'll find in college bookstores) on how to take oral histories on tape and how to interview people from any beginning course in journalism, interviewing, or producing interviews on tape in a news video course at a local community college.

Attend video conventions. Take seminars and workshops offered by video associations such as local chapters of the International Documentary Association, videographer organizations or clubs, and video suppliers that focus on creating videobiographies. Join the International Documentary Association or a local chapter of a documentary video group, sometimes listed in video trade magazines. Consult the Encyclopedia of Associations to find new national video organizations. Read the publications of associations and the usual video trade magazines (trade journals) and newsletters.

GENERAL APTITUDE OR EXPERIENCE:

You'll need a knack for interviewing people and putting them at ease in front of your camera. It helps to practice interviewing people in video. Sometimes adult education courses offer workshops on how to interview for a job. They tape the student job applicants to help them feel more at ease in front of a camera and during a job interview. It may be helpful to sit in such a course.

You can always get in touch with an actor's support group and inquire whether anyone will volunteer to be interviewed in front of your camera in a mock biography. In summarized point, the actors may want to keep the tape after you study or copy it to be edited for their video portfolios.

The best aptitude is a nose for news or a flair for video journalism, experience making interviews easy for someone to tell their life story on tape, and practice in composing a list of questions.

EQUIPMENT NEEDED:

You'll need a video camera, tripod, tape, editing and dubbing equipment, and sound props. You may want to use some props and special effects in your studio or interview setting, which may be outdoors showing the person walking, in which case, you'll need to hold the camera or pan in a vehicle. You may want to cut in scenes of the person's wedding, bar mitzvah or confirmation, a relative's funeral, childbirth, or any life event your clients want cut to tape.

Avoid talking heads by using many cuts and montages or outdoor scenes of the person in action, working, gardening, cooking, walking along the waterside, bicycling, driving, working, or in some kind of constant motion or action doing a variety of tasks.

If you make videbiographies of scientists or doctors, you'll have to set up studio in a laboratory, operating room, hospital, or medical office, and may need special micro-video recording equipment supplied by the scientist for videotaping what's seen through an electronic microscope.

If you videotape the biographies of astronauts, you'll have to get clips and stills of their missions in space from NASA, the government, or private archives and edit the stock footage onto your videotape. Obtain written permission for anything that's not public domain.

OPERATING YOUR BUSINESS:

Decide what kind of videobiographies you'll specialize in. They could be executive's corporate histories, autobiographies, senior citizen's life experiences, children interviewed every seven years to document them from early childhood into adulthood, public history, celebrity interviews, scientist's videobiographies, inventors, artists and writers interviewed on tape for schools, genealogy/family history documentation and memoirs, life stories, legal depositions, an individual's war, disaster, and holocaust recollections to document and preserve history for future generations, or anyone's life story on videotape.

You'll have to compose a list of questions for the interview. Ask your client what questions should be asked in order to compose the list while you do a preliminary interview on tape to gather information.

Set up your props in the person's home, senior center, or studio, and vary the scenes by showing the person at work, outside, in play, travel, driving, swimming, community service, or whatever they want to do in order to create a variety of scene changes and cutaways. Use backlighting to create a less harsh image of the person's face under bright lights. Use some television makeup on your client to create a matte rather than a shiny face, as people tend to sweat on their face during a video interview.

In the usual video interview, you sit next to your client and ask a variety of questions while someone else turns the video camera mounted on a tripod to catch interviewer and interviewee having a dialogue. As your client talks about specific life events, you can edit in scenes of the person performing some activity. The effect is the client's voice-over, while clips of your client in action outdoors or at a variety of settings shows the person in action, moving from one place to another, or actual footage of stock video or film on video scenes (such as war documentation) are cut in.

The result is your client's voice over speaking about the experience and answering your questions, while the viewer sees cuts and flashbacks to the particular events, war scenes, or news events. You can rent or buy the video/film stock footage from video and film libraries and archives.

Videobiographies, like instructional videos, are inspirational or motivational and end on an upbeat, optimistic note. Autobiographies of senior citizens are people's final comments on their own life purposes, experiences, relationships, and values. So train yourself to ask pertinent questions to help your clients put on tape their life purpose clarifications by asking the following questions of your clients:

1. What do you love to do?

2. What do you enjoy?

3. What do you do well?

4. What, in your own opinion, are your 10 greatest successes?

5. What do you feel enthusiastic or passionate about?

6. What are the 10 most important lessons you've learned in life?

7. What issues keep coming back?

8. What do you daydream about doing?

9. What do you want to be remembered for?

10. What would you do if you knew you could never fail?

Train yourself to help your client look beyond self-imposed limitations by focusing on asking your client to speak only in the client's own opinion, not in the opinion of friends, relatives, employers, co-workers, or criticizers, on the client's life successes. Attend video store or studio workshops given by traveling lecturers who are professional videographers, and view their videos. Producers may re-edit a corporate history videobiography.

Anything you edit to your videotape can also be cut into a computer disk or CD-ROM so the client can access the video clip or scene on a computer or watch it on video tape. Video footage combined with computer text and music sounds are useful if you're planning to create interactive software for students and market your videobiographies to schools.

Videotapes can also be marketed, either as interactive or plain videos. If you plan to cut segments of your video on software, there are many options available.

You can use the latest computer software to create fascinating biographical videos. In summarized point, you can not only create videobiographies and corporate histories on videotape, you can put the video tape on CD-ROM, computer disk, or laser disk. Adobe Systems, Inc. provides an update for Adobe Premier, a video editing software program for Windows.

Create multimedia biographical, genealogical, corporate, educational, or historical graphic presentations in video or on CD-ROM computer disk. Put your autobiography on videotape and then cut segments of it onto computer disks to combine your talking, live action, family photos, film and home movies, or corporate histories.

Adobe Premier Software captures video-at-large. Select a version that supports direct video capture using Adobe Video Capture software. It's included in the package, which also has sample video, audio, and still images on CD-ROM.

You use a video capture board and the capture program. You can digitize analog video and audio signals directly from your VCR, video camera, or laser disc player. Specify options for capture type, frame rate (how many frames you want captured per second), image size, video format, and audio format. Customize your videos by controlling the output data rate for optimizing your CD-ROM playback. To keep your colors consistent throughout your video, there's a color palette.

Also, you can import still images onto your video as a single video clip. For information, call Adobe Systems at (415) 961-4400 or 1(800) 833-6687. Put your videobiographies on CD-ROM so they can be played on a computer as videos or as videotape segments or "movies" combined with text, pictures, animation, illustration, still photos, music, and other sounds.

TARGET MARKET:

Work with genealogy books for specific audiences and ethnic groups. You want to reach anyone interested in putting an interview, oral history, or life story on videotape. Videobiographies are becoming popular among corporate executives who want to document corporate history or a family business on videotape. Many senior citizens centers offer courses in how to create videobiographies with your video camera.

Older people want to find ways to put life stories and messages or even confessions on video to give to their grandchildren to preserve their memories for future generations. You can even market your videobiographies to parents of young children and approach parenting classes. Many parents would like a videobiography of their child at different stages of life.

Some people want to create a tape every seven years to mark the rites of passage or stages of life. A tape should be made of everyone at birth, at age seven, 14, 21, 28, 35, 42,49, 56, 63, 70 and every decade after to mark all the stages of life. We all change every seven years, physically and in many other ways. Send out flyers to mailing lists of people at various ages seven years apart from birth to a hundred announcing your videobiographies to document them and their memoirs every seven years.

You can buy mailing lists of people at the various ages or stages of life spaced seven years apart. You can also advertise their age number and explain why a tape is made to document and celebrate a rite of passage marking change and growth every seven years of a person's life span. Documenting life passages on tape creates a library of tradition and change to be preserved by every future generation, hopefully, in a family time capsule.

RELATED VIDEO OPPORTUNITIES:

Teach senior citizens at adult education centers and senior centers how to create beautiful and professional-looking videobiographies. Offer your services as a video consultant in the schools. You don't need a credential or degree to offer your videotape to schools or approach teachers with your flyer.

You can volunteer to show children how to use the school's camcorders or other video cameras to create their life stories on tape or to document their growth, activities, and childhood creativity. Apply to the state government for a paid grant to be a visiting video artist in residence in the schools for a year.

Teach teenagers in neighborhood community centers how to make a teen video magazine or run their own video news and events video production team to discuss events with their peers or other generations for a meeting of the minds. You can start your own videobiography workshops in the YMCA or YWCA, in adult education classes, at community centers, or schools and senior centers or in children's hospitals or work with disabled teens or adults showing them how to put their biographies on videotape.

Volunteer to work with gifted high school students or community college students showing them how to compile biographies of celebrities or famous people in science or their vocational field of choice by putting together stock video footage or interviewing people on the job in their chosen occupations.

ADDITIONAL INFORMATION:

The Association of Music Pod casting
http://www.musicpod casting.org/

Digital Video Professionals Association
28 East Jackson Bldg #10-D572
Chicago, IL, USA 60604
http://www.dvpa.com/default.aspx

INFO Links (List of Video-Related Associations)
http://www.nonlinear4.com/info.htm

International Documentary Association
1551 S. Robertson Blvd. Suite 201
Los Angeles, CA 90035
http://www.documentary.org/

The Internet Movie Database (Movie-Related Urls)
http://www.imdb.com/links

National Association of PhotoShop Professionals
http://www.photoshopuser.com/

NYC Pod casting Association
http://pod casting.meetup.com/33/

Pod casting News
http://www.pod castingnews.com/

The Hawaii Association of Pod casters
http://www.hawaiipod casting.com/page/2/

Promoting Your Genealogy Books

Multi-Ethnic Genealogy Web Sites:

(Usually, there are several genealogy sites on the Web for each ethnic group.)

Acadian/Cajun: & French Canadian: http://www.acadian.org/tidbits.html

Afghanistan Genealogy: http://www.kindredtrails.com/afghanistan.html

African-American: http://www.cyndislist.com/african.htm

African Royalty Genealogy: http://www.uq.net.au/~zzhsoszy/

Albanian Research List: http://feefhs.org/al/alrl.html

Armenian Genealogical Society: http://feefhs.org/am/frg-amgs.html

Asia and the Pacific: http://www.cyndislist.com/asia.htm

Austria-Hungary Empire: http://feefhs.org/ah/indexah.html

Baltic-Russian Information Center: http://feefhs.org/blitz/frgblitz.html

**Belarusian—Association of the Belarusian Nobility:
http://feefhs.org/by/frg-zbs.html**

Bukovina Genealogy: http://feefhs.org/bukovina/bukovina.html

Carpatho-Rusyn Knowledge Base: http://feefhs.org/rusyn/frg-crkb.html

Chinese Genealogy: http://www.chineseroots.com.

Croatia Genealogy Cross Index: http://feefhs.org/cro/indexcro.html

**Czechoslovak Genealogical Society Int'l, Inc.:
http://feefhs.org/czs/cgsi/frg-cgsi.html**

Eastern Europe: http://www.cyndislist.com/easteuro.htm

Eastern European Genealogical Society, Inc.:
http://feefhs.org/ca/frg-eegs.html

Eastern Europe Ethnic, Religious, and National Index with Home Pages
includes the FEEFHS Resource Guide that lists organizations associated
with FEEFHS from 14 Countries. It also includes Finnish and Armenian
genealogy resources: http://feefhs.org/ethnic.html

Ethnic, Religious, and National Index 14 countries: http://feefhs.
org/ethnic.html

**(Finland) Genealogical Society of Finland: http://www.genealogia.fi/
indexe.htm**

Finnish Genealogy Group: http://feefhs.org/misc/frgfinmn.html

Galicia Jewish SIG: http://feefhs.org/jsig/frg-gsig.html

German Genealogical Digest: http://feefhs.org/pub/frg-ggdp.html

Greek Genealogy Sources on the Internet: http://www-personal.umich.edu/~cgaunt/greece.html

Genealogy Societies Online List: http://www.daddezio.com/catalog/grkndx04.html

German Research Association: http://feefhs.org/gra/frg-gra.html

Greek Genealogy (Hellenes-Diaspora Greek Genealogy): http://www.geocities.com/SouthBeach/Cove/4537/

Greek Genealogy Home Page: http://www.daddezio.com/grekgen.html

Greek Genealogy Articles: http://www.daddezio.com/catalog/grkndx01.html

India Genealogy: http://genforum.genealogy.com/india/

India Family Histories: http://www.mycinnamontoast.com/perl/results.cgi?region=79&sort=n

India-Anglo-Indian/Europeans in India genealogy: http://members.ozemail.com.au/~clday/

Irish Travellers: http://www.pitt.edu/~alkst3/Traveller.html

Japanese Genealogy: http://www.rootsweb.com/~jpnwgw/

Jewish Genealogy: http://www.jewishgen.org/infofiles/

Latvian Jewish Genealogy Page: http://feefhs.org/jsig/frg-lsig.html

Lebanese Genealogy: http://www.rootsweb.com/~lbnwgw/

Lithuanian American Genealogy Society: http://feefhs.org/frg-lags.html

Melungeon: http://www.geocities.com/Paris/5121/melungeon.htm

Mennonite Heritage Center: http://feefhs.org/men/frg-mhc.html

Middle East Genealogy: http://www.rootsweb.com/~mdeastgw/index.html

Middle East Genealogy by country: http://www.rootsweb.com/~mdeastgw/index.html#country

Native American: http://www.cyndislist.com/native.htm

Polish Genealogical Society of America: http://feefhs.org/pol/frg-pgsa.html

Quebec and Francophone: http://www.francogene.com/quebec/amerin.html

Romanian American Heritage Center: http://feefhs.org/ro/frg-rahc.html

Slovak World: http://feefhs.org/slovak/frg-sw.html

Slavs, South: Cultural Society: http://feefhs.org/frg-csss.html

Syrian and Lebanese Genealogy: http://www.genealogytoday.com/family/syrian/

Syria Genealogy: http://www.rootsweb.com/~syrwgw/

Tibetan Genealogy: http://www.distantcousin.com/Links/Ethnic/China/Tibetan.html

Turkish Genealogy Discussion Group: http://www.turkey.com/forums/forumdisplay.php3?forumid=18

Ukrainian Genealogical and Historical Society of Canada: http://feefhs.org/ca/frgughsc.html

Unique Peoples: http://www.cyndislist.com/peoples.htm **Note: The Unique People's list includes: Black Dutch, Doukhobors, Gypsy, Romani, Romany & Travellers, Melungeons, Metis, Miscellaneous, and Wends/Sorbs**

General Genealogy Web sites

Ancestry.com: http://www.ancestry.com/main.htm?lfl=m

BMD Certificates, London, England, UK: http://www.bmd-certificates.co.uk

Cyndi's List of Genealogy on the Internet: http://www.cyndislist.com/

Cyndi's List is a categorized & cross-referenced index to genealogical resources on the Internet with thousands of links.

DistantCousin.com (Uniting Cousins Worldwide) http://distantcousin.com/Links/surname.html

Ellis Island Online: http://www.ellisisland.org/

Family History Library: http://www.familysearch.org/Eng/default.asp

http://www.familysearch.org/Eng/Search/frameset_search.asp

(The Church of Jesus Christ of Latter Day Saints) International Genealogical Index

Female Ancestors: http://www.cyndislist.com/female.htm

Genealogist's Index to the Web:
http://www.genealogytoday.com/GIWWW/?

Genealogy Web: http://www.genealogyweb.com/

Genealogy Authors and Speakers: http://feefhs.org/frg/frg-a&l.html

Genealogy Today: http://www.genealogytoday.com/

My Genealogy.com: http://www.genealogy.com/cgi-bin/my_main.cgi

Scriver, Dr. Charles: The Canadian Medical Hall of Fame http://www.virtualmuseum.ca/Exhibitions/Medicentre/en/scri_print.htm

Surname Sites: http://www.cyndislist.com/surn-gen.htm

National Genealogical Society: http://www.ngsgenealogy.org/index.htm

United States List of Local by State Genealogical Societies: http://www.daddezio.com/society/hill/index.html

United States Vital Records List: http://www.daddezio.com/records/room/index.html or http://www.cyndislist.com/usvital.htm

Bibliography for Genealogy and Memoirs Book Authors and Publicists

Making Memory Books by Hand—by Kristina Feliciano, Rockport Publishers. 1999.

Easy Book Binding. Nathan De Stephano. 2005. See: http://www.easybookbinding.com/.

Making Books and Journals: 20 Great Weekend Projects. Constance E Richards. Lark Books, Div. Sterling Publishing Co. 2000.

More Making Books By Hand: Exploring Miniture Books, Alternative Structures, and Found Objects. Peter Thomas, Donna Thomas—Crafts & Hobbies—Rockport Publishers. 2004

Genealogy Books, General

A Bintel Brief: Sixty Years of Letters From the Lower East Side to the Jewish Daily Forward. Metzker, Isaac, ed Doubleday and Co. 1971. Garden City, NY

Climbing Your Family Tree: Online and Offline Genealogy for Kids. Ira Wolfman, Tim Robinson (Illustrator), Alex Haley (Introduction)/Paperback/Workman Publishing Company, Inc./October 2001

Complete Beginner's Guide to Genealogy, the Internet, and Your Genealogy Computer Program. Karen Clifford/Paperback/Genealogical Publishing Company, Incorporated/February 2001

Complete Idiot's Guide(R) to Online Geneology. Rhonda McClure/Paperback/Pearson Education/January 2002

Creating Your Family Heritage Scrapbook : From Ancestors to Grandchildren, Your Complete Resource & Idea Book for Creating a Treasured Heirloom. Nerius, Maria Given, Bill Gardner ISBN: 0761530142 Published by Prima Publishing, Aug 2001

Cyndi's List: A Comprehensive List of 70,000 Genealogy Sites on the Internet (Vol. 1 & 2) Cyndi Howells/Paperback/Genealogical Publishing Company, Incorporated/June 2001.

Discovering Your Female Ancestors: Special strategies for uncovering your hard-to-find information about your female lineage. Carmack, Sharon DeBartolo. Conference Lecture on Audio Tape: Carmack, Sharon DeBartolo.

Folklife and Fieldwork: A Layman's Introduction to Field Techniques. Bartis, Peter. Washington, DC: Library of Congress, 1990.

Genealogy Online for Dummies. Matthew L. Helm, April Leigh Helm, April Leigh Helm, Matthew L. Helm/Paperback/Wiley, John & Sons, Incorporated/February 2001

Genealogy Online. Elizabeth Powell Crowe/Paperback/McGraw-Hill Companies, November 2001

History From Below: How to Uncover and Tell the Story of Your Community, Association, or Union. Brecher, Jeremy. New Haven: Advocate Press/Commonwork Pamphlets, 1988.

My Family Tree Workbook: Genealogy for Beginners. Rosemary A. Chorzempa/Paperback/Dover Publications, Incorporated/

National Genealogical Society Quarterly 79, no. 3 (September 19991): 183-93

"Numbering Your Genealogy: Sound and Simple Systems." Curran, Joan Ferris.

Oral History and the Law. Neuenschwander, John. Pamphlet Series #1. Albuquerque: Oral History Association, 1993.

Oral History for the Local Historical Society. Baum, Willa K. Nashville: American Association for State and Local History, 1987.

Scrapbook Storytelling: Save Family Stories & Memories with Photos, Journaling & Your Own Creativity. Slan, Joanna Campbell, Published by EFG, Incorporated, ISBN: 0963022288 May 1999

"The Silent Woman: Bringing a Name to Life." NE-59. Boston, MA: New England Historic Genealogical Society Sesquicentennial Conference, 1995.

The Source: A Guidebook of American Genealogy. Alice Eichholz, Loretto Dennis Szucs (Editor), Sandra Hargreaves Luebking (Editor), Sandra Hargreaves Luebking (Editor)/Hardcover/MyFamily.com, Incorporated/February 1997

To Our Children's Children: Journal of Family Members, Bob Greene, D. G. Fulford 240pp. ISBN: 038549064X Publisher: Doubleday & Company, Incorporated: October 1998.

Transcribing and Editing Oral History. Nashville: American Association for State and Local History, 1991.

Using Oral History in Community History Projects. Buckendorf, Madeline, and Laurie Mercier. Pamphlet Series #4. Albuqueque: Oral History Association, 1992.

Unpuzzling Your Past: The Best-Selling Basic Guide to Genealogy (Expanded, Updated and Revised) Emily Anne Croom, Emily Croom/Paperback/F & W Publications, Incorporated/August 2001

Writing a Woman's Life. Heilbrun, Carolyn G. New York: W.W. Norton, 1988

Your Guide to the Family History Library: How to Access the World's Largest Genealogy Resource. Paula Stuart Warren, James W. Warren/Paperback/F & W Publications, Incorporated/August 2001

16

DESCRIPTION OF BOOK PUBLICITY BUSINESS:
Book News and Author Interviews Monitoring Service or Media Tour Guide

Combine planning writers' conferences at hotels, schools, or community centers with creating video, audio, multimedia, and/or print news clippings from all types of other conferences and news releases promoting your book and the books of other authors. Or offer media tour guides to writers coming to unfamiliar cities. Combine both services, or collect news clips only for authors to help promote their books and your own creative works.

If you plan conferences, charge enough to cover your expenses and make you a little profit, such as $175-$200 per person for your writers' conference that usually runs three days. For one day conferences, charge about $50 to $100 per day, depending upon where you locate your conference and the rent and expenses you paid for the space. Library and university conference rooms usually are lowest in rental price, but it various as do auditorium rental charges.

News clips may come from press releases—print and electronic, and video news releases sent to the media to use with permission and with all credits given to the news release organization, writers and researchers. Similar to the media tour monitor is the entrepreneur who creates video news clippings from video news releases (VNRs) and other types of news, drama, and product advertising broadcasts. Some news monitors will be asked to compare news broadcasts and look for discrepancies, conflicts, and other irregularities.

According to the American Marketing Association's Dictionary of Marketing Terms, a video news release is defined as "a publicity device designed to look and sound like a television news story. The publicist prepares a 60- to 90-second news release on videotape, which can then be used by television stations as is or after further editing. It is more sophisticated than a news clip."

Video pod casts might emphasize how competing businesses compare products broadcasted for test markets. You also might compare how the competition advertises a variety of similar products in your pod cast. You'll be asked to check to see whether ads are broadcasted at specific times and whether there are problems, conflicts or products, or other irregularities.

Review advertisements and infomercials for ad agencies in your pod casts and do more than monitor broadcasts and send reports back to the sponsors as to the quality and consistency of the TV program or advertisement you're asked to monitor. Video pod casts also can act like news clipping services for video segments rather than print articles clipped from newspapers or magazines. Audio pod casts can monitor and comment on or review various radio shows and advertising.

Specialize in news or in advertising or combine monitoring services across the board. Monitor and record television broadcast news. Pick up news from all over with use of a satellite dish. News monitors specialize mainly in taping and comparing a variety of news broadcasts, sometimes on the same subject. You're a video librarian, news clipping bureau, comparison checker, and researcher rolled into one monitoring service.

Air-checking also is a specialization. It's defined as monitoring and recording television commercials, infomercials, and other broadcasts. Your goal is to create a news, segment, and commercial advertisement clipping business using video and/or other electronic media. It's the electronic side of operating a newspaper, coupon, and magazine clipping service bureau.

Publicists who send out press releases frequently want the news clipped to send back to their clients. Some public relations agents, book publicists, and advertising media buyers send electronic press releases and want to know if and when they moved their client into the media. Or publicists and their clients want videotapes of their clients appearing on television talk shows or broadcast news interviews.

INCOME POTENTIAL:

Charge about $175 an hour to sit at home or in your own studio with your satellite dish and pick up the news around the world, recording the news and any commercials or infomercials or special broadcasts. If you work for other monitoring companies or air checkers, they will pay you a small hourly fee or a small fee per each broadcast you tape.

It's better to work for yourself doing television news monitoring than to sit at home and wait for someone to hire you to record at home. However, if you can't afford video recording equipment yet, working for a video monitoring service is one way to learn hands-on and acquire experience and training.

You'll find several classified or small display advertisements asking for people to record on videotape at home in entrepreneurial type magazines on your news or book store magazine display racks.

For example, more than a decade ago, in the summer 1994 edition of <u>Small Business Opportunities</u> magazine, a small display advertisement appeared on page 74 entitled, "Record Videotapes At Home For Profit." The advertisement stated that there…are no copyright violation or pornography involved and stated some of the details of recording videotapes at home for profit, including how much profit is possible.

Write to advertisers, advertising agencies, and marketing firms for information on how you can record commercials or other videotapes at home. Each of us has different business and income requirements. Learn as much as you can.

Remember, that recording videotapes at home is different from ***monitoring*** live or taped news broadcasts, commercials, infomercials or talk show segments. Other opportunities exist such as recording cable channel and pay television feature film broadcasts. Check with your client and the broadcaster to make sure you are not recording copyrighted material without written permission to record it.

BEST LOCALE TO OPERATE THE BUSINESS:

With a satellite dish, you can pick up hundreds of television stations around the world. You need to subscribe to the cable stations or purchase the type of satellite where you get everything out there, around the world or at least around the nation. The more stations you can receive, the better your chances are of finding clients who will pay you to monitor the news or commercials.

TRAINING REQUIRED:

It has been said that all you need to know to get started is how to sit at home in front of your television set, record, dub, and edit on your VCR and other television monitoring equipment what you are told to monitor on your television screen. However, you need to know how to tune in your satellite dish, dub a television program on your VCR or other monitoring equipment, and make video news clippings on a videotape.

Ask at your local video supplies store what you'll need to get set up at industrial quality to compete with local news monitoring services. Your video camera capabilities need to be at industrial quality. Any news clippings on video are played so many times that anything less than industrial quality camera and tape will wear out fast.

You could get training from a video supply store or take an adult education class in how to do news monitoring or "air checking" (recording television commercials). Sometimes seminars are offered in air checking or news monitoring by local chapters of national video associations, advertising organizations, and groups of media professionals. Inquire at your local community college or university's department of broadcasting and television, or join a business association for people in the video business.

GENERAL APTITUDE OR EXPERIENCE:

News monitoring and air checking are for people who really enjoy sitting home all day recording television news, commercials, infomercials, and other broadcasts for clients. If you rent a studio and fill it with equipment, you'll need room for your satellite dish so you can pick up all the stations. You also can record radio broadcasts on audio tape.

You'll need patience with people. It helps to have an aptitude for getting along with a variety of clients, including advertising agency executives, demanding media/broadcast people in a hurry, and video news clipping bureau competitors who insist on perfection on tape. You don't have to stay up all night anymore to record commercials or news if you program your VCR and recording equipment in other formats to turn on and off at certain times.

EQUIPMENT NEEDED:

Eventually, you will be asked by different clients to record in all formats. A satellite dish is necessary to pick up all the television stations around the nation and/or around the world. You'll need to get all the cable or satellite stations. An industrial quality video camcorder, VCR and DVD equipment is required for recording at industrial quality, dubbing or editing equipment for clipping the tapes at the right moment, and video tape of the client-specified length.

If you work at home, you'll need a backyard to put your satellite dish. Check to see whether your home is zoned for satellite dishes in case your neighbors complain. If you rent a recording studio, it should have enough space to put your satellite dish and recording equipment.

Find out whether your clients want broadcast quality or industrial quality videocassettes. That determines whether your camera will be broadcast or industrial quality, what kind of tape and editing or dubbing equipment you'll use, or what kind of packaging is preferred.

Industrial quality video can be copied many times without losing resolution. Broadcast quality video is more expensive and better, because it will stand up to more copying without losing quality. It's generally is used for network television broadcasting. It's what you see on the local TV news station.

Industrial quality tape or DVDs are used for non-broadcast television training purposes and to make industrial videos that will appear on corporate training videos rather than be broadcast nationally or locally to the public on television stations. Choose your format according to where your client wants to broadcast. Communication channels could be industrial, on national network television, or cable TV, non-broadcast media, via phone lines, Internet, or by satellite videoconferencing.

How many copies will be made from the tape or how much will it be played? Choose the best quality for your client, and bill accordingly.

Check with your video supplies store and the competition to see what they are using. You'll have to record in all formats. Look in video and television newsletters coming from local chapters of the International Television Association to see what the most popular formats are, and what supplies you'll need.

Talk to video equipment suppliers, especially at the booths during video and electronic trade conventions. Attend as many video-related industrial equipment conventions as you can because you learn the most by chatting with video outfitters who are not in competition with you.

Check what equipment your more silent competition has by networking at local chapter meetings of pod casting, television, and broadcast-related trade associations. Go on tours of the competition's businesses which are often sponsored by these professional broadcast industry associations, local chapters.

Study your local markets. Check out businesses that will buy your services, not the average person in the street.

OPERATING YOUR BUSINESS:

What you'll be offering to clients primarily is television news monitoring. You'll be recording from all formats. You'll record from film to tape. You'll edit videos, dub videos, and do video production.

Join the trade organizations for networking and mutual support. There are several national organizations with local chapters also who publish newsletters, such as the International Television Association or NATAS. Some of their ads are for television news monitoring companies. Call these businesses and chat with the owners.

Clients will ask you to monitor news broadcasts and tape or record to DVD, the entire program or certain segments, such as the commercials. You may be asked to tape educational or cultural broadcasts, public television presentations, or special cable television cultural broadcasts. What you are running is a news clipping service, and instead of clipping articles from newspapers, you are monitoring and recording the news, special broadcasts, commercials, and infomercials.

Sometimes you'll find clients appearing on television talk shows frequently, such as authors on book tours, speakers for special causes or associations, or celebrities, who want you to record all the shows on which your clients appear.

You'll send the client the requested video news clippings and keep a copy for yourself for your videobrary (video library). If the client's tape is destroyed, you can always copy from your original tape and send another to your client in the future.

Monitoring the news on videotape also can be made into computer software. Using multimedia software, you can transfer the entire videotape or edited scenes to computer disk, or use it in a videophone conference (or televised videoconference) on non-broadcast television by satellite around the globe.

If you transfer your video taped news or commercial segment to computer disk, you can add text, music or other sounds, and illustrations, animation, or other graphic images along with the text, video, and music. You can even make the disk interactive. So you have a choice of monitoring the news in the following ways on:

1. Video or audio tape.

2. Computer disk as a multimedia presentation

3. Text only in a computer database or, the old fashioned way, as a photocopied news clipping cut from a publication.

4. Interactive multimedia, as on an interactive cable television shopping channel, or in a video computer game.

5. Interactive laser disk to be played on a special laser-disk player, for example Philip's "Imagination Machine" for family entertainment and

learning, making the living room the learning room and entertainment center of the house.

How Do You Package A Video News Clipping Or Air Check?

When you package an air check of a broadcast television commercial or infomercial (28-minute cable informational television commercial), or a video clipping of a monitored news broadcast—the name of the show, the date, time, names of persons appearing, and any other pertinent information must be included on your labels. Send a sheet stating all information requested in addition to what appears on your labels, and keep your information in your database or files.

Advertisements in a variety of entrepreneurial magazines include selling videos for profit or learning VCR repair. Some ads offer information about little known home businesses and include audio cassettes and booklets. Use these ads as inspiration for you to consider making videos on related themes.

You can even make a video about how to earn money monitoring the news and commercials. Accompany the video by your own 50-page how-to booklet. Sell your video package to readers of home-based business and entrepreneurial magazines for a fee that includes all your expenses with enough of a margin left for at least a 15 percent profit.

A lot of people watch the news and would love to become involved in some way with the media. Monitoring the news gives anyone the chance to expand their knowledge of current events and issues.

TARGET MARKET:

Advertising agencies, television stations, publicists and public relations agencies, clients who advertise on television, cable television companies, persons in the news, celebrities, authors, researchers, talk show hosts, talk show guests, the government, corporations, hospitals, educational foundations, nonprofit agencies, schools, and broadcasters are all potential clients.

Anyone who ever appears on television or in the broadcast news would probably like to be monitored on videotape and sent a copy of the tape. Clients and business owners who pay for advertising want to know whether their ads were aired at certain times of the night or day.

Your target audience eventually may reach the point where you want national assignments from businesses. The chances of getting national assignments are based on your visibility, publicity, and advertising in a variety of broadcast industry trade journals.

Include yourself in direct marketing mail inserts. Expose your qualifications to businesses that use video monitoring services by advertising in the newsletters of professional associations, trade journals, and business newspapers read by your potential clients.

Advertise on video, including cable television, non-broadcast television, video-phone, videoconference ads, on shopping channels, and on radio. Share the costs of television spot advertising and trade show/convention non-broadcast television demonstration screen ads with other advertisers. Your clients are broadcast viewers themselves. That's where you're likely to reach them.

If you decide to make a video about how to earn money at home recording video tapes, news broadcasts, or commercials, be aware that many broadcast news monitors enjoy working alone in home-based studios. Your market would include readers of entrepreneurial publications.

RELATED VIDEO OPPORTUNITIES:

Offer a news clipping bureau on video. Monitor news and commercials. You do production, film to tape, editing, dubbing, cable, and satellite recording. What else can you offer? Clip newspaper and magazine articles, stories, ads, announcements, coupons, notices, photos, and other material and offer them to clients as news clippings or put them on tape or on computer disk.

Specialize in doing attorney's legal presentations for the courtroom, including forensic evidence recording, or medical video for attorneys, for the courtroom, or for hospital training or technical presentations. Or you can specialize in monitoring/recording those 28 1/2 minute infomercials broadcasted late at night on the cable television stations.

You can even make money on the side videotaping weddings. If you're mechanical, you can learn by correspondence courses to repair VCRs at home.

ADDITIONAL INFORMATION:

Video Monitoring Services of America, Inc.
http://www.vmsinfo.com/

EIN News-World News Media Monitoring (a news service, not an association)
http://www.einnews.com/?afid=73

Broadcast Education Association
http://www.beaweb.org/96news/itva.html

International Television Association
http://itvadc.org/itvadc/index.cfm/fuseaction/about

National Academy of Television Arts and Sciences
http://www.natasdc.org/

Association of Independent Video and Film Makers
http://www.aivf.org/

Public Relations Society of America
http://www.prsa.org/

American Marketing Association's "Dictionary of Marketing Terms."
http://www.marketingpower.com/mg-dictionary.
php?Searched=1&SearchFor=video%20news%20release

17

What Are the Best Ways to Promote Your Book at Minimal Cost to You?

Are you willing to go to any extreme to get attention? Or would you rather earn media recognition and credibility points through merit? How do you attract attention from reliable media that's not based only your book's current sales figures?

You find free publicity in the media and with other businesses by helping people get what they pay for, make improved choices, and solve problems. Gather an audience to watch your book promotions as informative video and audio pod casts and also as articles detailing your community service and volunteerism. Send this "volunteer of the year" type press release about your service and your book to the print media as press releases, fillers, or features.

Audiences also may be recruited by renting library or university conference rooms, set up in churches, or gathered from speakers' panels at conferences and conventions of national associations or particular industries—with advance notice. Don't take a fee from your audience to attend an event where you talk about your book. Invite the press to your conference on a related issue that you cover in your book.

Find higher quality for less money for your readers and the press by directing them to information they don't know about that you found in hidden, niche, and wholesaler's markets. Use the research to promote your book and the books of other authors. Promotion and publicity of books and instructional audio or video materials can be run at minimum cost online and at home.

The purpose of your business is to show people step-by-step how to transform their lives, grow, build, gain skills, solve problems, achieve results, and obtain at lower cost higher quality food, clothing, shelter, healthcare, education, and career opportunities. While doing all this, you can showcase your talent as a communicator or video pod casting artist, writer, producer, or engineer.

Your goal would be to broadcast your book's news, research, opinion, sermon, or course online or get more items and services of higher quality for less money. In showing others these techniques and strategies, you are training them to share what they know with others.

Your business would have the potential to turn into a franchise-like group of trained seminar leaders starting their own classes or groups. Begin a publishing and production service to provide training materials to share with others how to make money from the frugal lifestyle. At the same time, you can spin-off business that have a commitment to simple, natural ingredients and the do-it-yourself attitude.

To start a business showing people how to cut expenses you begin by interviewing and recording many different and/or competing businesses on the step-by-step methods business owners use to cut expenses and get higher quality items as well as how they avoid the pitfalls.

You learn how to cut expenses by interviewing people who have cut expenses in the area and products in which they work. Then you organize the ways they cut expenses on files, on cards, and in your computer. Your goal is to find the hidden markets and show others how to do the same.

Compile and analyze how people cut expenses and list the ways. Then list the ways they avoid pitfalls. When you have this information in front of you, it becomes part of your repertoire that you present to others showing your audience how to cut expenses and get more for their money by focusing on higher quality, hidden markets, shelf-pulls, overstocked items, and wholesale prices.

People pay for information they can use to make choices and decisions, especially information so new the media hasn't made it available to the public yet. These fresh angles on universal items or new applications become ancillaries. You can make a business by showing others how to spend less and get more because you get what you pay for.

Make use of proverbs and universal 'sayings' that are true. Make a business out of showing people how to get more quality for less money and still 'get' what they pay for in the lifetime of the product and its ability not to break down quickly. If you don't do public speaking, put your information on other media, such as on DVDs, CDs, or broadcast/pod-cast in MP3 audio files on the Internet and on disks.

You can also make pamphlets and booklets, or create Web sites. Another avenue would be to start a national association and franchise chapters in various cities whereby other people take a course you compile and qualify to start groups showing others how to open businesses showing people how to cut expenses and get higher quality rather than how to "live on less."

Show people not only how to live the frugal lifestyle, but how to live better, get better nutrition or health products, cleaning compounds, or pet care by doing it yourself is a business that helps people cut expenses to set up their own businesses. Here's how to start your home-based online business showing others how to cut expenses.

Where are the best and yet least costly cities to live? Show people who are relocating for specific reasons the most appropriate place for them to move. Research a variety of studies and reports, including Web sites that list the best and cheapest areas to live. Find out why the city had been recommended by reputable magazines and sites. Where did the research originate? Are the facts current and reliable?

When you've checked the facts, then you can let people know this valuable information and develop a budget for your clients about to relocate. To open a business showing others how to cut expenses, you need to be a listener and observer of current, credible research. Think of yourself as a mini-think tank. Your own budget can be minimal, and you can operate at home and online. What you're compiling and marketing is information so current that the media may not have seen it yet.

If you can find information for one client, you can do the same for a corporation that has decided to relocate. Keep your eye on the goal—showing others how to cut expenses and still get what they pay for—quality. Everyone wants more for less money. Your job is to reveal to clients and/or the public those places where people can find what they need at an affordable price.

If the item is a product, find out through customers who have used the product about how long it will last before the item wears out. You're book promotion campaign could be about searching for durability as well as quality and less expenditure or getting information on the newest trends. Maybe you've found hidden information that's so new the media hasn't touched it yet. Planning budgets for clients also is part of the picture of showing others how to cut expenses. Does your book offer escape or show people how to accomplish some service, learn a new subject, or make an item or product? Are you showing people the best places to live, work, or vacation?

If you're helping people relocate to inexpensive-to-live cities, consider what your client wants. The Web site called "Cheap Stingy Bastard.Com at: http://cheap.typepad.com/cheapster/2004/09/cheapest_cities.html offers a link to the

Forbes' Magazine site where the 60 cheapest cities to live are listed in that Forbes magazine research piece dated 2004. There are categories of individual needs to consider.

The *"Cheap Stingy Bastard.Com"* Web site notes that Forbes magazine divides communities into the following categories: "Porch-Swing, Happy Hootervilles, IQ Campuses, Steroid Cities, Bohemian Bargains, or Telecommuting Heavens." The *Forbes* magazine link is at: http://www.forbes.com/home/bestplaces/2004/08/09/life2land.html. You'll have to consider individual needs when customizing information on the cheapest cities to live in for your particular client.

The cheapest cities to live in reports update annually, and the cities change. Also see the 2005 CNN Money site that notes a new report from Salary.com looks at the relationship between salaries and cost of living in 188 large, metropolitan areas in the USA. See the Salary.com site at: http://www.salary.com. Whether you choose Tulsa, Oklahoma, or Huntsville, Alabama, or another city, you can find the cheapest city to live in for one year, but what happens when the various reports on the cheapest city to live in changes the following year?

Note that addresses and Web sites listed in this book may change over time and/or change frequently. To keep updated, check your Internet's search engine for new mailing addresses and Web site changes. The companies may have recently moved or changed their names and addresses. Check the Web before you write to anyone listed to see whether their address has changed. Also, see my Web site at http://www.newswriting.net for articles and various links.

What You Need to Get Started in Promoting and Marketing Your Book

Let action verbs direct you how to publicize your book. To connect with credible media, you need to show the media that you're a person who does the following:

1. Sees patterns in everything.

2. Makes connections between two unrelated subjects and brings them together creating a whole new third subject or object.

3. Sees symbols in nature and makes them concrete and easy to grasp. Takes the abstract and applies it to what is of universal interest to all people.

4. Makes the hard-to-understand symbols clear, useful, and practical.

5. Uses intuition (imagination based on experience and judgment) plus feeling to move the video forward. The forward action creates a measurable range of change from beginning to end known as growth.

6. Knows how to communicate, inspire, persuade, and motivate with video clips that reach people at their feeling/gut/emotional level while appealing to and respecting the viewer's logic/intellect.

7. Knows how to fill a void/need in the community with material that has universal appeal, even in a niche or specialty video.

8. Caters to the majority of pragmatic, down-to-earth viewers who want timely, useful information to make important life decisions, do something better, or improve themselves.

9. Presents learning as entertainment. Shows viewers how to have more fun with escape while learning new skills at the same time.

10. Shows the viewer without preaching how to reach his/her maximum potential or how to grow from the inside out. Works for a cause. Shows the viewer why and how to become involved.

11. Improves the quality of the viewer's lives while making the audience feel important and respected. The video leaves the viewer feeling good/positive at the end.

Does Book Publicity Show How Your Writing Improves Readers' Lives?

Two people improve each others' book promotions by paring words down to the bare bones. Use as few words as possible to pitch your book's concept and main points. Begin promoting your how-to book by interviewing competing businesses related to your book's topics on how competing businesses cut expenses and still find higher quality items. Record the step-by-step instruction or other information.

Use plain language that your readers or listeners can follow to see how others found results. Write down what you have learned from former mistakes and from other people's mistakes. Promote your book by showing people *what pitfalls to avoid*. Show how your book can help others to do at least one kindness each day. Make sure what you put in your book publicity is informative and directive. The publicity in whatever format needs to show how your book helps others to be healthier, happier, or improves the quality of lives.

You best promote your book and find free publicity in the print media through starting with video, radio, and the online media as a home-grown broadcaster. Web logs and pod casts are being reviewed in the media—audio, video, and print. Position yourself first to gain media visibility long before you publish in print.

Book publicity and book packaging—the *promotional* ends of the businesses of writing, publishing, and marketing—use technology and branding to capture audiences that have interests in specific subject areas. Here's where the hidden markets appear.

The narrower your niche, the broader your audience…For example, if you've written a book on how to build miniature palaces and castles as indoor-outdoor houses for cats and dogs, your audience is broader than you might think…

Try gift stores, home building super stores, and doll manufacturers. Then approach schools' shop classes, parents' publications, and do-it-yourself satellite TV networks. Your book is perfect for a garden supplies market workshop and for that real estate and architect's association convention. Ask for a press conference under the headline, "Building Palaces for Pets."

18

How to Write a Course Syllabus and Teach Online to Market Your Book

One of the best ways to publicize, promote, and market your book is to write a syllabus. Teach an online or in-person course related to the topic of your book. Require students to purchase the book. Teach the contents of the book in a how-to course. What's your hobby or field of expertise? My usual full-time working day emphasizes genealogy journalism and personal history research. My hobby combines visual anthropology and producing, viewing, and reviewing documentaries.

If your field relates to personal history or genealogy, here's how to write a syllabus to teach online (or in person) a genealogy course. You can train or teach at a variety of levels.

Starting your own classes and reserving a conference room in a library, church social hall, or community center don't require degrees or credentials, only expertise. Nothing lets you learn a subject better than if you have to teach it to beginners. If you don't like teaching face-to-face or training employees in a work setting, teach online from your Web site. Or apply to teach a course in something you can do well at online educational sites such as blackboard.com. Read online education publications such as the Virtual U Gazette. Check out GetEducated.com at: http://www.geteducated.com/vug/index.asp.

You learn more from your students' feedback than you ever learned from books in a variety of areas related to writing and publishing. The first step is to write a great syllabus that convinces others to hire you to teach a subject related to the information in your book. This technique works well with nonfiction, how-to or self-help books.

If your book is a novel, your course syllabus might emphasize plotting the novel or marketing and promotion. To sell your book in this type of class, you'd use each chapter to teach how to write "tag lines," emotions and behaviors in a novel, or portions of your novel as tools for fiction writers in the genre of your book—such as plotting the mystery or romance novel.

You'd use passages to teach consistency and transitions that move the plot forward and show how the characters grow and change or the romantic tension. A similar technique of "teaching the process" would be used if you wrote plays, poetry, or cinematic scripts. A syllabus helps you get hired and/or to recruit students so you can sell your book and teach a class or train a group of people either online or in person.

You can adapt this syllabus plan and format to the subject of your book in nearly any field. Instead of 'genealogy,' just substitute the concept and framework of your own book. Here's how to write a syllabus.

A short course may be taught online or arranged in any room available from a church basement to a library conference room. A seminar can last a few hours. A lengthy course can be planned for an entire semester at any level in adult education, for college extended studies programs, or at community centers. You need experience in your area of expertise, and a published book helps your credibility. If you're teaching a course in a community college or university for college credit you'd need a graduate degree. For public school you'd also need a teaching credential unless your expertise level is the equivalent. Teaching vocational education and using your book as instructional text is more flexible. You can teach in the extended studies (not for credit) department of universities and community colleges based on experience. Credentials in your field of work are helpful to get you hired, but without them, start your own course online or from an available room.

You can share a rented room to teach the course with other trainers or teachers. Least expensive is to teach at your Web site and sell your book online to students. At the end of the course, give them a certificate in the subject you've taught related to your book. Require students to buy your book, and use it throughout the course.

One of the easiest ways to get hired to teach a course is to offer one in genealogy and/or personal history, if you have done your research on how genealogists find their information. Since you have written a book, can you now call yourself an expert?

If genealogy, personal history, oral history, social history, anthropology, sociology, psychology, creative writing, early handwriting, or journalism interests you, a beginner's course in genealogy attracts people interested in where their ancestors came from and how they lived, ate, and played. Classes often fill up quickly.

People like to take courses where they can learn about themselves and their families' life styles. Genealogy courses work well online, at social, ethnic, and religious clubs, and at senior centers. So here's how to begin writing a syllabus for a genealogy course.

Your first genealogy course syllabus expands the four keys of genealogy research: identity, name, date information was recorded, locality, and kinship. How you organize, edit, and write a genealogy course syllabus often determines whether you'll be hired to teach a course in genealogy for beginners.

If you're a genealogist or want to promote your genealogy-oriented book or journalistic skills, teach a course in genealogy. Genealogy courses rely on verifiable details. Accidental or intentional alterations by scribes can dramatically affect information. Courses that go on year after year are evaluated by students as excellent.

Genealogists are concerned about accurate reproduction of texts or entry of information. For generations, most public family history entries were hand copied by government record clerks, clergy, and scribes deeply influenced by cultural, political, and theological disputes of their day.

Your syllabus can help students look for mistakes and intentional changes in surviving records. Can the original names be reconstructed? Genealogy course content also includes the social history of where and why these changes were made and how family historians go about reconstructing what might be the original names, relationships, and records as closely as possible.

Use your syllabus as a tool to outline your course. Students want an easy-to-follow syllabus. The *American Heritage Dictionary* defines the word 'syllabus' as an outline of a course of study. It's a table of contents with a schedule of topics, not a book proposal.

Your syllabus also needs to cover how to find records of hard-to-trace people, such as clergy. How would you direct students who want to trace nuns, priests, ministers, or rabbis?

Genealogy courses given in churches' social halls sometimes attract those who want to trace difficult-to-find genealogy records of clergy. Old books make excellent genealogy sources. Other primary sources to trace clergy or religious educators include College Alumni Records, The Clergy Lists, Crockford's Directories, Fasti Ecclesiae, Anglicanae, Parish Registers, Bishop's Records, Censuses, and County Directories.

A genealogy course syllabus for beginners includes answers to one of the most frequently asked questions: How do you find female ancestors and solve identity problems when maiden surnames didn't appear on the death certificates? Before you try to organize and write a syllabus, first list topics you'll cover in your syllabus.

Planning Your Syllabus

List all obvious items. Keep this list next to your blank syllabus page. Then list items often omitted from a syllabus for a beginning course in genealogy. Compare your syllabus with other genealogy course outlines that have received great student evaluations. Your clue is whether the course is repeated year after year. There are several copyrighted genealogy course outlines on the Internet to peruse. Use them only for comparison and motivation. Keep your syllabus unique to your own course. Make a list of resources to be used in your own course before you begin writing your syllabus.

Resources List

Social History (brief)
Genealogy sources created by women:
Diaries, journals, letters, postcards, family Bibles, heirlooms, artifacts, oral history, legislative petitions, atypical sources, published family histories, cemetery records, tombstone inscriptions or rubbings, church records, censuses, military records, hospitals, orphanages, institutions, sanitariums, passenger arrival lists, city directories, notaries' records, voter lists/registrations, pensions, widows' pension applications/civil war, orphans and guardianship records, land records, marriage records, medical records, Eugenics Record Office, (ERO), social data, midwives' journals, doctors' journals, asylums, divorce records, wills, probate, court records, school records, ethnic sources, codicils, ethnic/religious hospital records, naturalization laws.

After you compile this list, put it aside to refer to as you write your syllabus. Begin outlining the syllabus by starting with the course information, instructor information, text or reading materials, course descriptions, course calendar or schedule, and references or bibliography.

Each category would get a one or two-sentence description summarizing what will be covered in the course and what assignments are required of students. Keep your syllabus short—about three pages or less. The syllabus in a semester-long college level, 3-unit genealogy course meant for beginners and taught online or in person would look like this in its layout:

Syllabus

Course Number/Title: **Genealogy and Family History 1**
Name of School or College
Year and Month:
Department:
Credit Hours 3
Required Text
Days/Time
Instructor
Location
Prerequisite: None
Course Placement: Adult Education, Extended Studies, Community College, University Undergraduate level.

Overview

In Genealogy 1, students will learn special strategies for uncovering hard-to-find information about their ancestors. By the end of this course, students will become more versatile in using interdisciplinary skills for researching family and social history resources.

Course Description

Genealogy 1 is an introductory course in family and personal history research *methods* that includes learning interviewing and recording skills. This survey course covers the strategies of genealogical research in North America and introduces the student to the techniques of genealogical research around the world. Students able to read other languages may work on genealogical records in other languages if they can translate their findings, projects, or assignments to the class in English.

Research Methods

Students are introduced to a survey of all the methods used to identify individuals and their ancestors, including paper records, online searches, surname groups online, and DNA-driven genealogy resources.

Learning Objectives for Genealogy 1
At the end of this course, students will have learned the following skills:

1.   Students will be able to research the following resources:

Original records

Family histories

Church records

Censuses

Passenger Arrival Lists

City directories

Family history libraries and genealogy sections of public and university libraries

Voter lists and registrations

Military records and pensions, widows' pensions

Land records and notary records

Marriage records

Medical records

Divorce records

Ethnic women and men

   African American

   Native American, Inuit, and South American

   Indigenous Peoples Genealogy

   Jewish American

   European Immigrants

   Chinese and Japanese Immigrants in California

   Latino Immigrants

   Pacific Islanders

Genealogy and Social History of New Zealand, Australia, and Oceania

South Asian Genealogy

Middle Eastern Immigrants

East Asian, Philippine, and Indonesian Immigrants

Unique People's Genealogy, including:

Amish Genealogy

Mennonites Genealogy

Doukhobors

Romany

Travellers

Melungeons

Metis

Miscellaneous

Wends/Sorbs

Working with Databases and Genealogy Lists

2. Methods for determining maiden names.

3. Solving identity problems in genealogy research

4. Methods for identifying women

5. Genealogy as social history

   a. child bearing and raising in genealogy research

   b. children born out of wedlock and genealogy research

   c. women's work and genealogy records,

   d. property tax records

   e. religion and genealogy information

   f. women's reform movements, rights, and genealogy records

26. Oral history, video and audio recording—what questions to ask.

How Students will apply the newly learned genealogy research skills:

1. Use the methods of scientific genealogical research.

2. Establish lines of descent for the person or family you select and develop a pedigree chart or family history tree of names and critical dates such as birth, marriage, and death for each ancestor on the family tree and/or pedigree chart.

3. Organize genealogy records.

4. Interview and record relatives or selected persons.

5. Research the past.

6. Use online technology to research or supplement written records and develop a pedigree chart or family tree.

Six Assignments and Projects: Due by End of 12-Week Course. (Insert Specific Due Dates) One assignment is due every two weeks.

1. Write a publishable 1,000-word researched family history/genealogy article and submit it to a publication.

2. Develop a list of 30 to 60 questions (chosen from a list of suggested questions to ask from the handout) to ask another person during a genealogy-oriented or life story-oriented personal or family history recorded interview.

3. Interview using critical and creative thinking skills one or more older adults and record on audio or video tape a half-hour to one-hour life story experience to submit to an oral history archive library. Obtain a signed release form from all persons interviewed to send the recording to an oral history library. Give all persons interviewed copies of the interview recorded on tape or disc, such as a CD or DVD.

4. Use written records and online resources/technology relevant to your personal interests or selected discipline. Genealogy has several areas of emphasis including archival records research, oral history, personal history, family his-

tory, video biography/life story recording, and DNA-driven genealogy/genetics for ancestry.

5. Understand opportunities, skills, and requirements for genealogy journalism and publishing concentrations.

6. Research the diversity of cultures in North America and other countries as related to how genealogy records have been maintained.

Course Competencies:

1. Learn how to perform scientific genealogical research.

2. Fill out and expand a pedigree chart and family tree—first by hand and then using technology or genealogy software.

3. Collect sources and resource information and organize the sources using records, legacies, diaries, letters, or journals.

4. Understand the value of journaling and archiving journals, letters, and diaries.

5. Read an article on how to restore old diaries and photos.

6. Write and record as audio or video a life story to keep for future generations or to put in a time capsule. One copy would be text for reading and another recorded in any format, including text and photos, audio or video. Be aware technology changes, and a text copy on acid-free paper is required just in case the recorded format can no longer play.

7. Learn how to correspond with relatives or friends and what questions to ask when asking for genealogical information.

8. Fill out family group sheets for recorded information to be transcribed or kept in text form.

9. Read an article on genealogical identification, orphan trains, and family skeletons or hidden facts on everything from how a person's race or religion was listed to name changes. Understand how some pre-1948 housing laws and codes excluded certain groups from buying property in various areas and

how some records were changed so people could buy homes. Research articles on this subject as related to genealogy records.

10. Understand the four keys of genealogy as research tools: identity, name, date information was recorded, locality, and kinship.

11. Research the American and/or Canadian trains when children were sent from the East to the West. These trains are separate from the orphan trains. Records with the children's names are in various archives. Find out where to find the records.

12. Learn organization, documentation, filing techniques.

13. Analyze, interpret, and present genealogy-related findings.

14. Keep a research notebook that cites each source of documentation.

15. Look at working files that organize genealogical documents.

16. Listen to a recording of oral history. Read an article on restoring or preserving keepsakes, heirlooms, photos, and scrap books that document family traditions.

17. Use oral history as a research method. Learn to record oral history in audio and/or in video using a camcorder or audio recorder.

18. Learn how items and traditions have been preserved by families, librarians, conservationists, archivists, or family and public historians.

19. Gather family folklore, recipes, superstitions, or traditions.

20. Record family rites of passage, celebrations, or traditions.

21. Search genealogy records on the Internet

22. Read published genealogy information online.

23. Survey genealogy published materials.

24. Enter family information and print-out computer-generated charts and family trees.

25. Learn how to use vital records, divorce and cemetery records, jurisdictions records, original records, Social Security Death Index records online, and specific localities searches of historical groups for an area. Look for transcriptions of original documents.

26. Understand handwriting changes and how to interpret early American handwriting. Translate documents recorded in early American handwriting.

27. Find out where to obtain court records used in genealogy research.

28. Use church data to fill in missing information.

29. Use newspapers in genealogy research

30. Trace ancestor's lives using a city directory.

31. Research information on the Family History Library, Salt Lake City, Utah. Locate the nearest Branch Family Center and research an ancestor or friend.

32. Learn to research immigration, emigration, and migration records, ships' passenger lists, Naturalization records.

33. Investigate the reason why your ancestor immigrated to America. Trace the migration patterns used. Use passenger lists and naturalization records and find out where these records are located.

34. Use land and tax records, school records, and ethnic records.

35. Research what records are available in the National Archives. Find out what military records are available to genealogists for research. Find out the addresses to write to for military, pension, and bounty land records.

36. Plan for and/or attend a genealogy-related seminar, research-oriented field trip, family reunion, or a meeting of a heritage, historical, or lineage association. Read an article on or view a documentary on a family reunion. Research what grants are available from various societies related to genealogy research.

37. Read an article on how to look at medical histories and genograms. A *genogram* is a schematic representation (drawing) of a family's medical history. A genogram describes the medical and/or genetic history of a family and

includes family boundaries, attitudes, values, beliefs and related psychological history of family members.

38. Look at a Web site or surname group online researching DNA-driven genealogy for deep ancestry research. Read an article or handout on the psychological aspects of studying one's own family history. Start a *genogram* of your family. Does DNA-driven genealogy appeal more to anthropologists or to genealogists?

Libraries and Field Trips

Visit a library that has records related to genealogy and/or oral history research or archives. Record in your notebook in two paragraphs what you learned from the field trip and what most interested you there.

Method of Instruction

Class discussion, lectures, field trips, video documentaries, class participation, individual Internet computer research, collaborative projects, handouts, videos, and personal history recording projects is used. This course may be taught online or in person.

Evaluation

Class participation and completion of projects/assignments is due by the end of the course. Assignments are due by the due date specified in the handout.

Equipment

Access to the Internet, a personal computer and printer, a tape or other audio digital recorder or camcorder using either tape or DVDs, and a DVD or CD recorder/R/RW disk drive in your computer or other device that saves a computer file to a CD and/or a DVD. Save your recorded projects on DVDs or CDs. Instruction will be provided on how to save any recorded material to a DVD or CD. Technical help will be available.

Length of Course

Adjust the syllabus content and assignments to the length of your own course. Genealogy courses may run for a 12, 16 or 18-week semester in adult education unified school districts or in extended studies or community college classes.

◆   ◆   ◆

Questions to Ask Relatives or Friends Prior to Recording Their Genealogy, Traditions, and Life Experiences

In the process of promoting your book, if you are going to teach a course in folklore, genealogy, or personal history, and record traditions, here's how to talk to relatives and friends before recording their life experiences for books, keepsake journals, or documentaries.

STEP 1: Send someone enthusiastic about personal and oral history to senior community centers, lifelong learning programs at universities, nursing homes, or senior apartment complexes activity rooms. You can reach out to a wide variety of older adults in many settings, including at libraries, church groups, hobby and professional or trade associations, unions, retirement resorts, public transportation centers, malls, museums, art galleries, genealogy clubs, and intergenerational social centers.

STEP 2: Have each personal historian or volunteer bring a tape recorder with tape and a note pad. Bring camcorders for recording video to turn into time capsules and CDs or DVDs with life stories, personal history experiences, memoirs, and events highlighting turning points or special times in people's lives.

STEP 3: Assign each personal historian one or two older persons to interview with the following questions.

1. What were the most significant turning points or events in your life?

2. How did you survive the Wars?

3. What were the highlights, turning points, or significant events that you experienced during the economic downturn of 1929-1939? How did you cope or solve your problems?

4. What did you do to solve your problems during the significant stages of your life at age 10, 20, 30, 40, 50, 60 and 70-plus? Or pick a year that you want to talk about.

5. What changes in your life do you want to remember and pass on to future generations?

6. What was the highlight of your life?

7. How is it best to live your life after 70?

8. What years do you remember most?

9. What was your favorite stage of life?

10. What would you like people to remember about you and the times you lived through?

STEP 3:

Have the student record the older person's answers. Select the most significant events, experiences, or turning points the person chooses to emphasize. Then write the story of that significant event in ten pages or less.

STEP 4: Ask the older person to supply the younger student photos, art work, audio tapes, or video clips. Usually photos, pressed flowers, or art work will be supplied. Have the student or teacher scan the photos onto a disk and return the original photos or art work or music to the owner.

STEP 5: The personal historian, volunteer, student and/or teacher scans the photos and puts them onto a Web site on the Internet at one of the free communities that give away Web site to the public at no cost…some include http://www. tripod.com, http://www.fortunecity.com, http://www.angelfire.com, http:// www.geocities.com, and others. Most search engines will give a list of communities at offering free Web sites to the public. Microsoft also offers free family Web sites for family photos and newsletters or information. Ask your Internet service provider whether it offers free Web site space to subscribers. The free Web sites are limited in space.

For larger Web site spaces with room for audio and video material and other keepsake memorabilia, purchase a personal Web site from a Web-hosting company. Shop around for affordable Web site space for a multimedia life story time capsule that would include text, video and/or audio clips, music, art, photos, and any other effects.

1. Create a Web site with text from the older person's significant life events

2. Add photos.

3. Add sound or .wav files with the voice of the older person speaking in small clips or sound bites.

4. Intersperse text and photos or art work with sound, if available. Add video clips, if available and won't take too much bandwidth.

5. Put Web site on line as TIME CAPSULE of (insert name of person) interviewed and edited by, insert name of student who interviewed older person.

STEP 6: Label each Web site Time Capsule and collect them in a history archives on the lives of older adults at the turn of the millennium. Make sure the older person and all relatives and friends are emailed the Web site link. You have now created a time capsule for future generations.

This can be used as a classroom exercise in elementary and high schools to teach the following:

1. Making friends with older adults.

2. Learning to write on intergenerational topics.

3. Bringing community together of all generations.

4. Learning about foster grandparents.

5. History lessons from those who lived through history.

6. Learning about diversity and how people of diverse origins lived through the 20th century.

7. Preserving the significant events in the lives of people as time capsules for future generations to know what it was like to live between 1900 and 2000 at any age.

8. Learning to write skits and plays from the life stories of older adults taken down by young students.

9. Teaching older adults skills in creative writing at senior centers.

10. Learning what grandma did during World War 2 or the stock market crash of 1929 followed by the economic downturn of 1930-1938.

What to Ask People about Their Lives before You Write a Play, Skit, or Monologue

Step 1

When you interview, ask for facts and concrete details. Look for statistics, and research whether statistics are deceptive in your case.

Step 2

To write a plan, write one sentence for each topic that moves the story or piece forward. Then summarize for each topic in a paragraph. Use dialogue at least in every third paragraph.

Step 3

Look for the following facts or headings to organize your plan for a biography or life story.

1. PROVERB. Ask the people you interview what proverb represents their life stories. Look at a book of proverbs, but develop an original proverb not copyrighted or cliché. Proverbs can be found in libraries or even on tee shirts and bumper stickers. Create your own as you work with your client.

2. PURPOSE, MOTTO, OR SLOGAN. Ask the people you interview or a biography, for what purpose is or was their journey? Is or was it equality in the workplace or something personal and different such as dealing with change—downsizing, working after retirement, or anything else? If your client had to create/invent a slogan or aspiration that fit that person, what would it be? One slogan might be something like the seventies ad for cigarettes, "We've come a long way, baby," to signify ambition achieved. Look for an original slogan, not a copyrighted slogan or a cliché.

3. IMPRINT. Ask what makes an imprint or impact on people's lives and what impact the people you're interviewing want to make on others?

4. STATISTICS: How deceptive are they? How can you use them to focus on reality?

5. How have the people that you're interviewing influenced changes in the way people or corporations function? How does your client share meaning (communicate) with others?

6. What is your client's goal in life? To what is the person aspiring?

7. What kind of communication skills does the person have and how are these skills received? Are the communication skills male or female, thinking or feeling, yin or yang, soft or steeled, and are people around these people negative or positive about those communication skills?

8. What new styles is the person using? What kind of motivational methods, structure, or leadership? Is the person a follower or leader? How does the person match his or her personality to the character of a corporation or interest?

9. How does the person handle change?

10. How is the person reinforced?

Summarize and Review Your Writing

Once you have titles and summarized paragraphs for each segment of your story, you can more easily flesh out the story by adding dialogue and description to your factual information. Look for differences in style among the people you interview. How does the person want to be remembered?

Is the person a risk taker or cautious for survival? Does the person identify with her job or the people involved in the process of doing the work most creatively or originally?

Does creative expression take precedence over processes of getting work out to the right place at the right time? Does the person want his ashes to spell the words "re-invent yourself" where the sea meets the shore? This is a popular concept appearing in various media. Another popular concept in the media is to use the words 'love' or 'peace.'

Search the Records in the Family History Library of Salt Lake City, Utah

Make use of the database online at the Family History Library of Salt Lake City, Utah. Or visit the branches in many locations. The Family History Library (FHL) is known worldwide as the focal point of family history records preservation.

The FHL collection contains more than 2.2 million rolls of microfilmed genealogical records, 742,000 microfiche, 300,000 books, and 4,500 periodicals that represent data collected from over 105 countries. You don't have to be a member of any particular church or faith to use the library or to go online and search the records.

APPENDIX

List of Writing Web Links

Training Beginners in the Business of Writing and the Writing of Business

Alexander Communications, Business Writing Seminars
Provides on-site, customized seminars in business writing skills. The seminars are practical and tailored especially for employee needs. Yvonne Alexander founded Alexander Communications, a San Francisco-based company, in 1986 to help her clients increase profits and persuasiveness by developing effective writing skills. Trainers will travel to your training site.
http://www.alexcommunications.com/

The Business Writing Center
Online, Instructor-Led Business Writing Courses Business Writing Workshops at Company Sites. Currently, over 400 students from 158 companies in 12 countries taking 15 online business writing courses to enhance their work performance and success
http://www.writingtrainers.com/

Business Writing Workshop Catalog
The Basic Grammar for Business Writing workshop is for people who have a good command of the English language, but need to make their sentences and paragraphs clearer, or who show a small number of consistent errors in grammar, syntax, punctuation, and spelling. It is suitable for non-native speakers of English as well as people who are native speakers.
http://www.writingtrainers.com/workshop/workcat.htm

Salary Wizard
Thousands of jobs are listed with free salary information as well as compensation packages, stock options, and bonus information. Select the Media designation.
http://www.salary.com

Copywriter.com
This is a Web site where words get results. Site is created by Al Bredenberg Creative Services.
http://www.copywriter.com

American Reporter
This magazine is the online cooperative "reporter's newspaper."
http://www.compumedia.com/~albowh/.

Executive Speech and Business Writing Internet And Marketing Strategies For Writers
Practical advice books on how to use the Internet to further your writing career and market your writing.
http://www.speechwriter.net/

Instructional Solutions: Instructional Solutions Online is a leader in online business writing training. Writing services and training materials at this training site for business writing. All of their training is instructor-led, providing personalized coaching and evaluation of writing tasks.

The training offered measures and improves skill gaps, tracks progress, and boasts a 96% completion rate across programs. Instructional Solutions is very proud to have been chosen by FedEx University and Liberty Mutual Insurance Company to provide online business writing training to their employees worldwide, including clients from 11 nations.
http://www.instructionalsolutions.com/

Internet Strategies for Writers
Moira Allen's new book, *Writing.com: Creative Internet Strategies to Advance Your Writing Career* offers practical advice with chapters on finding markets online, electronic rights, netiquette, joining online discussions, Web site construction and online publishing, including at the end of each chapter, lists of relevant online resources for writers.
http://www.washwriter.org/resources/membersonly/archive/netstrats.htm

Rules of Punctuation for Business Writing
The rules are excerpted from "The Perfect Letter" published by Scott Foresman, with a link to the book.
http://www.smartbiz.com/sbs/arts/tpl4.htm

Writing Successful Business Proposals
Skills are taught at this site to prepare successful business proposals for potential customers or clients, structure of a business proposal as a series of slots into which you put persuasive information. The training also teaches methods of persuasion and effective, clear, correct writing. Grant writing is also taught at the Business Writing Center as is public relations writing and copywriting.
http://www.writingtrainers.com/center/bwc360.htm

Writers Conferences and Seminars

E-book World
Offering conferences, networking, and information on writing and publishing as well as all other business aspects of the e-book marketplace.
http://www.e-book-world.com/ebook-fr.shtml.

Newspaper Association of America
Conferences, marketing resources, circulation data, surveys, and events.
http://www.naa.org

Finding Paying Markets for Freelance Writers

Finding Writing Markets Online:
Online sources for finding the latest print markets: electronic newsstands, publication Web sites and guideline databases. Electronic newsstands help you find e-markets for writing.
http://www.NewsDirectory.com.

Writers Guideline Databases.
Online listing of writing markets and databases on marketing your writing.
www.Marketlist.com

Writers Guideline Publications
These may link you to guidelines on a publication's Web site.
www.writersdigest.com

Media Directories

To send review copies of books and freelance article queries to publications listed in media directories.

General Major Media Directories for Freelance Writers

Gebbie Press

> The All-in-One Media Directory
> PR Media Directory: Newspapers Radio TV Magazines: Press releases, Faxes, e-mail, publicity, and freelance. Media directory includes TV and radio stations, daily and weekly newspapers, and consumer and trade magazines.
> http://www.gebbieinc.com/
> http://www.gebbieinc.com/presto1.htm

Gebbie Press:

> Magazine Publishers on the Internet
> An alphabetical listing of leading publishers in the United States, and links to their web sites.
> http://www.gebbieinc.com/publish.htm

Electronic Media Directories

> Press Flash
> Distribute your Web firm's press releases to media outlets throughout the world using the services and resources provided by Press Flash. Press release writing services are also provided.
> http://www.pressflash.com/

E-zine directories

> E-Publications Directors Resource List
> If you want to write for electronic publications, see these e-publications directories. At this site you can find out information on writing for electronic markets.
> http://www.zinebook.com.

E-Zine Advice Publications Online

> > Contentious
> > This publication is the e-zine that advises and offers information for people who write or publish content on the Web. Find out where

to write for other electronic magazines. Offers online options for frustrated journalists.
http://www.contentious.com/.

Ethnic Media Directories

American Minorities Media
American Minorities Media is a subsidiary of Market Place Media, the leading
media placement company reaching specialized markets.
http://www.marketmedia.com/amm

Specific Markets

MarketMedia.com
Media and promotions solutions for reaching specialized markets such as senior citizens, minorities, military, students, and others. Also media analysis is offered.
http://www.marketmedia.com/

Freelance Editorial Association
(Includes desktop publishers)
The current online *Yellow Pages,* published annually since 1997, includes listings by skills as well as a specialties index. This association published the hardcopy, *Yellow Pages*, a listing of Association members who wished to advertise their skills and specialties, between 1989 and 1999.
http://www.tiac.net/users/freelanc/YP.html

International

International Journalists' Network
If you write about overseas subjects or travel, you'll find the International Center for Journalists' online source full of training information and media directories.
http://www.ijnet.org

SAJA: South Asian Journalists Association
Writers interested in South Asian features, covering the people, businesses, and processes that impact South Asia will find excellent resources in this association and its publications.
http://www.saja.org/job.html

International Women's Writing Guild
The International Women's Writing Guild, headquartered in New York and founded in 1976, is a network for the personal and professional empowerment of women through writing.
http://www.iwwg.com

Pressbox—UK
Pressbox is the UK online press center offering press release and copywriting services providing a professional resource for news, press releases, and postings to carefully targeted audiences.
http://www.pressbox.co.uk

Associazioni ed Enti Professionali—America
List of South American, Canadian, and US writers' organizations. This site contains a fine list of writers' associations and language translation firms.
http://www.alice.it/writers/grp.wri/wgrpame.htm

Rural Press Interactive
Rural Press Interactive outlines opportunities to target specific markets throughout Australia, includes metro, regional and rural. The association brings press and Internet together with a network of publications and sites.
http://www.rpinteractive.com.au

Electronic Pages and E-Marketing for Writers

The development journal of the International Informatics Institute is called Electronic Pages. It offers at the site, articles, forums, and announcements of conferences as well as great advice on writing for the electronic market
http://www.electric-pages.com/.

Tailwind.com
Responsible e-mail marketing, help for small businesses, help for the small business owner such as freelance writers.
http://www.tailwind.com/db/y.asp?hid=90&nid=1

Marketing Strategies and Techniques for Writers

101 Marketing Tips for Writers.
This site offers a list of 101 marketing tips, Cassell Success Guide, and some links for writers, such as if you "want to break into advertising, go to church." Pub-

lished by Cassell Network of Writers, Cassell Communications, Inc.
http://www.bitcave.com/101tips.htm

Elaine's Marketing Suggestions for Writers.
Writers Information Network (WIN). Christian writers information network
and advice. Excellent site for writers interested in writing for the Christian markets and quality Christian writing.
http://www.bluejaypub.com/win/ElaineTips.htm.

Associations—National

American Business Press
The American Business Press is the industry association for business-to-business
information providers, including producers of magazines, CD-ROMS, Web
sites, trade shows and products that build upon the printed product. The association has a staff of specialists in government affairs, marketing, communications,
promotion and finance.
http://www.salesdoctors.com/directory/dircos/3103a03.htm

American Society of Business Press Editors
(ASBPE) is the professional association for full-time and freelance editors and
writers employed in the business, trade, and specialty press.
http://www.asbpe.org/

American Society of Journalists and Authors.
Links on how electronic publishing allows a writer to create a parallel product
line to profitably meet more needs in a different way. This site contains links and
resources for the organization called American Society of Journalists and Authors
and features books by members and speakers. ASJA Writer Referral Service is at
(212) 398-1934 or writers@asja.org.
http://www.asja.org/index9.php

American Copy Editors Society
The society focuses on improving the quality of journalism. Writerly resources
include editorial advice, job openings, discussion boards and conference updates.
http://www.copydesk.org/

The American Society of Composers, Authors and Publishers (ASCAP)
More than 80,000 composers, songwriters, lyricists and music publishers belong
to this society. ASCAP protects the rights of its members by licensing and paying

royalties for copyrighted works. The job board and Resource Guide to the Music Business are excellent resources for writers interested in the business of writing lyrics or song and music publishing.
http://www.ascap.com/ascap.html

American Society of Journalists and Authors
This organization for professional freelance nonfiction writers whose career focus is writing offers online job resources.
http://www.asja.org

American Jewish Press Association
Founded nearly 50 years ago as an association for the English-language Jewish press in North America, today more than 150 newspapers, publications and individual journalists are members. Excellent job bank. Publishes a directory of members.
http://www.ajpa.org/

Academy Of American Poets
Provides information, events, publications, education, and professional services to people writing poetry as a profession. The Academy of American Poets offers poetry exhibits online and biographies, photographs, and selected poems.
http://www.poets.org/LIT/poet/kkochfst.htm

Writers Guild of America
Association of screenwriters and animation scriptwriters who work for union wages for the film and TV production industry. You may register scripts here, find a list of agents, WGA news, online mentor service, and research links.
http://www.wga.org/

Society for Professional Journalists
    This society offers local chapters, a code of ethics in journalism, and professional membership events, contests, and awards as well as meetings covering the business of journalism to any working journalist, freelance or staff.
    Maintains local and student chapters nationwide. The society offers ethics news, publications, job referrals, and continuing education seminars for journalists and grants scholarships in journalism. SPJ publishes Quill magazine, a trade journal for journalists. Maintains a site called The Electronic Journalist for online writers.
http://spj.org/

National Writers Association
Foundation partnerships, courses, publications, services for writers. Excellent site for contract reading, critiques, and help for all types of writers. National Writers Press, a leader in self-publishing of books.
http://www.nationalwriters.com/

American Society of Media Photographers,
Offers an online gallery of work done by members of this professional association for photographers. The links of this national organization includes a directory and links to members' Web pages. Useful for writers seeking a media photographer to work with them on an article or book that needs media photography work.
http://www.asmp.org/

Society of Children's Book Writers and Illustrators (SCBWI)
SCBWI is dedicated to serving those who write, illustrate, or share an interest in children's literature. The site offers conferences, regional newsletters, a bi-monthly bulletin, writing and publishing links and tips, including other informational publications.
http://www.scbwi.org/

Writersclub.com
Links to clubs, socials, and partying in different cities at the Writersclub.com site. Party weekends at the Club Media Ventures site with links to Writersclub.com.
http://www.writers.club.com/

California Writers Clubs
List of writers clubs and resources with links to seminars, training, magazines, groups, conferences, career centers, area writers organizations, book cafes, and directories of newspapers.
http://pw1.netcom.com/~mcrowe1/cwcsbb/resource.htm

Society for Professional Journalists
Their New Way Journalism Page is excellent.
http://www.journalism.sfsu.edu/

Society of American Business Editors and Writers
Members of the Society of American Business Editors and Writers have joined together in the common pursuit of the highest standards of economic journalism,

through both individual and collective efforts.
http://www.sabew.org/sabew.nsf/home?OpenPage

Technical Writers Associations

Society for Technical Communication
STC is the largest professional organization serving the technical communication profession.
http://www.stc.org/

Society for Technical Communicators
Technical writing information, grants, salary surveys, loans, and book listings.
http://www.stc-va.org

HTML Writers Guild
International association of Web Authors, tips on good Web writing, design information and technology resources for writers of html.
http://www.hwg.org

Hypertext Writers Guild
If you write content in hypertext or want to learn, you can benefit from the resources, tips, and networks at the Hypertext Writers Guild.
http://www.mindspring.com/guild/

Computer Press Association
The Computer Press Association (CPA) was established to promote excellence in the field of computer journalism. Members include working editors, writers, producers, and freelancers who cover issues related to computers and technology.
http://www.computerpress.org/

Associations for Business or Marketing Journalists and Copywriters

American Business Press
Non-profit, global association for business-to-business information
Providers, including databases, conventions, and other media.
http://www.americanbusinesspress.com/

American Society of Business Press Editors
(ASBPE) is the professional association for full-time and freelance editors and writers employed in the business, trade, and specialty press.
http://www.asbpe.org/

Associated Business Writers of America
This site contains an excellent list of writers' associations.
http://www.poewar.com/articles/associations.htm

Association of Professional Communication Consultants
APCC creates a "professional community where communication consultants increase their knowledge, grow their businesses, and achieve high standards of professional practice." APCC's mission is to "support members as they help clients reach their goals through better communication."
http://www.apcc-online.org/

Freelance Editorial Association
Freelance Editorial Association
(Includes desktop publishers)
The current online *Yellow Pages,* published annually since 1997, includes listings by skills as well as a specialties index. This association published the hardcopy, *Yellow Pages*, a listing of Association members who wished to advertise their skills and specialties, between 1989 and 1999.
http://www.tiac.net/users/freelanc/YP.html

Selected List Of Multimedia Publishers/Producers/Distributors
Kay E. Vandergrift has compiled an excellent list in order to facilitate easy access to contact media publishers, producers and distributors.
http://www.scils.rutgers.edu/special/kay/mediacatalog.html

Society of American Business Editors and Writers
Members of the Society of American Business Editors and Writers have joined together in the common pursuit of the highest standards of economic journalism, through both individual and collective efforts.
http://www.sabew.org/sabew.nsf/home?OpenPage

Software Publishers Association
Are you a multimedia developer or publisher? Or do you own multimedia content that you want to license? See The Software Publishers Association *Legal Guide to Multimedia*. It's a guide to the legal issues of developing, protecting, and distributing multimedia products.
http://www.awl-he.com/titles/0201409313.html

Women In Scholarly Publishing
Women in Scholarly Publishing (WiSP) is a professional organization serving the educational and professional advancement of its members. WiSP is committed to achieving equal opportunity and compensation for all those employed in the field of scholarly publishing.
http://www.wispnet.org/about.html

Writers Guild of America
Association of screenwriters and animation script writers who work for union wages for the film and TV production industry. You may register scripts here, find a list of agents, WGA news, online mentor service, and research links.
http://www.wga.org/

Truck Writers of North America
This site lists a glossary of trucking terms for writers and a list of freelance writing jobs available for writers specializing in writing about trucking and the truck industry. Excellent freelance writing job postings listed in their job bank. TWNA is an organization of professionals who are involved in gathering, writing and reporting news and information about trucks, trucking and the trucking industry.
http://www.twna.org/job_postings.htm

Advertising/Multimedia
Association of Independent Commercial Producers
Kaufman Astoria Studios
This association specializes in photo-real visual effects. It's a job bank on site for programmers, artists, and other creative people interested in working on photo-realistic projects.
http://www.telefilm-south.com/index.html

International Chain of Industrial and Technical Advertising Agencies
http://www.thevines.com

National Writers Association (NWA)
Foundation partnerships, courses, publications, services for writers. Excellent site for contract reading, critiques, and help for all types of writers. National Writers Press, a leader in self-publishing of books.
http://www.nationalwriters.com/

Academy Of Television Arts And Sciences
News, activities, committee events, publications, and awards related to the TV production, marketing, and scriptwriting industry.
http://www.emmys.tv/

Advertising Club Of New York
Strives to elevate the understanding of marketing and advertising communications by providing a common forum.
http://www.adclubny.org/index_home.shtml

Advertising Production Club of New York (APC)
Has products, manufacturers, and associations database and information at site.
http://www.arcat.com/arcatcos/cos36/arc36681.cfm

Advertising Women of New York
Holds events and has mentoring program. AWNY'S mission is to provide a forum for personal and professional growth; to serve as a catalyst for the advancement of women in the communications field; to promote and support philanthropic endeavors through the AWNY Foundation.
http://www.awny.org/

Science Writers Associations

American Medical Writers Association
For freelance and staff writers focusing on medical issues in the news, pharmaceutical copywriting, healthcare articles, health and nutrition, and related medical writing. Also see American Medical Writers Association Job Market for freelancers and full-time staff, for members.
http://www.amwa.org/about/about.html

National Association of Science Writers.
For writing, marketing, publishing, job information, and legal issues discussion of writers and journalists in all of the sciences such as pharmaceutical, life sciences, physical sciences, social sciences, and archaeology/anthropology.
http://nasw.org/

Aviation/Space Writers Association (AWA)
This professional association has publications, events, and tips for freelance and staff writers or journalists who cover the space and aviation industries.
http://brad.net/aero_outlook/other_resources/orgs.html#awa

Council of Biology Editors
Council of Biology Editors offers documentation. The 1994 CBE (Council of Biology Editors) manual, Scientific Style and Format, describes two systems of documentation in the handbook they offer in this association for editors working on biological documentation.
www.wisc.edu/writing/Handbook/DocCBE6.html

D.C. Science Writers Association
Washington, DC area science writers group for local science writers in Washington and surrounding states.
http://www.nasw.org/dcswa/

Georgia Area Science Writers Association—GASWA:
Local science writers group in the state of Georgia, USA.
http://www.nasw.org/users/GASWA/

New England Science Writers Association:
Science writers in the New England states have this organization.
http://www.umass.edu/pubaffs/nesw/

Canadian Science Writers Association
For science writers in Canada, an association offering networking and education in science writing as well as writing tips.
http://www.interlog.com/~cswa/

Canadian Farm Writers' Federation
Founded in 1955, The Canadian Farm Writers' Federation (CFWF) serves the common interests of agricultural journalists, editors and broadcasters as well as those in business and government whose primary responsibility is agricultural communications.
http://www.uoguelph.ca/Research/cfwf/

Penn State Association of Science Writers
An association for science writers in Pennsylvania.
http://nasw.org/users/cpnasw/cpnasw.htm

Society of Environmental Journalists.
The world's largest organization of journalists, students, and teachers who write about the environment and are interested in the business of writing and selling writing covering the environment.
http://www.sej.org/.

Indexers, Editors, Proofreaders, and Copywriters Associations

American Society of Indexers
ASI is a nonprofit educational and charitable organization, serving and dedicated to the advancement of indexers, librarians, abstractors, editors, publishers, database producers, data searchers, product developers, technical writers, academic professionals, researchers and readers, and others concerned with indexing of books and periodicals.
http://www.asindexing.org/goals.shtml

The Editorial Freelancers Association
The professional resource for editorial freelancers, EFA, is a national, non-profit, professional organization of self-employed workers in publishing and communications. The Freelance Editorial Association merged with the Editorial Freelancers Association in June 2000 and is now known as EFA.
The association offers jobs listings, marketing, setting fees information, a Yellow Pages of freelancers, skills listing, and the e-publication, Freelance Editorial Association News.
http://www.the-efa.org/ or http://www.tiac.net/users/freelanc/index.html or the newsletter http://www.tiac.net/users/freelanc/Newsletter.html

Writing Help Resources with Links

Children's Book Council
Resource site for children's books with a guide to children's writing and material on forthcoming books.
http://www.cbcbooks.org

Associated Writing Programs
Offers lists of university writing programs, conferences, and resources. Publishes *The Writers Chronicle*.
http://www.awpwriter.org

Absolute Write
Writing links offered on how to write or publish novels, nonfiction, plays, poetry, and scripts.
http://www.absolutewrite.com

Writers Toolbox
Resources for fiction and nonfiction writers, screenwriters, journalists, and technical writers. Excellent resource for writing help.
http://www.geocities.com/Athens/6346

Proofreaders
List of names and addresses of freelance proofreaders, from the Editorial Freelancers Association (EFA).
http://www.tiac.net/users/freelanc/YP/proofreaders.htm

Biology Editors, Rates and Payment, Editing and Proofreading
Biology editors and proofreaders charge upwards of $35 an hour. Biology Editors Company has an excellent Web site discussing how much to charge for technical writing or proofreading and editing scientific material, or proposal development and technical writing.
http://www.biologyeditors.com/rates_and_payment.html

Marketing Associations Writers Use for Resources

Writers Market Online
Writers Market book listing publishers and their needs is now online if you subscribe to the updated market information.
http://www.writersmarket.com

Fiction Writer Online
Answers to questions about writing fiction from novelists, agent, and editor.
http://www.fictionwritermag.com

American Marketing Association
The American Marketing Association is an organization for those interested in marketing. Network with marketing professionals to get timely and factual information for business articles or read marketing research publications.
http://www.ama.org/.

Artslynx: International Writing Resources
If you want more listings of writers' associations with links, including information for poets, these are excellent resources.
http://www.artslynx.org/

Hollywood Creative Directory
Job board for the entertainment industry, directories, and places to contact.
http://www.hcdonline.com

Publishers Marketing Association
For writers thinking of self-publishing, the Publishers Marketing Association (PMA) is the largest non-profit trade association representing independent publishers of books, audio, video and CDs. Their mission is to advance independent publishing through professional development, creative marketing, and global affiliation.
http://www.pma-online.org/

The Market Research Industry
Information on what the Market Research Industry is doing, special interest for writers seeking trends and marketing behavior. Market Research. A full-service market research and consulting firm.
http://www.asiresearch.com/mri/mri.htm

Market Research Organizations
Market research conference schedules and links to other market research sites. Study the latest market trends.
http://www.wsa.com/wsa/directories/membership/MarketTrend/info.html

Center For Research In Marketing
Bridging the gap between Marketing theory and practice through rigorous and relevant research.
http://www.csom.umn.edu/CSOM/MktgCenter/MktgCenter.html

Content Exchange LLC
Content creators online list their resumes and job opportunities are listed as well. Mailing list also.
http://www.content-exchange.com

PubList.com
Reference of more than 150,000 publications and contacts for writers or those who need permissions.
http://www.publist.com

Book Marketing Update
Self-published authors may subscribe to access independent book publishers, booksellers, and self-publishing feedback.
http://www.bookmarket.com/index.html

The Slot
Style points not in most stylebooks for copy editors or those who want to be freelance copy editors.
http://www.theslot.com

Software Publishing Association
Find any software or computer book publisher or games. A good resource for writers looking for publishers.
http://www.shopforacomputer.com/software/
software_publishing_association.html
Software and Information Industry Council

Many press release articles, news and conferences on trends shaping digital content and the educational technology market. Excellent link to keep current on news and resource material, especially about protecting privacy during the evolution of the digital economy.
http://www.siia.net/

Copyright, ISBN Number, and Library of Congress Registration Information for Self-Publishing Writers and Publishers

U.S. Copyright Office.
All the information you need to know in order to learn how to copyright your writing before you market your work. A link also features information on registration of copyright procedures and instruction.
http://www.loc.gov/copyright/
http://www.loc.gov/copyright/circs/circ1.html#rp

Library of Congress
Learn how to get a Library of Congress registration number for your self-published book, pamphlet, or booklet and other services to publishers and self-publishers
http://lcweb.loc.gov/loc/infopub/

International ISBN Agency.
How to Get an ISBN Number. Does your self-published book need an ISBN number? Find out how to receive an ISBN number at this Web site.
www.isbn.spk-berlin.de/html/howtoget.htm

International Standard Book Numbers (ISBN)
The International standard numbering system for the information industry is administered by R.R. Bowker. The U.S. Agency for ISBN assignment can be contacted at: 121 Chanlon Road, New Providence, NJ 07974, Tel: 908-665-6770—Fax: 908-665-2895.
http://www.bowker.com/standards/home/

International Standard Serial Numbers
    Do you write and self-publish serials or would like to publish serials written by other authors? Perhaps you need an International Standard Serials number. Serials are print or non-print publications issued in parts, usually bearing issue numbers and/or dates.
    A serial is expected to continue indefinitely. Serials include magazines, newspapers, annuals (such as reports, yearbooks, and directories), journals, memoirs, proceedings, transactions of societies, and monographic series.
http://lcweb.loc.gov/issn/ and http://lcweb.loc.gov/issn/issnbro.html

Resources for Business, Technical, and Humanities Writers

Internet Resources for Business and Technical Writers
This site provides excellent resources for the business writer. Links to resources for business writers. Internet Technical Writing Course Guide and career links.
http://www.english.uiuc.edu/cws/wworkshop/ww_tech.html.

Hypertext Writer's Guide and the Research and Documentation Online List of Style Manuals and Glossary of Internet and Library Terms
Helpful resources for business writers and others who want to learn about how to write in hypertext.

http://hildegard.engl.uvic.ca/writers/resources.htm
http://www.bedfordstmartins.com/hacker/resdoc/.

Researching Humanities Links
The humanities links are useful to the writer learning the business of writing from any genre of writing business, science, art, nutrition, or your own specialty.
http://www.bedfordstmartins.com/hacker/resdoc/humanities/overview.htm

Finding Writing Jobs Online

Techwriters.com
Technical writers will find Techwriters.com the best place to look for a technical writing job, other than through membership in technical writer's organizations.
http://www.techwriters.com/.

Technical Writing Jobs
Find current technical writing jobs here, including both staff and contract job listings. Excellent site for technical writing and similar communications media jobs.
http://www.techwriters.com/placement/writer_nationwide_jobs.asp

JournalismJobs.com
This the job board for finding jobs if you're a media person. Post your resume, look at recent job listings, or receive job notification by email at: http://www.journalismjobs.com/.

Journalism Jobs Page
The Journalism Jobs site lists current journalism jobs around the nation. It has links to other journalism job listing sites.
http://www.towson.edu/~bhalle/jjobs.html.

Sun Oasis Jobs
Good site for freelance writers, also staff journalism and tech writing jobs offered. Search by location. Updated frequently. Contains classified ads from editors.
http://www.sunoasis.com

Truck Writers of North America
    This site lists a glossary of trucking terms for writers and a list of freelance writing jobs available for writers specializing in writing about trucking and the truck industry. Excellent freelance writing job postings listed in their job bank.

TWNA is an organization of professionals who are involved in gathering, writing and reporting news and information about trucks, trucking and the trucking industry.
http://www.twna.org/job_postings.htm

All Freelance
Links to resources, articles, and job listings for freelance writers, illustrators, designers, programmers, and other independent contractors.
http://www.allfreelance.com/

Hire Minds
Job postings, e-newsletter, message board, and gatherings in New York City for media, publishing, or creative people.
http://www.hireminds.com/

Net Read
Publishing jobs listed along with content on publishing industry employment.
www.netread.com/jobs/jobs/

Monique's Newsjobs
Monique's Newsjobs is a comprehensive list of jobs for journalists. Working journalists highly recommended this site. It's recommended by Writer's Digest as the best list for journalists around to date.
http://www.news.jobs.net

Creative Freelancers
Submit your resume and samples, or look at the help-wanted area offering freelance writing, editing, or proofreading employment.
http://www.freelancers.com

Writing Employment Center
You'll find a daily updated listing of jobs here for writers and related editorial workers.
http://poewar.com/jobs/htm

Creative Nonfiction
Creative Nonfiction is a magazine of essays and literary nonfiction that offers job opportunities on the magazine from time to time. The publication is dedicated solely to the creative nonfiction genre. It offers different themes with each publication such as diversity, what men think, what men write, and emerging women

writers.
http://www.creativenonfiction.org/thejournal/opportunities.htm

Broadcast-Related Links:
Finding Radio, TV, and Film or Film School Jobs, Airchecks, and Talent

TVand radio Jobs.Com lists timely jobs and talent, including radio, TV, and film school, as well as links to real audio airchecks, available talent, and you can post an air check. You can find broadcast-related links here.
at http://tvandradiojobs.com/

All Starr Radio
An excellent site sampling what writers write about when they speak on the radio. Includes information on comedy, such as a link where you can list the weird things that happened to you.
http://www.allstarradio.com

TV and RadioJobs.com
TV andRadioJobs.com has 13,000+ Unique Visits a day. Almost half their visitors are radio management types looking for fresh talent. Available for a small fee: post your 6-minute aircheck on their streaming server for 5 months.
http://tvandradiojobs.com/.

Air Newslink Job Link for journalists
Search JobLink ads for journalists. Links to resources, publications, or interact with their search engine. Fill out their online form to narrow your job search in journalism.
http://ajr.newslink.org/joblink.html.

Reference Books/Sites for Writers

Allwords.com
Word definitions, origins, and translations. Look up works in five languages. Some audio pronunciations available, and information for crossword puzzle enthusiasts.
http://www.allwords.com

Guinness World Records
Guinness Book of Records for entertainment.
http://www.guinnessworldrecords.com

Rare Diseases Information
If you're a health or medical writer interested in writing about rare diseases and
support groups or need to find more information, try this health site.
http://www.rarediseases.org

Fundraising
If you need to raise funds for a worthy cause, or to publish your own book, look
at these tips on how to pan a fundraiser by an excellent Internet fundraising company.
http://www.fundraising.com

Mystery Writers

Sisters in Crime
Sisters in Crime combats discrimination against women in the mystery field, edu-
cates publishers, the public, and mystery writers and readers as to the inequalities
in the treatment of female authors, and raises the awareness of their contribution
to the field.
http://www.netaxs.com/~sincdv/sincnatl.htm

MysteryNet's Mystery Organizations
Mystery Network. Mystery entertainment and information for mystery fans and
enthusiasts
http://www.mysterynet.com/organizations

ClueLass
Network with other mystery writers here for news, mystery releases, and look at
the resource directory for mystery writers, Deadly Directory.
http://www.cluelass.com

Romance Writers Associations

Romance Writers of America
RWA is a non-profit professional/educational association of 8,400 romance writers and other industry professionals.
http://www.rwanational.com/

eHarlequin.com
Harlequin publishers runs this site for romance readers and writers. Gives writers a picture of what readers expect as it focuses on readers.
http://eharlequin.women.com/harl/

Young Writers

The Writing Corner
Writers under 18 may publish their writing on the site.
http://www.writingcorner.com

The Quill Society
Free writing club for young writers from 12 to 24 with online publishing resources, help, and forums.
http://www.quilll.net/home/index.htm

Templates for Feedback
Flashbase.com
Templates available on site to help writers track reader feedback or responses from proofreaders or agents and editors.
http://www.flashbase.com

Writers' Unions

National Writers Union
Excellent, timely informational articles on preventing your written work from being used without your permission electronically. Offers articles on all aspects of prevention of abuses to writers at work, including independent writers. Job referral listings and other services as union.
http://www.nwu.org/

Communications Workers of America
This is the largest union in America of journalists, printers, publishers, telecommunications workers, broadcast workers, and others involved in communications from writers to telephone company employees and broadcasters.
http://www3.cwa-union.org/

Articles:

Training in the Business of Writing and the Writing of Business

How to Get Publicity (Buzz Appeal) in the Media for Your Writing (before or after publication)

Here's how to get buzz appeal, that is, achieve visibility, credibility, and respectability in the media before or after you find a publisher for your work by making it possible for a popular media person to write about you and discuss what you write in a feature or news article. Published in the *Internet Writing Journal.*
http://www.writerswrite.com/journal/jul99/hart1.htm

Writing Inspirational Books, Articles, Columns, or Scripts

How to write, promote, market, and publish inspirational material, also religious and motivational works. Writing for the inspirational markets. Published in the *Internet Writing Journal.*

http://www.writerswrite.com/journal/sep99/hart2.htm

What is Creative Nonfiction?

(Audio excerpts) from the magazine, *Creative Nonfiction*
Audio excerpts online on the definition and discussion of what is creative nonfiction for writers interested in writing for this genre.
http://www.creativenonfiction.org/thejournal/whatiscnf.htm

Eastgate Systems, Inc.

"The primary source for serious hypertext,"—Robert Coover, The New York Times Book Review. The role of narrative in the Web experience is a pressing concern throughout the Web world, from entertainment to e-commerce. Subscribe to electronic roundtable newsletter, E-Narrative.
http://www.eNarrative.org/1/news.html

E-Lance Economy Not Happening

Read how and why the decline in self-employment has accelerated since 1997.
http://www.asja.org/newspub/x0101b.php

Hungry Minds, Red Hat, Join to Form Press

Hungry Minds Inc, (Nasdaq: HMIN) (formerly IDG Books Worldwide) and Red Hat Inc. (Nasdaq: RHAT) announced a joint multi-title publishing agreement to produce books around Red Hat's extensive product line, including Red Hat(R) Linux.
http://www.authorlink.com/pubnews.html#redhat

Niche Marketing Via the Web

This article is a case history of interest to journalists working online or those who want to Niche Marketing Via the Web: A Case Study Creating a Parallel Electronic Publishing Line by Gordon Burgett, from the December 2000 issue of the ASJA Newsletter, is an excellent article on electronic publishing by the author of Publishing to Niche Markets, by Gordon Burgett. Find a need and fill it.
http://www.asja.org/newspub/x0012a.php

Grant Proposal Writing Instruction

How to Write a Research Grant

How to get grant guidelines and sample proposals so you can write a research grant proposal.
http://www.ialc.wsu.edu/ialc/faculty_teaching/grants/
WtngGrantProposal.html#research

How to Write an Institutional Grant

Instruction and techniques in writing great institutional grant proposals adapted from Bob Lucas's workshop.
http://www.ialc.wsu.edu/ialc/faculty_teaching/grants/WtngGrantProposal.html#institutional

The Intensive American Language Center's site on Grant Proposal Writing
How to write proposals for grants. Methods of how to implement your idea. Article and free instruction site offered by the Intensive American Language Center of Washington State University. Excellent article on how to write grant proposals. The Intensive American Language Center's site on Grant Proposal Writing is adapted from a workshop by Bob Lucas.
http://www.ialc.wsu.edu/ialc/faculty_teaching/grants/WtngGrantProposal.html

Creative Nonfiction

This magazine offers excellent articles online or by subscription. See archived articles online specializing in creative nonfiction, including essays.
http://www.creativenonfiction.org/thejournal/articles/issue14/14contents.htm

"Traps," by Lee Martin.
Also issue #14, *Creative Nonfiction*, "What Men Think, What Men Write," contains two articles than can be read online.
http://www.creativenonfiction.org/thejournal/articles/issue14/14martin_traps.htm

See issue #12, *Creative Nonfiction,* Emerging Women Writers II, "The Old Sort: of Connemaras & Sweet Corn," by Caroline Nesbitt.
http://www.creativenonfiction.org/thejournal/articles/issue12/12nesbitt_theoldsort.htm

◆　　　◆　　　◆

Training Beginners in the Business of Writing and the Writing of Business

How to Get Publicity (Buzz Appeal) in the Media for Your Writing (before or after publication)
Here's how to get buzz appeal, that is, achieve visibility, credibility, and respectability in the media before or after you find a publisher for your work by making it possible for a popular media person to write about you and discuss what you write in a feature or news article. Published in the *Internet Writing Journal.*
http://www.writerswrite.com/journal/jul99/hart1.htm

Writing Inspirational Books, Articles, Columns, or Scripts
How to write, promote, market, and publish inspirational material, also religious and motivational works. Writing for the inspirational markets. Published in the *Internet Writing Journal.*
http://www.writerswrite.com/journal/sep99/hart2.htm

Writing Personal History
http://www.newswriting.net

Audio (MP3) and Video Files for Writers and Personal Historians
http://www.newswriting.net/writingvideos.htm

Anne Hart's Web site and links: http://www.newswriting.net or http://annehart.tripod.com. Audio and video files are at http://www.newswriting.net/writingvideos.htm.

Index

978-0-595-39221-6
0-595-39221-0